EDUCATING RITA, STAGS AND HENS, BLOOD BROTHERS

Two plays and a musical

WILLY RUSSELL was born in Whiston near Liverpool and left school at fifteen. He went through a succession of jobs before, at the age of twenty, he decided to take 'O' and 'A' levels and become a teacher. At about the same time he saw John McGrath's play *Unruly Elements* at the Everyman Theatre, Liverpool, and decided he wanted to become a playwright. Since then he has written *Blind Scouse* (Edinburgh Festival, 1972), *John Paul George Ringo . . . and Bert* (Everyman; Lyric Theatre, London; winner of the Evening Standard's and the London Theatre Critics' award for Best Musical, 1974), *Breezeblock Park* (Everyman; Mermaid, London, 1975), *One for the Road* (Contact Theatre, Manchester, 1986, on tour, 1978, revised for Lyric Theatre, London, 1988), *Stags & Hens* (Liverpool Playhouse, 1978) and *Educating Rita* (RSC Warehouse; Piccadilly Theatre, 1980; RSC tour, 1982; winner of the Society of West End Theatres' award for Best Comedy in 1980; made into a film, for which Russell wrote the screenplay, directed by Lewis Gilbert and starring Michael Caine and Julie Walters, in 1983). The musical *Blood Brothers* (Liverpool Playhouse; Lyric Theatre, London, 1983, Albery Theatre, London, 1988) for which he wrote the music and lyrics as well as the book. *Shirley Valentine* (Everyman, Liverpool, 1986; screenplay, 1987; Vaudeville Theatre, London, 1988). His television work includes *King of the Castle* (BBC 'Second City Firsts', 1973), *Break-In* (BBC TV play for schools, 1974), *Death of a Young Man* (BBC 'Play for Today', 1974), *Our Day Out* (BBC 'Play for Today', 1976; subsequently adapted for the stage and seen at the Everyman, Liverpool, in 1983), and *The Daughters of Albion* (Yorkshire TV, 1978). In June 1983 the Open University awarded him an Honorary M.A. in recognition of his work as a playwright.

EDUCATING RITA
STAGS AND HENS
and
BLOOD BROTHERS

Two Plays and a Musical
by Willy Russell

Methuen Drama

METHUEN MODERN PLAYS

This collection first published in 1986 in Great Britain
by Methuen London Ltd
Reprinted 1987
Reprinted 1988 by Methuen Drama,
an imprint of Reed Consumer Books Ltd
Michelin House, 81 Fulham Road, London SW3 6RB
and Auckland, Melbourne, Singapore and Toronto
Distributed in the United States of America by HEB Inc.,
361 Hanover Street, Portsmouth, New Hampshire NH 03801 3959, USA
Reprinted 1989, 1990 (twice), 1991 (twice), 1992, 1993
Educating Rita: Copyright © 1985 by Willy Russell
Stags and Hens: Copyright © 1985 by Willy Russell
Blood Brothers: book copyright © 1985 by Willy Russell;
                  lyrics copyright © 1983 Timeact Ltd t/a
                  Willy Russell Music.
This collection and the essays 'Not really An Introduction',
'I Want to Write a Musical' and 'Educating the Author'
copyright © Willy Russell
Set in IBM Press Roman by Words & Pictures Ltd,
Thornton Heath, Surrey
Printed and bound in Great Britain by
Cox & Wyman Ltd, Reading

British Library Cataloguing in Publication Data
Russell, Willy

   Educating Rita, Stags and hens, and Blood
   brothers: two plays and a musical.
   I. Title   II. Russell, Willy. Stags and hens
   III. Russell, Willy. Blood brothers
   822'.914   PR6068.U86/

ISBN 0–413–41110–9

CAUTION
All rights whatsoever in these plays are strictly reserved.
Applications for performance etc by professionals should be made
before rehearsals begin to Casarotto Ramsay Limited, 60 Wardour
Street, London W1V 3HP, and by amateurs to Samuel French Ltd,
52 Fitzroy Street, London W1P 6JR.
No performance may take place unless a licence has been obtained.

Contents

Not Really An Introduction

And because I've promised the publisher of these plays I sit here trying to write what is called an introduction. It hasn't been an easy week because I hate introductions. Indeed if I open a book which sports an introduction I often close it again and leave it unread. Have I got an unnatural prejudice against the innocent introduction? Well, the problem is, I don't really know exactly what is the point of an introduction. Will it, for example, heighten your experience of reading my play if you know that I am thirty-eight years of age, have a slight bump in my nose (which, family legend has it, is a result of my being extracted from the womb by a drunken midwife whose skill with forceps was not what it might have been) and that when not working my favourite pastime is to get out the guitar and write a song whilst polishing off a bottle of claret? Is anybody really interested that I consider the influences on the making of these plays to be (not necessarily in this order) Bob Dylan, The Beatles, my wife, my parents, Alan Dosser, Chris Bond, Henry the Fifth, A.L. Lloyd, John McGrath, Mike Ockrent, Danny Hiller, Bob Swash, Bill Morrison, *Death Of A Salesman*, Cagney and Bogart in *The Roaring Twenties*, Enid Blyton, Jimi Hendrix and British traditional music? Unless you are a critic these facts (some of which, anyway, are only part fact, part myth) have no relevance to your reading of my plays because if you need more information than that contained within the plays then the plays are failures and you should write to Methuen demanding your money back (don't worry — since publishing the brilliant *Adrian Mole*, they can well afford it).

Perhaps my introduction should be an attempt to win your sympathy at the outset by outlining the agony I endured, the sleepless nights I spent, the terror I knew and the emptiness I sometimes felt when struggling to realise each of these plays. But why inflict any of that on you? No doubt you too have your own struggles, your own terror and here you are, you've just got through the door after being sacked from your job, your spouse has recently left you, the dog's got worms, the Tories are still in power, the telly's bust, the radio's full of programmes about the nuclear winter (apart from the local commercial station, which just *sounds* like a nuclear winter) and you open this slim volume, just to read a few plays, and what do you get? Some pillock called the author whingein' on about the agony of writing a play, the deprivation of being alone with just his typewriter and his mind, neither of which are in good working order. And what do you do then?

In a mad and final rage you rip out these pages and gleefully dousing them in petrol you use them to fire and burn down what's left of your crumbling second-mortgage house, screaming as you do, 'Christ save me from the mind-numbing, self-justifying, irrelevant, sympathy-seeking INTRODUCTION!'

Now how can I risk doing such a thing to you when all you have done is buy, borrow or rob a book of my plays (probably under the mistaken assumption that they were written by one Willie Rushton)? Simply, I can't. I have your welfare at heart and, besides, I am aware again, that if I need to elicit your sympathy for my plays with anything other than the plays themselves then these plays cannot stand for themselves and therefore do not deserve your sympathy.

It occurs to me that with this chronic introduction phobia of mine I might have got it all wrong. What if . . . what if these introduction things are simply not intended for the general reader but for the specialist, for the critic? Perhaps that's it. Perhaps I should, for his benefit, be outlining my motives, discussing my themes, dropping biographical hints which will help him develop his essay, tentatively titled *'The Playwright As Lush* – A Study Of The Works Of A Northern Playwright With Particular Reference To The Influence Of Selected Premier Cru Clarets On His Formative Work'.

The problem with this approach to the introduction is that I am rather shy of outlining my motives for the benefit of critics and commentators. This reluctance of mine probably stems from the time I was being interviewed for radio's most prestigious arts programme. The interviewer, an established critic and arts commentator, was asking me about my play *Educating Rita*; specifically, he put it to me that in the final moments of the play, when Rita sets about cutting off Frank's hair, I was alluding to a passage in the Bible in which Delilah cuts off Samson's hair, thereby robbing him of his power, of his strength. Now I've never read the Bible. I saw a film once in which Victor Mature, all lips and lurid Technicolor, played Samson. And I did seem to remember that, improbably, once he got a haircut he was done for (I supposed it was just like how Superman would lose his power if he ever came into contact with kryptonite). The interviewer, mistaking my blank look of disbelief and assuming it to be failure to understand the question, put it to me again, 'Wasn't the end of my play an allusion to Samson and Delilah?'

I explained that no, this was not the case, and that in fact I'd chosen to end my play with the haircut because theatrically my instinct told me to close the play on a comic moment, with a joke, a gag. Frank is in his chair, Rita says she knows what she can give him, what she can do for him, leading Frank (and, hopefully, the audience) to expect some sexual favour but, instead, reaches for the scissors and gives him . . . a haircut. She is, after all, a trained hairdresser. Now it might not be a gag to rank with the best of the Marx Brothers but it was certainly what I intended when I wrote the scene and, as I explained to the interviewer, old Samson and Delilah never came into it. But he wouldn't believe me. His actual words were, 'Oh no, come on, that can't be it.' I felt rather accused, as if I was being determindly lowbrow, which I wasn't. I was telling the truth to the best of my knowledge and belief but he wouldn't have it. (This section of the interview was edited out of the final broadcast.) Perhaps the problem was that he wanted my play to be less easily explained, wanted mystique in place of communication, wanted evidence of serious and noble intent which would then justify the use of comedy. Perhaps it's just that amongst those who pass judgement on writing there is a belief that something which is easily communicated and understood is somehow inferior to that which requires profound analysis and explanation. Whatever, that and subsequent similar experiences led me to the conclusion that the plays must speak for themselves, that nothing I have to say will deter you if you're bent on finding Samson and Delilah dancing with Pygmalion in Frank's study, Tennessee Williams and Sam Shepard out with the boys in *Stags and Hens* or Francis J. Child and Raoul Walsh up there in a window, hovering above the streets of *Blood Brothers*.

But then again, why should I attempt to deter you from anything? Does it necessarily follow that as the author of these plays I know more about them than you the reader, you the audience? I certainly hope not and hope that once you have read or seen these plays you will know as much about them as I.

And suddenly, I'll stop. This is beginning to feel dangerously like **An Introduction**.

WILLY RUSSELL

STAGS AND HENS

Stags and Hens was first produced at the Everyman Theatre, Liverpool, in October, 1978, with the following cast:

LINDA	Anne-Louise Wakefield
MAUREEN	Barbara Peirson
BERNADETTE	Cecily Hobbs
CAROL	Donna Champion
FRANCES	Lola Young
DAVE	
ROBBIE	Philip Donaghy
BILLY	Christopher Martin
KAY	Chris Darwin
EDDY	Edward Clayton
PETER	Richard Clay Jones
ROADIE	

Directed by Chris Bond
Designed by Billy Meall

Stags and Hens was subsequently produced in London at the Young Vic in July 1984, with the following cast:

MAUREEN	Eithne Browne
BERNADETTE	Noreen Kershaw
CAROL	Gilly Coman
FRANCES	Kate Fitzgerald
LINDA	Ann Miles
ROBBIE	Nick Maloney
KAY	Graham Fellows
BILLY	Ray Kingsley
EDDY	Matthew Marsh
PETER	Peter Christian
ROADIE	Andrew Secombe
DAVE	Vivian Munn

Directed by David Thacker
Décor by Shelagh Killeen

AUTHOR'S NOTE

Although the use of music is not specified in the text, I envisage that in production, as the main doors are opened and closed, we would hear snatches of the music being played in the dance hall.

References to media people — e.g. Rod Stewart, Mick Jagger etc. can be updated.

W.R.

ACT ONE

The Ladies and Gents in a Liverpool dance hall. Evening. Stevie Wonder's "Superstition" is playing. The song fades and we hear, coming in over it, the sound of girls singing.

GIRLS (*off*):   She's gettin' married in the morning
                   Ding dong the bells are gonna chime
                   Pull out his chopper
                   Oogh what a whopper
                   Get me to the church on time . . .

The girls come into the Ladies. LINDA, *the obvious subject of their song, goes straight into a WC and closes the door. The remaining girls begin to make-up.*

MAUREEN (*crying*): Congratulations Linda. Congratulations.

BERNADETTE: What's up with you now?

MAUREEN: I don't know.

BERNADETTE: Cryin'! On a hen night! It's supposed to be a happy night.

MAUREEN (*bawling*): I am happy. I'm very happy . . . for Linda.

CAROL (*calling out to* LINDA): We're all happy for y'Linda. Ogh Lind, you lucky sod!

FRANCES: Just imagine Lind, after tomorrow you'll have your own flat, your own feller. You'll be a married woman.

BERNADETTE: You'll have your own front room, your own Hoover, your own telly.

MAUREEN (*crying*): Your own husband . . .

CAROL: Agh yeh. He's great Dave isn't he? He's a great feller. He's really dynamic isn't he?

FRANCES: He's good lookin'.

BERNADETTE: An' he's a worker isn't he? I mean he's not like some of them is he?

CAROL: They wouldn't lift a finger some of them, would they?

BERNADETTE: Her feller's not like that though, is he?

CAROL: I'll bet he helps in the house an' that. I'll bet y'he does.

BERNADETTE: Some fellers wouldn't, would they? My feller doesn't. Wouldn't lift a bloody finger. He wouldn't get out that chair if the roof was comin' through. Idle, y'know, that type! The kids call him the reluctant plumber . . . never does a tap!

FRANCES: Her Dave won't be like that though.

CAROL: Agh no, Dave'll be great in the house.

MAUREEN: I'll bet he even helps when the little ones come along. (*She cries.*)

FRANCES: Will you shut it!

BERNADETTE: For Christ's sake Maureen, tonight's supposed to be a celebration, not a wake.

MAUREEN: I am celebrating. I'm celebrating for Linda. It's just . . . just that I wish it was me . . .

FRANCES: Well never mind Maureen . . . your turn'll come.

MAUREEN (*brightening*): D'y'think so? D'y'really think so?

FRANCES: Yeh . . . you'll be all right. You've just got to meet the feller who appreciates your sort of looks.

MAUREEN: What sort of looks?

FRANCES: Well y'know sort of er, y'know . . . (*Looking round for assistance.*) . . . er . . .

CAROL (*calling*): Agh God . . . I'm so happy for y'Lind.

BERNADETTE: I can't wait t'see her in church tomorrow.

CAROL: Agh I'll bet she looks lovely in white as well. Have y'seen her dress Mo?

MAUREEN: When I was round there last week her mum said she'd show it me. But I couldn't bring meself to look. I would have cried. I cry very easily.

FRANCES: We wouldn't have known.

CAROL: I saw it. Oh it's gorgeous, y'know, just off the shoulder.

FRANCES: It's the new length, isn't it?

CAROL: Y'know, with the lace, across here Mo.

FRANCES: The back's lovely isn't it Carol?

CAROL: Oh the back's superb. It's got no back. Haven't you seen it Berni?

BERNADETTE: No . . . I like to save it for the actual day. I like to get me first glimpse of it in Church.

CAROL: Agh that's nice isn't it eh? That's really nice Bern.

BERNADETTE (*calling*): We're all so happy for y'Linda.

FRANCES: What makes it really special is that it's Linda.

CAROL: Ogh I know. I always thought Linda'd be the last one to get married, if she ever got married at all. Oh not 'cos she isn't eligible. She is, she's very eligible.

BERNADETTE: She could have been a model if she's wanted to.

CAROL: Ogh I know. No I'm not saying that. What I mean is . . .

Linda was always like sort of independent wasn't she? Y'know what I mean?

Murmers of agreement.

Like she wouldn't take things seriously would she? An' then she just announces that she's getting' married. An' she's not in the club or anythin' like that, is she?

BERNADETTE: Love, Carol. Love changes you. Love makes you grow up.

CAROL: Tch. Ah . . . I'm glad. I'm so glad for y'Linda.

BERNADETTE: I know she'll be very happy with Dave. Now it'd be a different matter if it was someone like my feller she was marryin'! Man? My feller? He's an apology! I said to him, last night, I was feelin' a bit turned on, y'know, an' he's lyin' there, snorin' again; that type he is, y'know, head hits the pillow an' he's straight asleep. I looked at him, lyin' there an' I said to him, I said . . . "Hey, it's a bloody good job they didn't have the Trades Descriptions Act when they christened you Dick!"

The GIRLS *laugh.*

FRANCES: Go away Berni. The poor feller's probably worn out with you. You'd be moanin' about not gettin' enough if y'were married to Rod Stewart.

BERNADETTE: You what? 'Ey I bet me an' Rod'd get on like a house on fire.

CAROL: Oh imagine bein' married to someone like Rod Stewart. You'd have your own big house, servants, a swimming pool, all the clothes y'wanted.

MAUREEN. It might all look glamorous Carol, but fame has its drawbacks though.

BERNADETTE: Eh, I'd risk it. Wouldn't you Carol . . . whoa, spit on me Rod!

MAUREEN: No, but honestly Berni, it's true y'know . . . the price of fame is a big one.

The GIRLS *shriek.*

What? . . . What's up? Oh 'ey . . . y'know I didn't mean it like that . . . that's awful . . . eh . . . look, I've smudged me eye now . . . I've got half an eye on me nose . . .

FRANCES: Oh come here. (*She does her make-up for her.*)

CAROL: 'Ey . . . what y'drinkin' tonight?

MAUREEN: I'm goin' on brandy an' Babychams. I could drink them all night.

FRANCES: Yeh, an'y' probably will knowin' you.

CAROL: You wanna try Pernod an' black, Mo. It's great.

FRANCES: Y'don't wanna drink too much tonight. Save y'selves for tomorrow.

CAROL: The fellers won't be doin' that will they?

BERNADETTE: Y'can bet they'll be pourin' it down them like it's goin' out of fashion.

MAUREEN: Where are they havin' the stag night?

FRANCES: Dave wouldn't tell Linda where they were goin'.

CAROL: I'll bet they've gone to a stag club, watchin' those films . . .

BERNADETTE: Tch. An' here's us come to a borin' dance.

CAROL: Go way Berni. We don't wanna be watchin' blue films.

BERNADETTE: 'Ey, you speak for yourself.

MAUREEN. What are they like Carol?

CAROL: Horrible. All sex.

BERNADETTE: Great!

CAROL: They're not like *Emmanuelle* Mo, that's a lovely film. But with the blue films it's just sex, y'know for the sake of it. With *Emmanuelle* it's like beautiful an' romantic, all in slow motion, now that's how sex should be. All soft an' in colour.

BERNADETTE. That's how it should be Carol, but it never is love.

CAROL: It can be. With the right man it can. I'm not interested in fellers who want to make sex. I want a feller who makes love, not a feller who makes sex.

MAUREEN: I just want a feller.

BERNADETTE: Y'know when my feller was young —

FRANCES: Young? Christ Berni he's only about thirty-two now, isn't he?

BERNADETTE: Yeah, but I'm talking about young inside; I mean he might be young on the outside, but he's a geriatric inside. No, when me an' him were first married we went on a holiday to Devon. We went the pictures one night and saw this film where this couple kept goin' down to the shore and making love —

MAUREEN: Ogh . . . I seen that . . . it's great — all the little waves are lappin' over them aren't they, an' the sun's setting', an' all the music an' that . . . It's a great film that . . .

BERNADETTE: Really beautiful. Magic. So when it was over we

come out the pictures an' me an' my feller walked down to the beach, an' honest to God it was just like the film, y'know, deserted it was, the beach. An' the sun was sinkin' into the horizon. There was nothin' but us an' the sound of the sea, just softly lappin' the beach.

CAROL: Agh isn't that lovely. It sounds like paradise.

BERNADETTE: That's what it was like . . . honest. That's just how I felt, like I was standin' on the edge of Paradise. (*She pauses.*) An' my feller's got his arm around me, an' he sort of squeezed me an' he said, I'll always remember it, y'know what he said?

All the girls are wide-eyed in anticipation, shaking their heads.

'Well are y'gettin' them off or what?'

The GIRLS *laugh.*

FRANCES: 'Ey . . . it'd be great on the films that wouldn't it? Imagine Ryan O'Neal to Ali McGraw? 'Ey girl, d'y' fancy a legover?'

Laughter from the GIRLS.

BERNADETTE: Y'see Carol, it's only half of it y'see in the films. I'll tell y'another thing the film didn't mention: the bloody sand gets everywhere!

MAUREEN (*laughing with the rest of them*): Agh we're having a great time aren't we? Aren't we eh?

BERNADETTE: We were gonna stay down there in Devon. We didn't though. But y'wanna hear my feller. He's always goin' on about movin' down there — y'know if we go out together an' he has a few jars y'can't shut him up about Devon. I say to him, "Well let's do it, come on, let's go" . . . but he wakes up the next day and pretends he never said it. I suppose we'll live and die round here.

CAROL: It's a dump isn't it eh? It's like this place — Christ look at it. Why didn't we go to a club?

FRANCES: Linda wanted to come here. It's her hen night, she chooses where we go.

CAROL: Why did she choose here though? God it's dyin' on its feet this place.

FRANCES: There's a group on after the disco though, isn't there? She said she wanted to dance to live music not just to records.

CAROL: I hate groups, they're not half as good as the records. What have they got a group for?

FRANCES: They tryin' t'bring some life back t'the place.

BERNADETTE: It's dyin' this place is.

FRANCES: It's dead.

CAROL: They'd have to do more than just stick a group on after the disco if they wanted this place to come alive again.

BERNADETTE: It's like everythin' else round here Carol, the life's just drainin' away from the place, but no-one ever does anythin' about it. It's like round our way, y'know what they do if a wall's fallin' down — they give it a coat of p̄aint. They do.

CAROL: Well I think we should've gone to a club.

FRANCES: Well we can do that afterwards. But Linda wanted to come here first.

MAUREEN: 'Ey . . . wouldn't it be awful if the fellers turned up as well?

CAROL (*shocked*): Oh God Maureen don't say things like that. If Linda saw Dave on her weddin' night, that'd be it, y'know.

MAUREEN: I know . . . that's what I'm sayin' — y'marriage would be doomed to perpetual bad luck if y'saw your feller the night before.

BERNADETTE: 'Ey . . . maybe that's what happened to me eh?

FRANCES: What's she doin' in there anyway? (*She bangs on the WC door.*) Linda . . .
No answer.
Linda! Linda are you comin' out of there?

LINDA: No!
We see the foyer doors swing open. ROBBIE, BILLY and KAV are struggling to get the legless DAVE into the Gents.

ROBBIE (*to BILLY*): Hold the door. Just hold the door will y'.
He does so.

KAV: Jesus!
They get him through the swing doors which BILLY continues to hold open.

BILLY: No . . . y'see the problem is that y'not manœuvring him right. You've got to manœuvre correctly. Yeh.

KAV: I'll manœuvre you in a minute.

BILLY: What?

DICK: What y'doing?

BILLY: I'm holdin' the door like y'said. Yeh.

ROBBIE: We're in now, dickhead! Come here will y'? Get hold.
He lets BILLY take his place. He looks down at the stain on

his trousers, holds open the door to the Gents. They begin to get him in.
Agh look at that. Jesus! Curried bleedin' chicken all over me.

KAV: It's disaster for you Robbie. Disaster.
ROBBIE begins to help get DAVE into the Gents.   ,
An' that little one was givin' you the big eye on the way in.

BILLY: It's all physics y'see. I read about it. Yeh.

ROBBIE: Was she? Which one?

KAV: Know that little one in the cloakroom?

ROBBIE: That little one? Looks like Bianca Jagger?

KAV: Yeh . . . that's the one.

ROBBIE: Was she givin' me the eye?
They try to get DAVE into the WC.

BILLY (*as they do so*): No, see . . . he's a dead weight . . . you've got to take that into account. Yeh.

ROBBIE: I thought she was givin' me the eye, that one.

KAV: Y'can forget now though can't y'? You've got no chance with spewed curry all over y'. Y'll stink all night like a Chinese chippy.

ROBBIE: All right, all right. I'll wash it off. Come on, get him sorted out, then I can get me kecks clean.
They get him into the WC.
Where's Eddy? He should be here givin' us a hand.

KAV: He went the bar.

ROBBIE: As long as he's not tryin' to chat up that little Bianca one.

KAV: No way, I know what Eddy's like. He never chats tarts.

BILLY: He gets one when he wants one though. Yeh.

KAV: Yeh, but he doesn't chat them up. He just waits till the end of the night, sees one an' says "Come here you!" An' they do y'know. But he won't waste his time chattin' them up.

ROBBIE: He'd have no chance anyway. Not with competition from me. See me when I get out on that floor. They can't take their eyes off me.

KAV: They will when they smell that spewed curry all over y'.

ROBBIE (*to* BILLY): That's you that soft lad! Gettin' us to go the Chinese before we start drinkin' instead of afterwards.

BILLY: No y' wrong there Robbie. Yeh. See, I said we should go to the Chinese first 'cos it puts a linin' on y'stomach.

ROBBIE: Yeh. An' it's put a linin' all over my suit as well!

KAV: Come on . . . lift him so his head's over the bowl.

BILLY (*as they struggle with* DAVE): I didn't know Robbie.
I didn't know he'd start drinking Black Velvets. An' he'd been
on double Southern Comforts before that y'know. I said to
him ' That's a lethal combination that Dave '. Yeh.

ROBBIE: Come one . . . lift him . . . an' keep him over that side.
If he gets me other leg I'm done for!
*They manage to get him arranged. We see only his legs sticking
out. They stand back.*

BILLY: You wanna put your fingers down your throat Dave.

ROBBIE: You wanna stick y'fingers down your throat. An' keep
them there. Give us all a rest.

BILLY: I'm only tellin' him Robbie. 'Cos if he got it all up he
could start drinkin' again. He's not gonna have much of a
stag night if he spends it all in here, is he?

KAV (*looking at* DAVE): 'Ey it's a good job his tart can't see him
now isn't it?

ROBBIE: She'd just laugh, her, she's mental.

KAV: She's a good laugh though isn't she? She's all right Linda is.

ROBBIE: She drinks as much as him y'know. I was goin' out with
this crackin' tart once, y'know, nice, smart girl she was. We
went out on a foursome with Dave an' his tart. I got the first
round in, asked them what they were havin'. This girl I'm with
she said er, a Babycham or a Pony or somethin', y'know, a
proper tarts' drink. Know what Dave's tart asked for eh?
A pint of bitter! That's dead true that, she wasn't jokin'.
I was dead embarrassed. I'm out with this nice girl for the first
time an' Dave's tart's actin' like a docker.

KAV: She is a laugh though isn't she?

ROBBIE: Laugh. The one I was with, she never came out with me
again after that. I said to Dave after, fancy lettin' your tart
behave like that. 'She's always the same,' he said. 'But she'll
settle down when she's married.' I wouldn't take the chance.

BILLY: They do calm down Robbie. Women, y'can't get a laugh
out of them once they've turned thirty.

KAV (*beginning to draw on the wall*): I like Linda.

ROBBIE (*wetting paper towels and beginning to try a repair job
on his trousers*): What y'doin' Kav?

KAV: Just me name. (*He is beginning an elaborate scroll which is
intended to form his name.*)

BILLY (*watching*): 'Ey that's dead good that. Yeh. I didn't know you could do that Kav. It's good that isn't it? (*He watches for a moment.*)

KAV *suddenly crosses it all out.*

KAV: Agh . . .

ROBBIE: He's a good artist Kav is.

BILLY: 'Ey don't cross it out. It's dead good that. Yeh.

KAV: It was crap.

BILLY: I thought it was cracker.

KAV: Useless. Y'shoulda seen the stuff I did in the Top Rank Suite. What was it like Robbie?

ROBBIE: Didn't y'see that Billy? It was smart that was. Y'know he did a big drawin', didn't y' Kav, on the back of a bog door, covered the whole door it was . . .

KAV: Took me weeks to do that y'know. Every time we went the Top Rank I spent longer in the bogs than I did on the dance floor.

ROBBIE: It was like abstract wasn't it? Not like that stupid abstract suff though — y'could see picture in it couldn't y'Kav?

KAV: Even Eddy said that was good, didn't he? But then we went in there one week an' they'd had the painters in to paint out all the writin' in the bogs. They stippled all over me picture with Artex an' put up a sign saying they'd prosecute anyone found defacin' the place.

BILLY: How d'y'draw like that eh?

KAV: I dunno. It's dead easy. I just do it.

BILLY: I wish I could draw like that . . . don't you Robbie.

ROBBIE: Too right. I'd spend all day drawin' me own porny pictures.

BILLY: Ogh I can do them . . . gis y'pencil Kav. Yeh. (*He takes the pencil and begins drawing on the wall.*)

ROBBIE (*inspecting his trousers*): Ah . . . look at that. It's gonna take ages to dry now.

BILLY: There's no rush anyway. We can't just leave Dave here can we?

ROBBIE: On y'bike. He'll be all right. We can keep nippin' in to have a look at him. Where's Eddy anyway? He should be here. Dave's his best mate.

KAV: Eddy doesn't like it when y'get pissed. It gets him narked.

BILLY: Eddy never gets legless himself though does he? It's 'cos he's captain of the team. He thinks he should set an example.

KAV: He's dead professional Eddy, isn't he? An' he's dead serious about his football. He's dead serious about everythin'.

ROBBIE: It's only Sunday League though isn't it? I mean it's not professional football is it?

KAV: Don't let Eddy hear y'say that.

ROBBIE (*showing his trousers to* KAV): That look all right or what?

KAV (*non-committal*): It's all right.

BILLY: Y'll never get that off properly with water Robbie. Y'need petrol. Yeh.

ROBBIE: Well I'll tell y'what . . . why don't you sod off down the garage an' get a can!

BILLY: What? No, listen. If there were still petrol lighers you'd be OK wouldn't y'? It's all gas though now isn't it? See that's an example of where technology makes significant advances an' losses at the same time.

ROBBIE: Yeh that's just what I was thinkin'.

BILLY: No listen, I read about it. See if they still had petrol lighters you'd be able to take the cotton wool out an' clean your kecks with it wouldn't y'? Yeh. You wouldn't be stinkin' of curry then.

ROBBIE: Yeh. I'd just be stinkin' of friggin' petrol wouldn't I?

BILLY: No. It'd evaporate. Yeh.

ROBBIE: I wish you'd bleedin' evaporate! (*He notices* BILLY's *drawing.*) What the fuck's that?

BILLY: It's a tart. With nothin' on! Yeh.

KAV: She's got no arms or legs!

BILLY: I know.

ROBBIE: An' where's her head?

BILLY: I don't do heads. I only do the important bits. I'm a primitive!

ROBBIE: You're a fuckin' idiot. Y've given her three tits!

BILLY: Where?

ROBBIE (*pointing*): There!

BILLY: That's her stomach.

KAV: Well why's it got a nipple on it?

BILLY: That's not a nipple — that's a belly button.

ROBBIE: Anyway soft lad, who told y'heads weren't important?

The way a tart looks, her face an' that . . . it's dead important.
There's nothin' better than a beautiful girl.

BILLY: They're all the same when y'get down to it though aren't
they?

ROBBIE: Get lost. When y'get married y'spend longer looking at
them than y'do screwin' them, don't y'? I'll tell y'la, when I
get married she'll be a cracker my missis will, beautiful.

KAV: She might be a cracker when y'get married to her Robbie
but she won't stay that way.

ROBBIE: She bleedin' will!

KAV: Go 'way Robbie. Y'know what the tarts round here are
like; before they get married they look great some of them.
But once they've got y'they start lettin' themselves go. After
two years an' a couple of kids, what happens eh? They start
leavin' the make-up off don't they, an' puttin' on weight.
Before y'know where y'are the cracker y'married's turned
into a monster.

EDDY *enters through the double doors and heads for the
Gents.*

ROBBIE: My missis isn't gonna be like that. If any tart of mine
starts actin' slummy she'll be booted out on her arse. A
woman has got a responsibility to her feller. No tart of mine's
gonna turn fat.

BILLY: I like a bit of weight. Somethin' t'get hold of.

EDDY *enters. He goes straight to the urinal.*

KAV: What's the talent like out there Eddy?

EDDY: I don't know about the talent. The ale's last!

BILLY: Yeh, y'know why that is Eddy? Eh? It's 'cos it's pumped
up with top pressure.

EDDY: Is that right?

BILLY: Yeh. I'm a real ale man I am.

EDDY: Who's smart idea was it to come here? We coulda stayed
in the pub.

ROBBIE: There's no talent in the pub Eddy.

BILLY: CAMRA. Y'know, the Campaign for Real Ale. I support
that. I've got a badge.

ROBBIE (*giving up the cleaning attempt*): What am I gonna do?
That little Bianca one's gonna be all over me in half an hour.
What's she gonna say if she can smell curry everywhere?

KAV: Tell her it's the latest aftershave.

EDDY: 'Madras: For Men'.

ROBBIE: 'Ey yeh . . . 'Things happen to a feller who uses Madras for Men.'

KAV: Yeh. Instead of gettin' y'oats y'get chicken byriani.

ROBBIE: No danger. I'm on I am. See her givin' me the eye did y'?

KAV: Yeh . . . it was me who told y'!

EDDY: Tarts! Women!

BILLY (*laughing*): He's always on about tarts him, isn't he Eddy?

EDDY: Y'know your problem Robbie . . . y'were born with y'brains between y'legs.
KAV *and* BILLY *laugh.*

ROBBIE: That's not a problem.

EDDY: Isn't it?

ROBBIE: What's wrong with likin' the women eh Eddy?

EDDY (*looking in at* DAVE): Look at him! You'll end up like him Robbie. See him, he's the best inside player I've ever seen. But it's all over for him. Well, it will be after tomorrow.

ROBBIE: Christ Eddy, he's gettin' married, not havin' his legs sawn off.

EDDY: You just watch him over the next few months. I've seen it before. Once they get married the edge goes. Before long they start missing one odd game, not turnin' up. You mark my words. The next thing is they stop playin' altogether. They have t'take the kids out on a Sunday, or they go down the club at dinnertime, drinkin'. Or they just can't get out of bed 'cos they've been on the nest all night. Nah . . . it's the beginnin' of the end for him.

BILLY (*approaching* EDDY): I'm not gonna get married Eddy I'm stayin' at home with me mam.

KAV: Don't you think that woman's suffered enough?

BILLY: I'll still be there, playin' in defence, when I'm forty Eddy. Yeh. I keep meself fit I do.

EDDY: I know y'do Billy. Y' not like Robbie are y'? Robbie's a tarts' man. You'll end up like Dave you will, Robbie.

ROBBIE: Ah give it a rest will y'Eddy. Sunday League football isn't the be all and end all is it? This is supposed to be a stag night, not a pre-match pep talk.

EDDY: Who the fuck are you talkin' to? I'll remember that Robbie, I'll remember that when I'm pickin' this week's team.

BILLY (*after a pause*): Are y'droppin' him Eddy?

KAV: Are y'Eddy?

ROBBIE: I don't care!

EDDY: Don't y'? Not even when there's an American Scout gonna be watchin' us?

KAV: Watchin' our game Eddy? On Sunday?

BILLY: I'm at the top of me form y'know Eddy. Yeh.

KAV: An American Scout Eddy?

EDDY: There's talent scouts from America combin' this country lookin' for potential.

KAV: 'Ey . . . we'll be without Dave. Dave won't be playin' on Sunday, will he?

EDDY: That's his hard luck isn't it? If he wants t'be in Spain when we've got a scout watchin' us, that's his hard luck!

ROBBIE: Ah come on Eddy . . . let's get out there . . . listen to a few sounds, it's great when the music's playin'. Come on, have a few jars an' a laugh an' that.
EDDIE *snorts and turns away.*
Look Eddy, I'm set up already with a smart little one, just like Bianca Jagger, isn't she Kav? She's bound to have a crackin' mate with her, Eddy. I'll have the little Bianca one, you take her mate.

EDDY: What? Spend all night chattin' up some dumb tart, two hours of sufferin' her talkin' an' drinkin' and dancin', just to get a poke at her. Sod off.

BILLY (*at* ROBBIE*'s shoulder*): I'll take her mate for y' Robbie.

ROBBIE: On y'bike! You're a bleedin' liability you are.

BILLY: Well. You always go after the smartest tarts in the place. I get nervous with that type.

ROBBIE: I've told y' haven't I? Always go for the crackers. Loads of fellers make that mistake, they see really smart tarts an' they think they've got no chance. But it's the opposite. If a tart looks really good, an' y'can see she's spent hours gettin' herself to look somethin' special it's 'cos she wants someone to tap off with her.

BILLY: But I just get shy Robbie.

KAV (*to* BILLY): Come on. Me an' you it is. But listen . . . no standin' at the side of the floor all night. When I say go in, we go in . . . right?

BILLY: All right.

ROBBIE: Come on.
The three of them move towards the door.

EDDY: 'Ey.
They stop.
Hold on!
Pause.
Where youse goin'?

ROBBIE: What Eddy?

EDDY: What about him? (*He indicates* DAVE.)

ROBBIE: What about him?

EDDY (*after a pause*): Just gonna leave him here are y'?
The three of them, on the spot, look at each other.
He's our mate isn't he?

KAV: Course he is Eddy.

ROBBIE: Yeh.

EDDY: An' y' just gonna leave him here are y'? Y'gonna leave
him like this while y' go off listenin' to cheap music an'
chasin' tarts?

ROBBIE: Ah 'ey Eddy . . .

EDDY: Ah 'ey what? Y' just gonna fuck off on y' mate when he's
incapable, needs lookin' after.
Pause. EDDY *looks at them.*

KAV: He'll be all right Eddy.

EDDY. That's loyalty for y' isn't it?
Pause.

ROBBIE: Well you look after him Eddy! We've had our turn.
Christ we got him in here didn't we? Look, spewed curry all
over me best suit.

EDDY: Haven't you heard of loyalty?
Pause. They can't move.
Go on then . . . piss off. I'll look after him. I'm stayin' in the
bar. I'll keep nippin' in to see that he's all right.
Pause.
Go on . . . sod off!
They don't move.
It's last out there anyway. All it is is music, fuckin' music.

BILLY: I like music Eddy.

EDDY: You would wouldn't y'. 'Cos y' fuckin' soft, like them!
Go on then, get out there, an' listen to it.
Pause.

KAV: What's wrong with music Eddy?

EDDY (*after a pause, looking at them*): Y'know what music does don't y'?

ROBBIE: It makes y' feel good Eddy.

EDDY: Makes y' feel good! Makes y' go soft.
Pause. EDDY looks at them.

ROBBIE: Come on Eddy, come with us. Dave'll be all right.

KAV: There's a live group on after, Eddy.

EDDY (*turning to look into the WC*): Is there? I'll bet they're shite as well!

ROBBIE: They're not a local band Eddy. They're up from London. They'll be good.

EDDY: They didn't look like Londoners to me. I just saw them comin' in. They looked local. I thought I recognized one of them.

ROBBIE: Nah . . . That'll be from off the telly Eddy. They're big league this lot, honest.

EDDY: What d' y' want me t'do Robbie? Rush off home for me autograph book?

ROBBIE (*to the others*): Tch . . . agh . . . come on . . .
They turn and go into the corridor. EDDY follows them.

KAV: Y' comin' with us Eddy?

EDDY: Nah — it's a stag night isn't it? Y' know what y' do on a stag night don't y'?

KAV: What Eddy?

EDDY: Get pissed!
They exit from the corridor.

CAROL (*shouting*): Linda . . . are you comin' out?

LINDA (*after a pause*): No!

BERNADETTE: Linda . . . Linda love . . . why not?

LINDA: Because, Berni love . . . you are getting right up my fucking nose!

CAROL: Linda d'you really think that's appropriate language for a bride-to-be?

BERNADETTE: Take no notice of her Carol . . . she doesn't mean it. They all go a bit funny when they're gettin' married. She's probably just havin' a little cry to herself. They do that on the night before.

CAROL (*whispering*): Agh yeh. Agh . . .

MAUREEN (*leaning in, joining the whispering*): What?

CAROL: She's havin' a little cry. Did you Berni, did you cry the night before you got married?

BERNADETTE: No love. I've just been cryin' ever since!

MAUREEN (*to* FRANCES): Come here . . . Frankie come here . . . leave her . . . she's just havin' a little cry to herself . . . Agh.

FRANCES: Cryin' . . . what for?

MAUREEN: Frances! She's crying for what she'll be losing tomorrow.

FRANCES (*laughing*): Oh 'ey Maureen, she lost that years ago, just like the rest of us.

MAUREEN: No . . . I didn't mean that. But y'do give something up when y' get married don't y'? You give up bein' a girl when y' get married.

FRANCES: What d' y' turn into instead — a feller? Her Dave's not gonna be too happy about that tomorrow night is he?

MAUREEN (*slow*): What?

FRANCES (*banging on the WC door*): Linda . . . come on . . . the night's gonna be over.

MAUREEN: Frances . . . leave her with her thoughts as a single girl. Come here. (*Whispering.*) What have y' bought for them?

FRANCES: Weddin' presents y' mean?

MAUREEN: Shush! Yeh. I thought I'd go for something functional. I mean it's nice having pictures an' ornaments but y' can't do anything with them can you? Apart from looking at them!

BERNADETTE: What have y' bought them then Mo?

MAUREEN (*delighted*): A pair of barbecue chairs! In saddle brown.

FRANCES (*aghast*): What are they?

MAUREEN: Barbecue chairs. Y' know for in the summer when you have friends round for a barbecue.

FRANCES: Oh that'll be very functional Maureen. They'll have a great time with a barbecue in a block of flats six floors high!

MAUREEN: Oh . . . oh . . . 'ey . . . (*Thinking.*) But they will have a balcony won't they?
The others look at each other in disbelief.
No . . . I don't mean they'll be able to have a barbecue on the balcony. But they'll be able to sit out there won't they?

FRANCES: An' watch the sun go down on the other blocks of flats!

MAUREEN: I'll tell her that they're balcony chairs. She won't know the difference will she? I'll tell her they're balcony chairs.

CAROL: We all clubbed together in work. We got them a coffee percolator. Y'know for real coffee.

BERNADETTE: Ah that'll be nice Carol. They'll be able to sit an' have coffee when their friends come round.

FRANCES: Or when they're sittin' out on the balcony! What have you got them Berni?

BERNADETTE: My feller knows someone at work who makes antique furniture, they're great. I've got them a coffee table in antique.

FRANCES: Christ I hope they like coffee! I've got them a coffee set!

MAUREEN: Ah that'll be really swish that, won't it? They will like coffee Frances. You might drink tea when you're at home with your mum, but when you become a couple you drink coffee together. An' that's worked out really lovely hasn't it? Ah . . . just think — they'll be able to sit at Bernadette's coffee table, drinking coffee out of Carol's percolator in the coffee cups that you gave them, sittin' on my balcony chairs. Agh. It'll remind them of us won't it?

FRANCES: They'll never be able to forget us Mo. (*She knocks on the WC door*) Linda!

BERNADETTE: Oh come on Linda love . . . all the good lookin' lads'll have gone home if they think I'm not here.

ROBBIE *and* BILLY *burst through the double doors and into the Gents.*

ROBBIE: The bitch . . . the stuck-up bitch . . .

BILLY (*checking out* DAVE): All right Dave. Yeh. She was dead fuckin' humpety anyway! She was destroyed when you got in close.

ROBBIE: I've told you three times haven't I? What d' y' want me t' do, write it out for y'?

BILLY: But I couldn't hear y' in there, with the music an' that . . . go on, what did she say?

ROBBIE: She said — 'I never dance with men in suits.'

BILLY: Is that what she said?

ROBBIE: I thought she was jokin' at first, y' know, comin' on with the laughs an' that. I give her a big smile an' said to her, 'I'll tell y' what love, if y' don't like suits why don't we go back t' your place an' y' can take it off for me'.

BILLY (*laughing*): Did y'? What did she say?

ROBBIE: She walked away. She walked away from me. What's wrong with suits, eh? Cost sixty-five quid this did, from Hepworths. No rubbish goes on my back. The stuck-up cow. She doesn't look like Bianca Jagger anyway. She looks more like Mick Jagger. I told her though. Should've heard me Billy . . . classic it was; 'Eh love,' I said, 'I don't waste my time on tarts who don't appreciate quality.'

BILLY: Is that what you said Robbie?

ROBBIE: Too right . . . ! 'This suit, this suit', I said, 'cost every penny of sixty-five notes.' See her face did y'? See her face when I told her that?

BILLY: Yeh Robbie. An' she said 'You were robbed.'

ROBBIE (*stung*): I thought you said you couldn't hear!
    EDDY *enters the corridor.*

BILLY: I couldn't hear what you said Robbie. I heard what she said though.

ROBBIE: Well y'wanna get y' friggin' ears tested don't y' 'cos she never said that.

BILLY: She did Robbie, I was standin' —
    EDDY *comes into the Gents.*

ROBBIE (*as EDDY enters*): All right Eddy. We were just keepin' an eye on Dave for y'.

EDDY: Good lad.

ROBBIE: Doin' y' a favour.

EDDY: Yeh . . . Kav's doin' the same for you out there!

ROBBIE: What?

EDDY: Know that tart who keeps givin' you the elbow, that really smart-lookin' one, Kav's dancin' with her. She's all over him as well!

ROBBIE: I don't care, I wasn't interested anyway . . . she was destroyed.
    EDDY *laughs.* ROBBIE *heads for the door.*

ROBBIE (*to BILLY*): Come on.
    ROBBIE *and BILLY go into the corridor, then exit.*

EDDY: Go on then . . . go on . . . piss off. Piss off t' y' dancin'. An' y' music. Music . . . bleedin' music makes me wanna spew! Eh Dave . . . is that what made you spew, the music eh (*laughing*) music! (*He produces a quarter bottle and takes the cap off.*)

In the Ladies. The WC door opens. LINDA *stands in the door frame.*

LINDA: 'But if we do not change, tomorrow has no place for us.' It says so . . . on the wall in there. (*She goes to the mirror and simply pushes her hair into place.*)

CAROL: Tch. There must have been a student's dance here. No-one with sense'd write somthin' like that.

MAUREEN: They write dead stupid things don't they, students.

CAROL: I went to a dance once, y'know at the students union. Y' should have seen the bogs, they were full of writin'. An' it was last. Y' couldn't understand any of it. Honest.

BERNADETTE: What was it like?

CAROL: Y'know all dead soft stuff. Somethin' about God bein' a woman. It was terrible. An' this thing that said 'a woman needs a fish like a feller needs a bike' y' know really stupid stuff like that.

BERNADETTE: An' the bloody tax my feller pays to keep them students. Wouldn't y' think with all them brains they'd write somethin' sensible on the bog wall.

FRANCES: Take no notice of her, Berni. There were some really good things. There was this great thing, it said 'Love is blind, marriage is an institution, who wants to live in an institute for the blind'.

MAUREEN: God Frances . . . that's wicked . . . don't say things like that.

LINDA: Come on . . . let's go.

FRANCES: You haven't done y' make-up.

LINDA: I can't be bothered. Come on.

FRANCES: Y' not goin' into a dance without y' make-up on!

LINDA: Why not?

BERNADETTE: We'll wait for y' Linda . . . go on, do y' make-up. Y' don't wanna look a mess.

FRANCES (*taking* LINDA's *arm*): Come on. I'll do it for y'. Be quicker then.

LINDA (*turning away*): Tch. I'll do it meself then. Go on, you lot have waited long enough. Go on, I'll see y' in there. (*She takes out her make-up.*)

CAROL: Linda, we're y' mates aren't we? It's your hen night.

Y' don't think we'd desert y' do y'?

LINDA: Y' not deserting me. I'll come an' find y' when I'm ready.

BERNADETTE: We never leave someone behind. We only go out when we're all ready.

CAROL: We stick together.

LINDA: Why don't y' all come on me honeymoon?

BERNADETTE: We would Linda love, but I'm afraid if I was there, you wouldn't get a look in.
The GIRLS, apart from LINDA, laugh.

LINDA: Look . . . I am a big girl now y'know. I can find me way out of the Ladies an' into the dance.

BERNADETTE: Linda . . . it's your hen night, we stick with you.

LINDA: Yeh, until some feller wants t' take you outside. Then you'll be off like a flash.

BERNADETTE: Well . . . you've got to get a bit of fresh air haven't you?

LINDA: Is that what you call it?

BERNADETTE: With some of them that's what it feels like!
Shrieks from the GIRLS.

LINDA: Well you'd better watch out tonight, Berni. You're gonna have a bit of competition.

BERNADETTE: Ooh. Tch. Who from?

LINDA: Well y' don't think I'm gonna end my hen night stuck in the bar like some old married woman do y'? I'm gonna get out on that floor an' forget about everythin' else. I'm gonna get real legless. If it's a last fling then that's what I'm gonna make it.

FRANCES: Well y' better get a move on or your last fling'll be already flung. Come here, let me do it. Go on, you lot go . . . y' can be gettin' the drinks in.

CAROL: Yeh . . . come on then . . . what y' havin'?

FRANCES: Get us a port an' lemon. What d' y' want, Linda?

MAUREEN: Come on, let's go then.

LINDA: Get me a pint of bitter.

BERNADETTE: Linda love, no come on. A joke's a joke. I've seen you do that before love and we all think it's a good laugh. But not tonight. It's a hen night you're on, not a stag night. Now come on, something a bit more lady-like.

LINDA: All right, I'll have a pint of mild!

BERNADETTE: Oh sod off . . .

CAROL: We'll get y' a Snowball Linda, y'like them.

LINDA: All right. With a nice little cherry on the top.

BERNADETTE: Come on. We'll be in the bar.

CAROL: We'll just have a drink an' listen to the sounds till you come out . . .

BERNADETTE: Ogh . . . come on. Give us some music. Music, music, music. It's an aphrodisiac to me.

LINDA: Bromide'd be an aphrodisiac to you.

BERNADETTE: Too right . . . ooogh . . . come on girls . . .
They go into the corridor and exit.
FRANCES is fixing LINDA's hair and make-up.

FRANCES: It's great the way music gets to y' though, isn't it? Y' can come to a disco or a dance an' be feelin' really last. But once y' walk into the music it gives y' a lift doesn't it? Makes y' feel special.

LINDA: Yeh. (*After a pause.*) I get lost in music I do.

FRANCES: Yeh I do that.

LINDA: I become someone else when the music's playin'. I do y' know.

FRANCES: Yeh I'm like that.

LINDA: D' y' know if it wasn't for music I wouldn't be gettin' married tomorrow.

FRANCES (*laughing*): Oh don't be stupid Linda. You're nuts sometimes. Y' are y' know.

LINDA: I'm not bein' stupid. We were dancin' when he asked me to marry him. 'When A Man Loves A Woman' it was. I heard this voice in me ear, like it was part of the music, sayin' 'Will y' marry me?' So I said yeh. I would've said yeh if I'd been dancin' with Dracula's ugly brother.

FRANCES: Linda stop bein' soft.

LINDA: When the music stopped I looked up an' there was Dave, beamin' down at me, talkin' about gettin' married an' I'm wonderin' what he's on about, then I remembered. An' the next thing y' know I'm here, tonight.

FRANCES: Linda!

LINDA: Oh come on, hurry up an' get me hair done. All I wanna do is get out there an' dance the night away. There mightn't be another opportunity after tonight.

FRANCES: Linda, you're gettin' married, not gettin' locked up!

There y' go. (*She begins putting her implements away.*)

LINDA (*looking at herself in the mirror*): Y' do get frightened
y' know. I mean if it was just gettin' married to Dave it'd be
OK, he's all right Dave is. But it's like, honest, it's like I'm
gettin' married to a town.

FRANCES: To a what?

LINDA: It's not just like I'm marryin' Dave. It's like if I marry
him I marry everythin'. Like, I could sit down now an' draw
you a chart of everythin' that'll happen in my life after
tomorrow.

FRANCES (*looking at her*): D' y' know something Linda, you're
my best mate, but half the time I think you're a looney!

LINDA (*going into an exaggerated looney routine*): I am . . . (*She
plays it up.*)

FRANCES (*laughing*): Linda . . . don't mess y' hair up . . .

LINDA (*quickly knocking her hair back into place, preparing to
leave*): Well . . . look at it this way, after tomorrow I'll have
me own Hoover, me own colour telly an' enough equipment
to set up a chain of coffee bars.

They go into the corridor and exit.

In the Gents, EDDY *is taking a swig from the bottle.*

EDDY (*laughing*): Ey, Dave . . . d' y' wanna drink? (*He laughs.*)
'Ey, can't y' hear me Dave? Jesus . . . you wouldn't hear if a
bomb went off would y'? It's your own fault Dave. Y' can't
blame me lad. It's all your own fault. Y' don't have to drink
do y'. See, y' don't have to do anythin'. (*He pauses.*) The
US, Dave, an' you coulda' been comin' with me . . . you
should've been comin' with me. Not with a wife though.
Y' can't travel when there's too much baggage weighin' y'
down. (*He pauses.*) She's OK your tart. She's all right. But
round here, if y' get married Dave, y' trapped then. It's the
end. Y' don't go anywhere, y' just stay forever in this fuckin'
dyin' dump. It's hard to get out anyway Dave, you know it
is. Look at all the scouts who've seen our team. But I'm still
here aren't I eh? It's hard to go. But once y' get married round
here, y' never gonna go at all. You've got t' fuckin' leave
y' self free Dave so that when the time comes y' can be off
without a word to anyone. Y've got t' leave yourself free
like me. I can go anywhere Dave, anywhere, at any time.
There's nothin' holdin' me down. (*He pauses.*) But if you
don't wanna come with me, if you wanna get married to some
tart, well you do it. Yeh you do it! Mate? Soft get . . .

ROBBIE *and* BILLY *enter from the foyer and go towards the Gents.*
EDDY *goes to take a swig from the bottle.* ROBBIE *and* BILLY *enter.* EDDY *quickly hides the bottle in his pocket.* BILLY *stands at the door.* ROBBIE *goes to the urinal.*

ROBBIE: All right Eddy. (*He sees* BILLY *holding the door.*) Come in an' close the bleedin' door will y'?

BILLY (*entering*): What have we come in here for? We told them we'd see them in the bar. Yeh.

ROBBIE: Yeh . . . soft lad . . . we told them that 'cos we wanted t' get rid of them didn't we?

BILLY: Did we? Mine was nice!

ROBBIE: Nice? Shoulda seen her Eddy, she could have had the star part in *Jaws*.

EDDY: Where's Kav?

ROBBIE: What?

BILLY: We saw him goin' out the back with that one who looks like Bianca Jagger.

ROBBIE: I hope he gets a dose.

EDDY (*moving to the door*): I'm goin' the bar. (*Snorting.*) Soft gets . . .

BILLY: Are you pissed Eddy?

EDDY (*wheeling and grabbing him*): Have you ever seen me pissed?

BILLY: No Eddy.

EDDY: No Eddy . . . I don't get pissed. I'm not like you. I'm not like him . . . I don't get pissed.

BILLY: No Eddy, what I meant was —

ROBBIE: Shut up Billy . . .

EDDY: Yeh, shut it. Soft arse! (*He pushes him away and goes to the door.*) Look after Dave. I'm goin' the bar.
Eddy goes into the corridor and exits.

BILLY: I think he is a bit pissed y' know Robbie.

ROBBIE: Well there's no need to go tellin' him is there? Eddy thinks he never gets pissed. I've seen him in a state loads of times. But I never tell him.

BILLY: Well why doesn't he just say, y' know, that he's pissed?

ROBBIE: I don't know, do I? He just likes to pretend, y' go along with him don't y'? It's like he pretends that one day he's gonna play big league football. Y' just go along with him.

KAV *enters. Sheepish.*

KAV: I'm sorry Robbie.

ROBBIE (*all innocence*): What about Kav? What's up son?

KAV: Y' know.

ROBBIE: What? What?

KAV: I'm sorry about gettin' off with your little Bianca one.
It wasn't my fault though, honest, she was —

ROBBIE: Did you get off with her? Christ y' didn't did y'? Did
you hear that Billy?

KAV: What? What's wrong?

ROBBIE: Ah no . . . you'll be all right though, y' didn't go
outside with her did y'?

KAV: Yeh . . . round the back, why?

ROBBIE: Yeh, but y' didn't slip her one, did y'?

KAV: Yeh . . . she couldn't get out there fast enough.

ROBBIE: Ogh Kav, Kav . . .

KAV: What's up?

ROBBIE: Come on Kav. Why d' y' think I gave her the knock
back?

KAV: What?

ROBBIE: Tommy Stevens told me didn't he? That one who looks
like Mick Jagger's got the clap! Come on Billy . . . those two'll
be up in the bar now. Ogh . . . wanna see these two we've
tapped off with Kav, stunners. What they like Billy?

BILLY: Y' wanna see them Kav. Ugliest boots y' ever saw in y' —

ROBBIE: Go way soft lad . . . take no notice of him, he's blind.
A coughing from the WC takes them over to DAVE.
That's it Dave, go on get it up.

BILLY: It might be a gold clock. Yeh.

KAV: Don't y' think we better get him sobered up? It's his stag
night isn't it?

ROBBIE: Christ you're considerate all of a sudden aren't y'?
I'll bet y' weren't thinkin' of him when y' were round the back
gettin' a dose off that tart.

KAV: I haven't got a dose. You were just messin' . . .

ROBBIE: You wait an' see pal. You wait.

KAV: Go away. Come on . . . let's try an' make him get it all up.

ROBBIE: Ah leave him. Christ it's not a proper stag night if the
groom's conscious.

BILLY: It's bad luck if the groom's sober the night before he gets married, yeh.

ROBBIE: That's right that is. Me dad told me. He was sober on his stag night an' look what happened to him the next day!

KAV: What?

ROBBIE: He married me mother! All right, come on, just get him right over the bowl an' he'll be OK.
In the corridor PETER *enters, carrying a pint. Passing him, carrying cable, is the* ROADIE.

PETER: Have y' cracked it?

ROADIE (*southern accent*): Have we fuck. Every socket we try's an antique. What a bleedin' dump. Every socket I try just blows.

PETER: Keep tryin'.

ROADIE: I'll keep tryin' but I'm tellin' y' it'll be a miracle if you get on tonight. What a place. What a fuckin' town.

PETER: 'Ey dickhead, I'll have you know you're talkin' about my home town.

ROADIE: Yeh . . . an' I can see why y' left it now. Where y' goin'?

PETER: There's no bogs workin' backstage.

ROADIE: See . . . see what I mean? Will I be glad when this one's over.

PETER: Get lost. You'd be moanin' about the state of the plug sockets if we were playin' the bleedin' Hollywood Bowl.

ROADIE: I'll tell you what Peter mate, after this place I'll never complain about a plug socket again.

PETER: Well comin' here's done some good then!

ROADIE: Huh!
The ROADIE *exits.*
PETER *goes into the Gents, pint in hand, smoking, goes into the urinal. He leans back and looks at what the fellers are doing.*

PETER: All right lads. Christ he's in a state isn't he?
They look at him.
What's up with him, one over the eight?

ROBBIE: No, it's his hobby, lookin' down bogs!

PETER (*laughing*): No accountin' for taste eh?
They stand and look at him. He zips up and returns the gaze.

KAV: 'Ey, d' y' get paid for wearin' boots like that?

PETER: What? (*Laughing.*) Good aren't they? (*He shows them off*) Like them?

BILLY: They look like tarts' boots to me.

PETER: They are tarts' boots. Good though aren't they?

ROBBIE (*laughing*): Tarts' boots.

BILLY: I wouldn't even wear them if I was a tart!

PETER (*walking through them and getting a look at Dave*): What's he been drinkin'?

ROBBIE (*aggressively*): Y' what?

PETER: You deaf?

ROBBIE: What the fuck d' you wanna know what he's been drinkin' for?

PETER: It's one of me hobbies, gettin' to know what people drink.

BILLY: He's been on Black Velvets an' Southern Comfort.

PETER: Ah. That type is he? Subtle palate?

KAV: Listen you — who the fuck d' y' think you're talkin' to?

PETER: Kavanagh isn't it? Erm . . . Tony Kavanagh.

KAV: How the fuck d' you know my name? How does he know my name? Listen you, you just . . . (*Pointing.*) Hold on . . . 'ey . . . it is, isn't it it is! You used to live round our way didn't y'?

ROBBIE: Ogh fuck. It's you isn't it?

PETER: I hope so.

BILLY: Who is it?

KAV (*excited*): You know . . . you know him . . . er hold on, hold on, don't tell me . . . it's erm . . . erm.

PETER: Peter . . .

KAV: That's it, that's it . . . I knew it was . . .

ROBBIE: 'Ey, you're famous aren't y'?

KAV: Are you with this group tonight? 'Ey . . . they're famous . . .

BILLY: Who is it?

KAV: 'Ey . . . I always said you were dead good on that guitar y' know, I did didn't I Robbie? Here, look, that's Robbie. Y' remember Robbie don't y'?

PETER: Hia Robbie.

KAV: An' Billy . . . y' remember Billy don't y', Billy Blake?

PETER: Erm . . .

KAV: Ah y' do . . . y' must do . . . his mam an' your mam were mates . . . remember . . .

PETER: Oh yeh . . . all right erm . . .

BILLY: Who is he?

KAV: Christ, is that really you? Look at y' now! An' you used to be just like us! Tch. 'Ey, here's Dave. Y' remember Dave don't y'? (*He leads him over.*)

PETER: Er, no I think er . . .

KAV: Ah y' do. You remember Dave. (*Shouting.*) 'Ey Dave, Dave, wake up . . . look who's here Dave! Dave'll be sick at missin' y'.

PETER: Maybe that's the best thing eh?

KAV (*laughing, too much*): Still kept your sense of humour eh? Great. (*He looks at him.*) I can't believe it.

ROBBIE: What y' doin' playin' in a dump like this?

PETER: It's work isn't it?

KAV (*to anyone*): Gis a piece of paper, where's a piece of paper? (*He goes into the WC.*)

ROBBIE: You're on the radio an' the telly an' that, aren't y'?

PETER: Now an' then.

ROBBIE: An' y' come back playin' in dives like this.

PETER: It's only one gig. It was arranged before the single happened.

ROBBIE: Well y' should've told them to fuck off. Y' don't wanna belittle y' selves do y', playin' holes like this when y' famous. Live in London now do y'?

PETER: Yeh.

ROBBIE: What's it like?

PETER: It's all right man, it's OK.

ROBBIE (*looking at him*): I'll bet it's fuckin' great!

PETER (*smiling*): It's OK.

ROBBIE (*looking at him*): Jesus!

PETER: Small world eh?

KAV (*coming out of the WC with the bog paper*): I'm sorry about the paper, I couldn't find any other . . . (*He offers pencil and paper.*)

PETER: Ah come on man, you don't want . . .

KAV: Put, erm . . . 'To Kav — an old mate'.

PETER: Look man, for Christ's sake you don't want me to do this . . .

KAV: You're jokin' aren't y'? Of course I do . . .

PETER: Look, for Christ's sake I used to live just down the road from you . . .

KAV: I know. I'm gonna show that to people.

PETER *looks at him.* BILLY *comes out of the WC with a piece of paper, joins the queue.* PETER *signs.*

ROBBIE: 'Ey is it true what they say about the tarts, y' know, the groupies.

PETER: A bit of it. Most of it's fiction.

ROBBIE: I'll bet it's not. Jesus I bet you can have anythin' y' want can't y'?

KAV (*looking at his piece of paper*): Ogh . . . look at that!

PETER *takes* BILLY's *paper, signs it.*

ROBBIE: 'Ey, what sort of a car d' y' drive now?

PETER: I haven't got one. Listen, what you lads doin' these days?

ROBBIE: Fuck all, us. Eh, have y' got a big house in London?

PETER: A flat. What, y' all on the dole?

KAV: Nah, we work.

ROBBIE: Got a big house in the country have y'?

PETER: What sort of work's that then?

KAV: Listen, we don't wanna talk about us, it's dead borin'. We just fuckin' work. Go on, tell us all about you. Tell us all about the, y' know, the thingy, an', what it's like an' all about it.

PETER: Go way. What d' y' wanna hear about me for?

KAV: Listen Peter. You're someone who's made it. We're proud of you. We are.

BILLY *has been studying his piece of bog paper.*

BILLY: Who is he?

ROBBIE: Can't you read?

PETER: Look lads . . . I've gorra go. We haven't even got the gear set up yet. Gotta tune up an' that . . .

ROBBIE: Aren't y' gonna come an' have a bevvy with us?

PETER: We're not even set up yet.

KAV: What about afterwards, y' know after the gig?

PETER: Yeh, maybe . . . that's a possibility. See y' lads. 'Ey, look after the Southern Comfort King won't y'?

He goes into the corridor and exits.

KAV: See y' Peter.

ROBBIE: Tarar.

BILLY (*looking up from his paper*): 'Ey . . . that was Peter
　　Taylor! Ogh . . . he's famous. Yeh.

ROBBIE: Imagine comin' back to this dive when y' as big as he is.
　　See his boots. They were smart weren't they?

BILLY: I'm gonna get a pair of them.

ROBBIE: They wouldn't look the same on you.

BILLY: Why won't they?

ROBBIE: They just won't.

KAV: They'll be custom-made anyway.

ROBBIE: Y' wouldn't get nothin' like that round here.

KAV: Christ . . . the way he must live eh?

ROBBIE: I'll bet his tarts never grow old, do they?

BILLY: Boots like that'd suit me.

KAV: I'll bet he's never bored is he? An' he used t' live near us!
　　EDDY enters.
　　Eddy . . . Eddy guess what?

EDDY: I know! Dave's tart's out there!

OTHERS: What?

EDDY: I've just seen her now. She's out there, dancin'!
　　Blackout

END OF ACT ONE

ACT TWO

BERNADETTE *and* CAROL, *laughing, enter the Ladies.*

BERNADETTE: Ogh . . . God! Did y' see the state of him. An' he was serious. He tried to get off with me! He was all of four foot nothin'.

CAROL: What about his mate? He was smaller. An' he had acne. (*Disgusted.*) Oogh, God the thought; four foot nothin' an' spotted all over. He was like a walkin' Eccles cake. Oogh . . .

BERNADETTE: At least you got rid of him after the first dance.

CAROL: I had to Berni. He made me feel ill, honest I hate ugly people. I feel sorry for them like, but no, I had to get rid of him. You should have given yours the elbow straight away.

BERNADETTE: Didn't y' see me tryin'? 'Are you stayin' up?' he says to me. All three foot six of him starin' up at me. I said 'I don't know about stayin' up, don't y' think y' better sit down before y' get trodden on.

CAROL (*shrieking*): Y' didn't . . . Berni . . . Y' could have hurt his feelings.

BERNADETTE: Y' jokin'. He didn't have any feelings. He just ignored everythin'. He wouldn't take no for an answer. I said to him, 'Look son, I'll let y' into a secret, it's no use tryin' it on with me, I'm a lesbian . . .'

CAROL: Berni . . .

BERNADETTE: It did no good. 'That's all right', he said, 'I like a challenge.' By this time I'm dancin' away again, hopin' no-one'd see me with him. And honest to God, he's so small he kept gettin' lost. I'm just walkin' away when he appears again. 'Goin' for a drink are we?' he says, I said to him, ''Ey you'd better run along, Snow White'll be lookin' for you.' Ey, he didn't get it though. 'Oh I'm sorry', I said, 'but I thought you were one of the Seven Dwarfs.' He started laughin' then, y' know, makin' out he's got a sense of humour. 'Oh yeh', he says, 'I'm Dozy,' I said 'You're not friggin' kiddin' . . .'

CAROL *and* BERNADETTE *laugh.*

I'm walkin' away an' he's shoutin' after me ' 'Ey I'll see y' in the bar, I'll be in the bar.' I said 'Yeh, an' that's the best place for you, along with every other pint that thinks it's a quart!' FRANCES *enters.*

CAROL: Frankie . . . have y' been in the bar?

FRANCES: Yeh.

CAROL: Is there a spotted midget in there?

FRANCES: Ogh him? He's destroyed isn't he? An' his mate, just been tryin' to chat me up.

BERNADETTE: Well the two-timin' sod!

FRANCES: Three-timin'. He's chattin' Mo up now.

CAROL: Ogh God.

FRANCES: She's made up!

CAROL: Go way!

FRANCES: She's just standin' there, beamin' down at him with big dreamy eyes. Mind you that might be the Pernod. She's had five in the last half-hour.

BERNADETTE: She'll need a bottle full if she's takin' him on.

MAUREEN, well away, enters. She's singing the chorus of 'Dancing Queen'.

MAUREEN: Whoa . . . hia . . . I feel great! . . . great! That's how I feel . . . great . . . I feel really . . . beautiful . . .

FRANCES: I thought you were off with someone.

MAUREEN (*laughing*): Big John Wayne . . . !

FRANCES: I thought it was all set up Maureen.

MAUREEN: He said, he did, he said to me . . . 'D' y' wanna drink?' So, so I said, 'Yeh, a double Pernod!'

CAROL: Tch. Maureen!

MAUREEN: He said, 'On y' bike.' 'On y' bike', he said, 'y' can have half a lager an' like it.' Honest, cheeky get; he said 'I'm not made of money y' know.' So I said (*laughing*) an' I was dead made up with this, I said to him, 'Listen you, to make you out of money would only cost about three an' a half pence!' (*Laughing.*) An' he got all dead narked then, an' said he was fed up 'cos people had been takin' the piss all night. So y' know what I said, I told him to go for a swim in his half of lager!

She laughs and goes into the song again. Raucous, pitched too high. The others join in.

LINDA enters. She joins in the singing.

We're havin' a good time, aren't we? Aren't we eh? We're all havin' another good time. Ogh sometimes . . . sometimes I feel so happy. Linda . . . Linda, are you havin' a good time?

LINDA: Great Mo.

FRANCES: God, can't y' tell she is? Haven't y' seen her, she hasn't stopped dancin' since she got out there . . . have y' Linda?

LINDA: I love this y' know. I love it when we're all out together an' havin' a laugh. It's good isn't it? It's great.

BERNADETTE: Y' can't beat it when there's a crowd of y'.

LINDA: Come on . . . let's all go out an' have a dance together . . .

FRANCES: Come on yeh, we'll have a line out . . .

CAROL: Agh yeh . . .

LINDA: An' if any fellers try to split us up we'll tell them to sod off . . .

FRANCES (*as she leaves*): Come on . . .

MAUREEN (*as she leaves*): I feel a bit sick . . .

BERNADETTE: Come on . . . (*Pushing* MAUREEN.) Get out . . . you'll be all right . . .
They all go down the corridor. Someone begins the 'Dancing Queen' chorus, they all sing.

In the Gents, the fellers are all as at the end of Act I.

EDDY: Talk about a rope round y' neck . . .

KAV: Yeh, but what I'm tryin' to tell y' Eddy is who's been *here*!

EDDY: She's not even married to him yet, an' she's spyin' on him! Couldn't she leave him alone eh? Couldn't she leave him with his mates on his last night?

KAV: Eddy . . .

ROBBIE: She won't know Dave's here Eddy. She'll just be here for the dancin'.

KAV: Eddy guess —

EDDY: Dancin', yeh, she's dancin' all right. I just seen her from the balcony, dancin' round with all different fellers, the bitch!

ROBBIE: Come on Eddy, it's only dancin'.

EDDY: Is it? An' what about him? (*He indicates* DAVE.)

ROBBIE: Christ Eddy, she's only dancin', isn't she?

KAV: Forget her Eddy . . . listen, y' know who's been here eh? Guess who's been standin' on that very spot you're standin' on.

BILLY: Y' should've seen his boots Eddy. Custom-made, yeh.

KAV: Go on Eddy, guess, guess who?

EDDY: I don't fuckin' know do I?

KAV: Peter Taylor.

EDDY: Who?

KAV: You know Peter Taylor. Remember? He used to live round our way, played the guitar. He's with this group that's on tonight. He's famous Eddy.

EDDY: Famous?

BILLY: He's got these great boots Eddy. I'm gonna get a pair. Yeh.

KAV: You'll be able to see him after Eddy. He's gonna have a drink with us, y' know after the gig.

EDDY: After the what?

KAV: The gig. That's what they call it Eddy, when they play somewhere.

BILLY: He's a real star y' know Eddy.

EDDY: I thought I told you to look after Dave.

BILLY: We have done Eddy.

ROBBIE (*to* DAVE): All right Dave? OK?

BILLY (*going across to join* ROBBIE): All right Dave? Yeh.

KAV: Ah he's fantastic Eddy, not stuck up or anythin' y' know.
(*He brings out his autograph.*) Look Eddy.
EDDY *takes it.*
See what it says Eddy . . . 'To Kav — an old mate' an' that's his name there.

BILLY (*coming over with his autograph paper*): He did one for me Eddy, look. Yeh.
EDDY *takes it and looks at it.*
I'll bet he'll do one for you Eddy. Yeh. If y' ask him.

EDDY: What are these?

BILLY: Yeh, it's dead hard to read at first Eddy, I couldn't read it at first but look it says . . .
He goes to point at the paper. EDDY *turns away, holding up the paper.*

EDDY: This? What's this?

BILLY: We didn't have an autograph book Eddy.

EDDY· You big soft tarts!

KAV: What Eddy?

EDDY: Kids get autographs. Are you little kids?

KAV: No Eddy, but he's famous!

EDDY: On y' bike! (*He crumples up the paper.*) Famous!
He goes to the WC, throws the paper down the pan and flushes it.

KAV (*transfixed*): Eddy, what have y' done?

EDDY (*coming out*): What have I done?

ROBBIE (*from the bog*): You've just flushed Dave's head, Eddy.

EDDY: Do it again. It might sober him up.

KAV: Eddy! That was my autograph!

BILLY: An' mine. But y' couldn't read it anyway.

KAV: Eddy, that was my fuckin' autograph!

EDDY (*swiftly grabbing him*): Who the fuck d' y' think you're talking to? (*He glares him into submission.*) Y' don't get autographs from people like him! He's just a fuckin' nomark! *He glares at* KAV *who stares back, helpless.* EDDY *lets him go.* Y' don't wanna waste y' time Kav. See, it's people like you Kav, runnin' around after people like him that make them what they are. You're as good as he is! Did he ask you for your autograph? Did he?

KAV (*quietly*): No.

EDDY: No. You wanna keep your dignity you do. You're as good as him. You could do that, what he does if you wanted to. You can do anythin' he can do. We all can. We can do anythin' we want to do, anythin'. He's nothin' special, so don't belittle y'self beggin' for a scrawlin' on a piece of bog paper. We can all write our names y' know. Here, here, give me that pencil. Give it me!
KAV *does so.*
Look, look, it's dead easy y' know. You want an autograph? I'll give y' a fuckin' autograph . . . here. (*He writes his name in huge letters on the wall.*)

KAV: It was great meetin' him though. Wasn't it Robbie?

ROBBIE: It was all right.

BILLY: Gis a go Eddy, Eddy . . . I'm gonna do my autograph. I am. I'm gonna do mine bigger than yours Eddy. Yeh.

ROBBIE: He's no bleedin' big shot is he? Hasn't even got a car.

BILLY (*doing his name*): Y' shoulda seen the stupid boots he had on Eddy, y' know, tarts' boots.

ROBBIE (*taking out a felt-tip pen and doing his own name*): He's nothin' special, anyone could do what he does.

KAV: Oh yeh. Anyone could do it. That's why later on, whilst he's standin' up on the stage with all the coloured spotlights on him, you'll be down on the floor, dancin' in the dark with all the other nomarks.

EDDY (*snatching the pencil from* BILLY): Gis that. (*He offers it to* KAV.) Go on!

KAV: What?

EDDY: Put y' name up.

KAV (*after a pause*): I don't want to Eddy.

EDDY: Why?

KAV: There's no point is there?

EDDY: The point, Kav, is that our names are up there. Where's yours?

KAV: What?

EDDY: Your name has got to be up there!

KAV: Why?

EDDY: So they can be seen, that's why. So that everyone'll know we've been here.

KAV: They'll only paint it out. They always do.

EDDY: Let them, we'll come back an' do it again.

KAV: Then they'll stipple over the walls so y' can't write on them.

EDDY: So. We'll come back again, an' carve our names out, won't we? I've told y' Kav, we can do anythin'. (*He pauses.*) Write y' name.
KAV *looks at* EDDY.

ROBBIE: Go on Kav. I wouldn't mind, but he can write better than any of us.

EDDY: Come on Kav. I want y' t' do it for me. Y' know the way y' do it in fancy scrolls an' that, that's clever that is Kav. You do it. For us. Come on.

KAV (*taking the pencil; after a pause*): All right Eddy.

EDDY: Agh . . . good lad Kav.

KAV (*stepping up to the wall, looking at their writings*): Who taught you lot t' write? Look at the state of that.

EDDY: You show us how it should be done Kav.

KAV (*beginning to write*): Go on, you'se lot go. It'll take a bit of time this. Go on, I can keep me eye on Dave, Eddy.

EDDY: Come on . . . (*He goes into the corridor.*)

ROBBIE (*following with* BILLY): Y' gonna go for a dance Eddy?

EDDY: Nah.

BILLY: Why not Eddy?

EDDY: 'Cos I'd rather just watch youse make fools of yourselves.
They exit.

As KAV *is doing his name, we see* BERNADETTE *and* CAROL, *followed by* MAUREEN, *come through the doors.*

BERNADETTE: Well the inconsiderate swines.

CAROL: Tch.

MAUREEN: What's up?

CAROL (*as they enter the Ladies*): You saw them didn't y'?

MAUREEN: Who? Oh me head . . .

CAROL: Robbie Smith's here. An' Billy Blake.

MAUREEN: Oh he's nice him, Billy Blake isn't he?

CAROL: Tch. God Maureen, that's not the point is it?

MAUREEN: What?

BERNADETTE: Maureen love, if Billy Blake an' Robbie Smith an' them are here, who else must be here?

MAUREEN: Dave! Dave? Oh God . . . get Linda in, get Linda in here quick . . .

CAROL (*pulling her back from the door*): Come here, Frances has gone to tell her . . .

BERNADETTE: We'll just have t' go somewhere else.

CAROL: Tch. I was dead made up when I first saw Robbie, I really fancy him.

BERNADETTE: Fancy him or not Carol, we can't take the risk, for Linda's sake.

CAROL: Oh God I know, I'm not sayin' we should take the risk, Berni.

MAUREEN: If she sees her Dave tonight that's it y' know. Her marriage has had it.

BERNADETTE: We'll go somewhere else. We'll have to.

MAUREEN: My Mum knew a couple who saw each other the night before they got married an' y' know what happened eh?

BERNADETTE: What?

MAUREEN: The next day, in church, they were standin' y' know in the archway, havin' their picture taken. And the archway collapsed on them. Killed outright, an' that's true that.

CAROL: That was in the paper wasn't it?

MAUREEN: Yeh, the picture was in the paper wasn't it? Y'know, just a pile of stones, Berni.

BERNADETTE: There was this woman by us y' know, she got an emerald engagement ring . . .

CAROL: Go way . . .

MAUREEN: Did she take it off for the weddin'?

BERNADETTE: Everyone told her . . .

CAROL: Y' should never wear green at a weddin' should y'?

BERNADETTE: Everyone told her. But she wouldn't listen, thought she knew best, that type y' know, thought she could make her own rules . . .

CAROL: Y' can't can y'?

BERNADETTE: 'Ey she wouldn't learn though, Carol. A couple of years later she got married again, an' y' know what colour her dress was?

CAROL: Green?

MAUREEN: Tch.

BERNADETTE: Everyone told her. I believe her mother was distraught about it. But she wouldn't listen, tried to make out that things like that didn't matter.

MAUREEN: What happened Berni?

BERNADETTE: Heart attack wasn't it? Three months married an' her feller had a cardiac arrest. Gone, finished!

CAROL: I'll bet she was sorry after that . . .

BERNADETTE: No, that's not the end of it. She got married again didn't she?

CAROL: God, y' wouldn't think a feller'd take a chance on her, would y'?

BERNADETTE: She was told, time an' time again she was told, everyone told her. An' she said all right, y' know no green this time . . .

CAROL: I'll bet her feller was relieved wasn't he?

BERNADETTE: They get to the church an' she hasn't got a patch of green, anywhere.

MAUREEN: Oh thank God for that! Did they live, y' know, happily an' that?

BERNADETTE: Yeh, for ten minutes. As she was walkin' out the church she slipped, knocked her head on one of the gravestones. Dead!

CAROL: Go way.

MAUREEN: But there was no green, Berni.

BERNADETTE: No, there was no green Mo, but as they picked her up, what did they see? Pinned to her dress?

MAUREEN: What?

BERNADETTE: An opal brooch!

MAUREEN: Agh . . . !

LINDA *enters, led by* FRANCES. *They head for the Ladies.*

CAROL: Tch, when y' think about it, gettin' married's a terrible liability y' know.

MAUREEN: Never wear an' opal unless it's y' birth-stone.

CAROL: She was askin' for trouble though, that one, wasn't she Berni?

BERNADETTE: Thought it didn't matter, y' see. Thought she could make up her own rules.

LINDA *and* FRANCES *enter.*

LINDA: For Christ's sake Frances. What's wrong with you lot? If y' wanted to talk to me why didn't y' come out there? Come on, I wanna get back t' the dancin'.

BERNADETTE: Linda love, we've got to go somewhere else.

LINDA: What's wrong with here?

CAROL: Give us y' cloakroom tickets, I'll go 'n get the coats an' make sure it's all clear.

LINDA: What's wrong?

BERNADETTE: Nothing. Apart from the fact that the man you're marryin' is here tonight.

LINDA: Who? Dave? Where?

FRANCES: He's here, somewhere. We've seen all his mates.

LINDA: Well?

BERNADETTE: Well what?

LINDA: Well why do we have to go?

BERNADETTE: Linda! You cannot see your future husband on the eve of your wedding!

LINDA: Who says so?

CAROL: Linda, you see your Dave tonight an' your marriage is doomed.

LINDA: Ogh . . . Carol. Get lost will y' . . .

MAUREEN: Linda, d' you want to end up under a pile of stones?

LINDA (*laughing*): What?

BERNADETTE: We don't want to go Linda. This is for your sake love. We're only thinkin' of you Linda.

CAROL: You can't afford to see Dave tonight, Linda.

LINDA: Y' don't really believe that do y'?

CAROL: Linda. Y've got to believe it, 'cos it's true.

LINDA: Y' do don't y'? You really believe it.

BERNADETTE: Yes, an' so should you. Now come on, let's have your cloakroom ticket, we'll get the coats an' —

LINDA (*to* FRANCES): You don't believe this do y'? Eh?

FRANCES: Well y' don't do y' Linda? Y' don't see each other the night before y' get married.

LINDA: For Christ's sake. Come on!

BERNADETTE: Linda, we don't want to see you put your future in jeopardy.

LINDA (*looking at them; after a pause*): If it wasn't for the fact that you're my mates, an' have been for a long time, I'd say you were all certifiable! (*She stares at them.*) Why don't y' do what y' *want* t' do? Why don't y' do what you think you should do? But y' won't will y'? That's the biggest sin of all to you lot isn't it? You'll just keep on doin' what you're told to, won't y'?

BERNADETTE: Nobody tells me what to do Linda. I do whatever I want to do.

LINDA: Oh do y'? Well look Berni, you came here tonight to get off with a feller. Well there's loads of them out there. Come on, come on out an' get one . . .

BERNADETTE: I could do Linda. I could. But for your sake —

LINDA: For my sake? Look, just forget about my sake, will y'? (*She opens the door.*) Now come on, all of y' come on, now . . . *She holds the door for them. They make no move.*
Well, sod off then! (*She turns and goes out. In the corridor she leans against the wall, takes out her cigarettes, lights one.*)

BERNADETTE: Well if you ask me I say she's not been herself all night.

FRANCES: But that's what she's like Berni. How long have I been her mate eh? An' I've seen her, she can be like this y' know . . .

BERNADETTE: It's the pressure isn't it? I know what's goin' through her mind.

CAROL: Yeh but if she's actin' like this now Berni, imagine what she'll be like tomorrow.

BERNADETTE: What we've got to do is to stop her doin' anythin' stupid, whether she wants to or not.

FRANCES: I say we go an' see the fellers. Tell them to go somewhere else.

CAROL: They won't though will they? Y' know what fellers

are like.

FRANCES: We were here first weren't we? Sod it. I'll go an' see
if I can find Eddy Ainsworth. He'll tell them what to do.
If he says leave they will do.
FRANCES *goes out to the corridor. In the Ladies they pass
around fags, smoking, thinking. In the corridor . . .*

LINDA (*as* FRANCES *passes*): Frances . . .
FRANCES *tries to ignore it.*
Frankie . . . !

FRANCES (*turning*): What?

LINDA (*after a pause*): Forget it.

FRANCES: Listen Linda . . . I don't know what's wrong with
you tonight but you can't half be an awkward bitch . . .
LINDA *turns away.*
FRANCES *continues on down the corridor and out through
the doors.*

From the other end of the corridor we see PETER *and the*
ROADIE *enter.*

ROADIE: Well I'll try this and I'm tellin' y', if it don't work
we've had it. We might as well throw the gear back in the van
an' piss off.

PETER: Not play at all?
LINDA *looks up, with recognition.*

ROADIE: Well y' can't play without power can y'? You show me
how t' get some power out to the —

LINDA: Hello . . .

ROADIE (*thinking it's for him*): Hello darlin', what y' doin' eh?

LINDA (*passing him*): 'Ey.

PETER (*looking at her, with recognition*): Christ! 'Ey . . . Jesus
. . . come here . . .
He hugs her, she breaks away smiling and looking at him.

ROADIE (*going down the corridor*): What the fuck. I wish I was
famous . . .
He exits.

LINDA (*looking at him*): Well the state of you!

PETER: What d' y' mean?
The ROADIE *sticks his head through the doors.*

ROADIE: 'Ey . . . an' don't be long. You're on in a minute . . .

PETER: I thought you said y' couldn't get any power!

ROADIE: I will now!

The ROADIE *exits.*

PETER (*of his gear*): Like it do y'?

LINDA: Where d' y' get y' boots?

PETER (*camp*): Tch. Chelsea Girl . . .

LINDA (*laughing*): They're great . . .

PETER: Did y' know we were on?

LINDA: No. How long have y' been with this lot?

PETER: 'Bout a year. Just out for a bop are y'?

LINDA: Sort of.

PETER: Christ, I would have thought you'd given up comin' to this sort of place.

LINDA: Same could be said for you.

PETER: Nah . . . it's different for me isn't it? I'll never grow up.
She laughs
Anyway, it's work isn't it? I don't come out of choice. (*He laughs.*) How are y'?

LINDA: All right. How are you?

PETER: I'm OK. Lovely. Tch. I'm all right.

LINDA (*looking at him*): The state of y'.

PETER: I thought y' liked it.

LINDA: I do but y' don't wanna go out like that round here. Y'll get locked up.

PETER: I know. We went over the road for a pint before. Should have heard them in there . . . 'All right cowboy' they kept shoutin'. 'Where's Tonto then?' (*He laughs.*) I dunno . . .

LINDA: Well what d' y' expect if y' come round here in women's boots?

PETER (*grabbing her in a mock headlock*): Agh . . . (*He turns it into a hug.*) You know better than that. (*He holds her and looks at her. Shaking his head*) I can't believe it.
FRANCES *comes through the corridor doors.*
LINDA *pulls away from him.* FRANCES *clocks it. She goes into the loo, closes the door, leans on it.*

PETER: Isn't that whatshecalled, your mate?

LINDA: Frances.

PETER: Frances, that's right. How is she?

LINDA: All right.

PETER: 'Ey it's great to see y' y' know.

LINDA: It's great to see you. I suppose.

PETER: Suppose? Tch. I'll say tarar an' go an' tune up if you like.

LINDA: Go on then.

PETER: Come off it. Fancy a dance?

LINDA: With you?

PETER: No, with Tonto! Who d' y' think?

LINDA: I didn't think fellers from famous groups went dancin', I thought they kept themselves apart from the rabble.

PETER: They do usually. But you're special rabble!

LINDA: Tch. Oh such flattery. Or was it an insult?

PETER (*leading her along the corridor*): Come on. What's the dance up here these days? Still do the twist?

LINDA: The Foxtrot actually . . .

PETER: Oh is it actually . . .
They go through the doors.
FRANCES moves from the outer door, through the inner door into the Ladies.

CAROL: What did they say?

BERNADETTE: Well?

CAROL: Are they goin' Fran?

FRANCES: No.

CAROL: Tch. Fellers.

FRANCES: Listen. Guess whose group it is that's playin'?

BERNADETTE: Y' what?

FRANCES: Peter Taylor. It's his group . . .

BERNADETTE: We don't wanna know about a group Frances, we wanna know —

FRANCES: Berni! The thing is Berni, in this group there's a feller called Peter Taylor. An' him an' Linda only had a thing goin' for about two years didn't they?

CAROL: You what?

FRANCES: They're right outside this door, now, arms round each other . . .

BERNADETTE: Oh . . . so that's why she wanted to come here is it?

FRANCES: Well we don't know that, Berni . . .

CAROL: Oh come off it, Frances.

BERNADETTE: Look Frances, if she went out with him for that long she's bound t' know what group he's playin' in . . . there's a poster outside isn't there?

CAROL: I wondered why Linda wanted to come to a dump like this. Well fancy doin' somethin' like this, on y' weddin' night . . .

MAUREEN: God . . . no good'll come of this . . . I'm tellin' y' I know . . .

FRANCES: Look . . . she is only talkin' to him . . .

BERNADETTE: Yes, an' we all know where talk leads . . .

MAUREEN: Don't Berni . . . don't . . .

CAROL: Y' don't see ex fellers the night before y' gettin' married do y'?

FRANCES: She could just have bumped into him y' know . . .

BERNADETTE: Well we can soon find out can't we Frances? We'll get her in here . . . (*She goes out to the corridor.*)

FRANCES (*sighing*): Ogh Christ . . .

CAROL: I knew we shoulda gone the Top Rank . . . I knew we shouldn't have come here.
BERNADETTE *comes in.*

BERNADETTE: Where did you say she was?

FRANCES: Just outside.

BERNADETTE: Well she's not there now . . .

CAROL: Well where is she?

BERNADETTE: How do I know? But I'll tell y' what, if y' ask me she's up to no good. That girl is playin' with fire. We're her mates, I reckon we better sort out a way to stop her gettin' burnt . . .

MAUREEN: Oh God . . . (*Beginning to cry, she rushes into the WC*)

FRANCES: For God's sake Maureen shut it will y' . . .

MAUREEN (*frantic*): Why can't everything be nice?

BERNADETTE: Who said everything won't be nice Maureen?

MAUREEN (*crying*): No good'll come of this . . . You mark my words . . . you see . . .

BERNADETTE: Maureen . . . we'll sort it out, don't worry. Everything will be nice Maureen. There's a wedding tomorrow; there's'll be a nice cake and a nice service, nice bridesmaids, nice presents. And a nice bride and groom. But Mo, we've just got to see that Linda doesn't do anything silly. We're her mates Mo. What are mates for eh? Eh?
MAUREEN *comes out of the WC.* BERNADETTE *puts her*

arm round her.

Everything will be nice love. We'll look after her . . . don't worry. Come on . . . everything'll be very nice.

The girls go into the corridor as . . .

BILLY *and* ROBBIE *come through the doors.*

ROBBIE: All right girls?

BERNADETTE: Come on girls . . .

CAROL (*stopping*): Hia Robbie . . .

ROBBIE: All right . . . er . . . Carol isn't it?

CAROL (*flattered*): Tch . . . y' good at names aren't y'?

ROBBIE: I'm good at most things Carol!

BERNADETTE (*from the door*): CAROL!

CAROL: Got t' go. See y' tomorrow eh Robbie . . . at the weddin' . . .

She dashes off through doors, following the others.

BILLY: You're on there Robbie. I could tell. Yeh . . .

ROBBIE: Don't fancy it much though . . .

BILLY: Don't y'?

ROBBIE: Nah. I'd screw it though. Come on . . . hurry up or them other two'll have gone.

'Ey they're crackers those two aren't they?

BILLY: Yours is Robbie. Yeh . . .

ROBBIE: Dead ringer for Britt Ekland isn't she? Whoa. Come on . . .

They enter the Gents. KAV is putting the finishing touches to an impressive drawing of his own name.

Ogh . . . look at that . . .

BILLY: That's dead smart that Kav.

KAV: It's all right isn't it?

ROBBIE: Yeh. 'Ey . . . y' wanna see these two we've tapped off with. Mine looks just like Britt Ekland, doesn't she Billy?

BILLY: Yeh. Mine looks just like Rod Stewart. That's great that, Kav . . .

ROBBIE: Come on Billy . . . what y' moanin' for? She's all right that one. Don't you go doin' a bunk on her will y'? I'm knackered with the Britt Ekland one if you give her mate the elbow.

BILLY: I can't stand her though, Robbie. That's smart, Kav.

ROBBIE: What's wrong with her?

BILLY: She's destroyed.

ROBBIE: Well it's dark in there isn't it? Keep her out the light an' no-one'll notice her hunch back. Ah come on Billy . . . I'd do the same for you wouldn't I eh? Wouldn't I Kav? I'm your mate aren't I?

BILLY: Yeh.

ROBBIE: Well, I'm askin' y' to do me a favour.

KAV: Robbie's right y' know Billy. You stand by y' mates an' they stand by you, don't they?

MAUREEN, CAROL *and* FRANCES *come through the corridor doors and into the Ladies.* BERNADETTE *follows them.*

BILLY: Yeh. All right.

ROBBIE: Good lad . . . come on . . . 'ey, it's smart that Kav. Eddy'll be made up with y'.

KAV (*as they leave*): Yeh . . . I'm gonna tell him.

BERNADETTE *enters the Ladies just before the fellers come into the corridor and exit.*

BERNADETTE: Well the brazen . . . ogh . . . did you see it . . . did y' see it?

MAUREEN: Dancin' . . . like that, with him . . .

FRANCES: An' ignored her mates.

MAUREEN: She was dancin' like she was stuck to him wasn't she?

BERNADETTE: She's makin' a spectacle of herself she is.

CAROL: An' it wasn't even a slowy was it?

BERNADETTE: Y' don't dance like that to a fast record unless you've got one thing in mind. It's written all over them what they've got in mind.

MAUREEN: What Berni?

BERNADETTE: Come on Maureen. It's patently obvious.

CAROL: God, he's got a cheek that feller hasn't he eh, comin' round here, dancin' like that. He must have no shame that feller.

LINDA *enters through the corridors and heads for the Ladies.*

BERNADETTE: Well I think she's immoral, I do. There's no excuse for that sort of behaviour. Not on the night before y' gettin' —

LINDA *enters. Immediate silence. She walks through them and into the WC, closing the door.*

Linda . . . Linda!

LINDA (*from the WC*): What Berni?

BERNADETTE: Linda, don't y' think you're bein' a bit inconsiderate?

LINDA (*all sweetness*): Why's that Bern?

BERNADETTE: I could say 'improper' Linda, but I won't. There is moderation y' know Linda.

LINDA (*from the WC*): Why don't y' tell me what's botherin' y' Bern?

BERNADETTE: Do you really think you should be carryin' on like this, with a stranger, the night before your weddin'?

LINDA (*from the WC*): He's not a stranger . . . he's someone I know very well. You could call him an intimate friend, Berni . . .

BERNADETTE: Don't you try and take the piss out of me Linda. *The WC flushes, the door opens and* LINDA *crosses to the basin.*

LINDA: Berni . . . I'm dancing, that's all.

CAROL: Yeh, but y' used to go out with him didn't y' Linda?

LINDA: Yes Carol, I did.

CAROL: Well don't y' think that makes it worse?

LINDA (*drying her hands*): No Carol, I don't think it makes it anything. I am dancin', with someone I used to go out with. I like him. I like him very much as it happens. An' I think it's got sod all to do with you, or you or you or any of you.

BERNADETTE: Have you forgotten that tomorrow you an' Dave will be standing in that church, getting married? *She finishes drying her hands, goes to the door, opens it, turns and looks at them.*

LINDA: An' what makes you think I'm still going ahead with it? LINDA *goes into the corridor and exits.*

MAUREEN: I knew it . . . I told you . . . I knew it . . . what did I say?

CAROL: God, I'm supposed to be a bridesmaid an' everythin' . . .

MAUREEN: I'm gonna be sick, I am, I'm gonna be sick. What am I gonna do with the barbecue chairs?

BERNADETTE: This is gettin' out of hand this is.

FRANCES: What we gonna do?

BERNADETTE: Y' know who y' can blame for this don't y', eh? This is Peter Whatsisname's doing isn't it?

CAROL: What we gonna do though Berni?

BERNADETTE: Well if y' ask me Carol I reckon the sooner she gets away from that Peter feller and comes to her senses the better it'll be for everyone.

FRANCES: She's makin' a fool of herself.

BERNADETTE: She's makin' a fool of everyone. I think the fellers should know about this. I think they've got to be told . . .

CAROL: Don't tell Dave, Berni . . .

BERNADETTE: I won't have to tell him if she carries on flauntin' herself out there. He'll see it for himself soon enough. No, come on, we'll tell the others . . .
They begin to exit into the corridor.

FRANCES: What y' gonna say Berni?

BERNADETTE: I'll tell them what she told us . . . that the weddin's off!
They go into the corridor and exit through the doors.

PETER and LINDA enter as if from the bandroom. PETER is carrying a pint.

LINDA: Does that mean you won't be able to play?

PETER: Doesn't look like it.

LINDA: Ah I was lookin' forward t' seein' y'.

PETER: It's not our fault. All the wiring's lethal. Every time they connect to a socket it blows. The place is fallin' to bits.

LINDA: It's like everythin' else round here. It's dyin' this place is. Didn't y' notice?

PETER: Huh. I didn't think I'd see y' y' know. I thought you would have left by now.

LINDA: Left for where?

PETER: Nowhere in particular. I just didn't think you'd stay round here.

LINDA: An' what's wrong with round here?

PETER: Come on, y' just said yourself it's dyin'.

LINDA: Well, that's no reason to leave is it?

PETER: I just never thought this place'd be big enough for you.

LINDA: Get lost!

PETER (*laughing*): I'm not takin' the piss, honest. I'm serious.

LINDA: Tch.

PETER: You should've come to London when I went. You

should've come with me.

LINDA: I couldn't, could I?

PETER: Wouldn't.

LINDA: All right, wouldn't.

PETER: Why?

LINDA: I didn't (*camping it*) erm, love you enough. (*After a pause.*) I didn't half like you a lot though.

PETER (*camping it*): You always were a smooth-talking bitch Linda.

She smiles.

Anyway, I didn't necessarily mean with me in that sense. What y' gonna do then, settle down here?

LINDA: I might.

PETER (*shaking his head*): Tch.

LINDA: 'Ey, it might have escaped your notice but there are a lot of people who like livin' in this town.

PETER: Including you?

LINDA: Yes.

PETER: Why?

LINDA: Oh sod off you. Just 'cos you live in London now it doesn't give you the right to come back up here an' start tellin' us we're all peasants y' know. We do know where London is. I mean it's only two and a half hours away on the train. Christ you'd think you'd gone to the other end of the world to hear you talk. It's only a train ride away.

PETER (*laughing*): Not when you've only got a single ticket.

LINDA: Comin' up here, tellin' everyone what to do.

PETER: I'm not tellin' you what to do.

LINDA: You think you can tell anyone what to do just 'cos you can get away with wearin' women's boots . . .

PETER (*laughing*): You do what you like. I'm not tellin' you. Stay around here if y' want to Linda. Have y' kids an' keep y' mates an' go dancin' an' go to the pub an' go to the shops an' do all those things you used to tell me you hated doing.

LINDA *goes to reply. Can't.* PETER *is waiting for her.*

LINDA: Get lost you! Well, I was young then. I mean y' do hate all those things when y' young, don't y'?

PETER: An' how old are y' now?

LINDA: Twenty-two.

PETER: A twenty-two year old geriatric.

He looks at her. She at him.

LINDA: You're a bastard y' know.

PETER: I know. I'm a selfish shitty bastard because I did what I wanted to do. I did the worst thing possible y' know, what I wanted to.

LINDA: An' why do y' think I should get out?

PETER: Come on lovely; because you want to! Because while you're doin' all this number you hate it. Y' do it, but while you're doin' it you hate it. You want out of it.

LINDA: D' y' know somethin'? You are the most arrogant big-headed . . .

PETER: I know. But I'm right aren't I?

LINDA: No. You're just so arrogant, you think you're . . . that you're right.

PETER *smiles and shakes his head at her.*

Think what you like. It doesn't matter.

PETER (*after a pause*): Why don't y' jack it in up here? When we finish tonight we're in the van and away — Scotland tomorrow, Newcastle on Sunday, day off on Monday, on to Norwich, Southampton, couple of gigs in Devon. Then back to London. Come with us.

LINDA: I gave you your answer a couple of years ago.

PETER: But then I was askin' you to come with me. This time, lovely, I'm just offerin' you a lift. You can get off wherever you want.

LINDA: I never accept lifts off strange men.

PETER: Yeh. Well you should.

LINDA: Oh should I? God has spoken has he? Listen, Mr Knowall . . . it'd be great wouldn't it, speedin' through Scotland with a second-rate band when there's a hundred an' twenty guests stood in the church tomorrow waitin' to see me get married.

PETER (*after a long pause; looking at her*): We are not a second-rate band.

LINDA *laughs. He puts his arm round her.*

Honestly?

LINDA: Yeh. Why d' y' think I came here tonight? It's the hen night.

PETER (*baulking*): Hen night! What? D' y' want us to play 'Congratulations' for y'? Or d' y' prefer 'Get me to the Church'?

LINDA: Neither. Just give us a kiss.
*He does so. She looks at him, hugs him, breaks away, turns to
the door of the Ladies.*
Thanks for lettin' me have me last fling with you.

PETER: Hey.
She stops.
D' y' love him?

LINDA: Accordin' to me mates I do. (*She opens the door.*)

PETER: Hey . . . do you?

LINDA (*stopping*): What's it to you Peter?

PETER: I'm tryin' to understand why you're stayin'.

LINDA: Look . . . don't you listen? I've told y', I'm gettin'
married tomorrow.

PETER: I wasn't askin' about that.

LINDA (*smiling at him*): Tarar Peter. (*She enters the Ladies.*)
*He stares at the closed door for a moment before turning and
going into the Gents. He heads for the urinal, sees KAV's
drawing, stops to look at it. In the Ladies, LINDA goes into
the WC.*

The corridor doors fly open, EDDY leading the others.

ROBBIE: An' the weddin's off is it Eddy?

EDDY: You're jokin' aren't y'? She might fuckin' say it's off.
But no-one makes a laughin' stock of my mate.

BILLY: Too right. Yeh.

EDDY: Thinks she's some sort of clever tart does she? We'll
fuckin' sort her out. An' we'll sort out her fancy feller as well.

ROBBIE: The fuckin' cheek of him — comin' up here an' nabbin'
Dave's tart. He thinks he can just take whatever he wants,
doesn't he?

EDDY: He'll think again when we've finished with him. We
wanna get him in here, right, away from the rest of his posin'
mates . . . Look Billy you go down the back an' see if y' can.
PETER *having finished in the bog and taken another look at
KAV's drawing opens the door of the Gents. He sees them.*

PETER: All right lads?
EDDY *blocks his exit, the others supporting him, crowding
PETER back into the Gents.*

EDDY: No sunshine, it's not all right is it?

PETER: What?

EDDY: In there. Go on.

PETER: Look the –

EDDY: In.

PETER *backs into the Gents. They stand looking at him.*

PETER: Well?

EDDY: You what? You just shut it. (*He looks at him.*) Are you a tart?

PETER *looks back, sighs. Pause.*

'Ey, I asked you a question.

PETER: No. I'm not a tart.

EDDY: Well why have y' got tarts' boots on?

PETER (*after a pause*): I like them.

EDDY: I don't!

PETER: No. Well . . .

EDDY: I don't like you either.

PETER: Yeh. Yeh I'd gathered that.

EDDY: Oh had y' now?

PETER: Well . . .

EDDY (*after a pause; pointing*): You've been dancin' with our mate's tart.

PETER: What?

ROBBIE: While he's fuckin' lyin' sick in there.

PETER (*glancing at the WC*): Look, I didn't know she was anythin' to do with –

EDDY: You've been messin' around with Dave's future missis.

PETER: Now hold on –

EDDY: NO! You just hold on! Comin' back here. Posin' all over the place. You can't just walk over us. Think y' someone special don't y'? Eh? You think y' can fuckin' do things that we can't, don't y'? Well I'll fuckin' show you what we can do . . .

PETER *backs away.* EDDY *grabs him, turns him and forces him to face* KAV*'s drawing.*

That's what we can do! Look at it. Look.

PETER: I'm lookin'.

EDDY: Good.

ROBBIE: That's fuckin' clever that is.

PETER: I know.

EDDY: Oh do y'?

PETER: Who did it?

KAV: Me.

EDDY (*to* KAV): Shut it.

PETER (*to* KAV): It's good.

EDDY: We can do anythin'. (*He pushes him away.*)

PETER: Yeh. (*To* KAV.) D' y' go to Art School?

ROBBIE (*laughing*): Art School! Listen t' the stupid get . . . (*He laughs.*)

EDDY (*laughing*): 'Ey Kav . . . y' could be an artist you could! (*Laughing.*) Picasso Kavanagh . . .

ROBBIE: Kav the artist . . . (*Camp.*) Oogh can I hold y' brush for y' ducky?

EDDY *and* BILLY *laugh.*

KAV (*joining the laughter*): Art School! The only artist I wanna be is a piss artist.

They laugh.

PETER (*to* KAV): You stupid cunt!

EDDY *wheels and grabs him.*

EDDY: Don't you . . . don't you dare! I'm gonna tell you somethin' for your own good — don't you come round here with your music, y' fuckin' music. Don't you come makin' people unhappy! Understand? We'll be watchin' you. You go near Dave's tart again an' your fuckin' number's up. Right?

PETER: Yeh. Whatever you say.

EDDY: She's our mate's tart. We look after our mates. We stick with them. (*He leans in close.*) You left this town. Y' walked out. You've got no claims here. You left this town, so when you've finished tonight just fuck off out of it! (*He pushes him away.*) Get out!

PETER *starts to go.*

BILLY (*shouting*): An' don't come back. Y' big poufter.

PETER *stops in the corridor and shakes his head. In the Ladies,* LINDA *comes out of the WC and washes her hands.*

EDDY: Right, come on. Let's find his tart.

They leave the Gents.

As they do so, the ROADIE *enters and sees* PETER.

ROADIE: It's no good Pete, the bleedin' place is —

PETER (*walking as if to the bandroom*): Good. Come on, let's get the gear packed and piss off.

EDDY *and the others approach the corridor doors.*

As they do, BERNADETTE *and the girls come through.*

BERNADETTE: We can't find her, Eddy . . .

EDDY: We will. Come on.
The fellers exit.
The ladies continue on their way to the Ladies.

BERNADETTE (*watching* EDDIE *go*): Ogh . . . I wish y' d find me Eddy.

CAROL: D' y' fancy him Berni?

BERNADETTE: I wouldn't say no to an hour with him. Come on.
They enter the Ladies.

LINDA: What you doin' here? Why aren't y' out dancin'. There's not a lot of fellers left y' know Berni.

BERNADETTE: You should be ashamed of yourself. (*Aside to* MAUREEN.) Go an' tell Eddy she's here.

LINDA: Why should I Berni?
MAUREEN *goes into the corridor and exits.*

CAROL: Ignore your mates Linda. We don't matter to you, do we Linda?

LINDA: For God's sake, what y' on about now?

BERNADETTE: Look Linda, you just listen to us for a minute.

LINDA: Tch . . . yes sir!

CAROL: See, see. Well don't listen Linda. Be selfish. You be a selfish bitch.

LINDA (*after a pause*): All right. Go on. I'm listening . . .

BERNADETTE: Listen to me Linda. Now I've been married quite a few years Linda. You're forgettin' that I've been through what's happening t' you. I understand.

LINDA: Well? Go on.

BERNADETTE: Linda, there isn't one woman who doesn't have doubts the night before she gets married —

LINDA: Berni —

BERNADETTE: Now don't interrupt me Linda! Every woman has doubts. But that's all they are, doubts. Y' don't act on feelin's like that. Just because you've got some doubts it doesn't mean you can go rushin' into the arms of some ex-boyfriend an' then disappear with him —

LINDA (*slightly warning*): Berni —

BERNADETTE: What would happen if every woman did that eh? Who'd be married today if we all took notice of how we feel? Eh? Eh?

LINDA: Berni. Can I get a word in now?

*She looks at them all. Their intensity is too much for her.
She laughs.*

We see the fellers come through the corridor doors, led by
EDDY.

ROBBIE: Eddy, don't be daft . . . we can't go in there . . .

CAROL: See . . . see . . .

LINDA: Look Carol . . . look, all of y'. For your information
I've got no intention of —
EDDY *knocks the door open, points at* LINDA.

EDDY: Right you, out. Now!

CAROL: She won't listen Eddy. (*Glancing out to the corridor.*)
Hia Robbie.
EDDY *and* LINDA *stare at each other.* ROBBIE *and others
hesitate outside the Ladies.*

ROBBIE: Come on Eddy, we can't go in there . . . It's the Ladies.

EDDY (*to* LINDA): Get outside I said!

CAROL: I've told y' Eddy. She won't listen.
They stare at each other.

EDDY: All right, all right. Stay in here. I'll stay as well. (*To the
others.*) Get in here.
They can't.
It doesn't bother me y' know. I don't care that it's the fuckin'
Ladies — rules mean nothin' to me! (*To the others.*) I said get
in here!
Reluctantly they do so.

ROBBIE: Come on Eddy . . . let's get out . . . we can't stay in
here . . .

KAV: Eddy, we're in the women's bogs . . . come on . . .

EDDY: You stay where y' are. What does it matter where it is.
Y' don't worry about names on doors do y'? Names on doors
don't bother me. I go where I wanna go. (*He turns to* LINDA.)
Now you just listen to me. You might be Dave's tart, yes. But
I'm his mate. I'm his best mate. He's our mate. You might try
an' treat him like shite but we don't.
LINDA *glares.*

CAROL: Eddy's right y' know Linda . . . you are makin' a
terrible show of Dave.

EDDY: Goin' round tellin' people y' not marryin' him — you!
(*Pointing at her.*) Don't you treat a man like that —
understand? You just learn a bit of respect an' loyalty an'
don't you go tellin' no-one that y' not marryin' Dave. 'Cos you

are. Tomorrow!

LINDA: Piss off little man!

*She quickly turns and goes into the WC, closing the door.
EDDY, fast, bangs it open and grabs her.*

EDDY: Don't . . . just fuckin' don't . . . you! Now you listen to
what I'm sayin' girl. You play awkward friggers with me, you
do it once more tonight an' I'll get that posin' bastard you've
been dancin' with an' I'll break every finger he's got. Did you
hear me, eh? We've already seen him. He's been warned. And
so have you. Did you hear me?

LINDA: Yes. All right. Yes. OK . . .

He lets go of her but stays close.

EDDY (*quietly*): He's crap y' know. (*He pauses.*) He can't even
play the guitar. (*He pauses.*) Y' think he's good don't y'?
Well he's not. (*He pauses.*) I know about guitars. I play the
guitar. Chords I play. G and F an' D minor.

ROBBIE: Come on Eddy . . . if we're seen in here . . .

EDDY: Y' don't wanna be impressed by him girl. He's all show.
I could've been in a group. A famous group. I play the guitar.
(*He backs out of the WC, turns to the other women.*) She's
all right now. She's come to her senses. Haven't y' eh?

LINDA (*dumb*): Yeh.

KAV: Come on Eddy, this is the Ladies.

ROBBIE: Come on . . .

EDDY: Right. (*To* LINDA): See y' in church! Come on.

They go into the Gents.

Come on. (*He begins running a bowl of water.*) Get him over
here, let's get him sorted out. I've had enough of this place.
We're goin' the club.

They begin to try and sober DAVE *up by dousing his head in
water.*

CAROL: Eddy was right wasn't he Linda?

LINDA: Yeh. Yeh.

BERNADETTE: Oh Lind . . . Linda . . . thank goodness you've
come to your senses.

FRANCES: I'm always tellin' y' about your moods aren't I Lind?

MAUREEN *comes through the corridor doors and heads for
the Ladies.*

BERNADETTE: Well I'm glad it's all been sorted out . . .

CAROL: Ah yeh. (*Arms around her.*) Come on now Linda eh?
I didn't mean anythin' harsh that I might have said, Lind.

All friends now eh?

MAUREEN *rushes in.*

MAUREEN: What's happenin'?

BERNADETTE: It's all right Mo. Everything's fine now.

MAUREEN: Ah I'm glad. Hia Lind.

BERNADETTE: Now we can get back to havin' a good night, eh?

MAUREEN: 'Ey, listen the group's not gonna be playin'.

FRANCES: Why?

MAUREEN: I dunno. They just announced it. There's not enough power or somethin', for their equipment.

BERNADETTE: 'Ey, I bet I could put a bit of power in their equipment, eh?

The girls, apart from LINDA, *laugh.*

Eh Lind?

LINDA (*smiling*): Yeh.

FRANCES: What we gonna do now?

CAROL: Why don't we go somewhere else?

FRANCES: What does Linda want to do?

BERNADETTE: Linda only wanted to come here 'cos there was live music. If there isn't gonna be any she won't mind movin' on. Will y' Linda?

CAROL: Let's go to a club.

MAUREEN: Ah shall we eh?

BERNADETTE: Come on eh. Eh Lind?

LINDA: If you like.

CAROL: I'll go get the coats. Hurry up. We'll get a taxi before the pubs start emptyin'

CAROL goes into the corridor and exits.

The others start preparing to go. In the Gents . . .

KAV: Come on Dave . . . Dave . . . we're goin' down the club . . . have another bevvy . . .

BILLY: We'll have t' get in before eleven y' know. Yeh.

The ladies leave the loo. They approach the corridor doors.

As they do so, CAROL *comes through with coats.*

They begin preparing themselves to leave. LINDA *leans on the wall, slightly apart from the rest of them.*

EDDY: Sod it. Come on. Let's get him out. We'll get a taxi.

FRANCES: I'll go see if there's any taxis passin' . . .

She goes through the doors.

BERNADETTE (*to* LINDA): All right love?

LINDA: Feel a bit sick.

BERNADETTE (*to the others*): That'll be all the drink. Don't worry love, you'll be OK tomorrow. Be all right on the big day.
The door to the Gents opens. The fellers come into the corridor, carrying DAVE.
Linda . . . close your eyes.
LINDA *does as ordered.* MAUREEN *crosses to her and turns her to face the wall.*

MAUREEN: Turn this way Lind. Y' can't be too safe. God Linda . . . count y' self lucky y' cant see him. What a state.

ROBBIE (*as they approach*): All right girls.

CAROL: Hia Robbie.

BERNADETTE: 'Ey . . . don't bring him here. We don't want tomorrow's bride seein' tomorrow's groom.

KAV: He can't see anythin'.

ROBBIE: He's blind.

CAROL: Hia Robbie . . .

ROBBIE: Here . . . put him down here till we get a cab . . . he'll be all right.
They put him down, propping him against the wall. ROBBIE *leaves the others to it and shoots across to* CAROL.
'Ey, I was hopin' I might get a dance with y'.

CAROL (*almost overcome*): Were y'?

ROBBIE: Who's er . . . lookin' after y'?

CAROL: No-one.

ROBBIE: No-one? Y' mean no-one's lookin' after a lovely young thing like you? (*He puts his arm around her.*) We'll have t' do somethin' about that won't we?
FRANCES *enters.*

FRANCES: There's no taxis anywhere.

EDDY (*looking at* ROBBIE): I'll er, I'll go see if I can see one . . .

BERNADETTE: Need a hand Eddy?

EDDY: What? (*He looks at her.*) Yeh. All right then.
EDDY *and* BERNADETTE *exit.*
MAUREEN *beaming at* BILLY *who doesn't know where to put himself.* KAV *goes up to* ROBBIE *who is now necking with* CAROL.

KAV: Eh Robbie . . . y' were only jokin' weren't y'?

ROBBIE (*breaking*): What?

KAV: Y' were only jokin' . . . about the clap? Weren't y'?

ROBBIE: Yeh. (*Aside*) Sod off will y' . . .

KAV: What?

ROBBIE (*breaking again; indicating* FRANCES): Go on.
   KAV *goes across to* FRANCES.

FRANCES: There's no taxis.

KAV: I know. It's terrible isn't it? Can't get one anywhere.

FRANCES: Your name's Kav isn't it?

KAV: Me real name's Tony. But they call me Kav.

FRANCES: Oh.

KAV: Hey.

FRANCES: What?

KAV: Come here.
   She does.

FRANCES: What?

KAV: Give us a kiss.

FRANCES: Tch. Sod off.

KAV: Come here. (*He gets a grip.*) Come on.
   He kisses her. She responds. Throughout the above, MAUREEN
   has been edging along the wall to BILLY. *She is now next to*
   him. He tries to ignore it.

MAUREEN: Hia.

BILLY (*not looking*): Hello. (*He coughs.*)

MAUREEN: I see everyone's made friends!

BILLY: Yeh.

MAUREEN: Has anyone ever told you you've got 'come to bed'
   eyes?

BILLY: I don't think so.

MAUREEN: Well you have y' know.

BILLY: Have I? Yeh.

MAUREEN: Tch . . . you're a real smooth-talker you, aren't y'?
   She goes to walk away. He quickly grabs her and starts necking
   with her. LINDA *turns and opens her eyes. Looks at the scene*
   before her. Looks at DAVE. *She crosses to him, bends down*
   to him and quietly shakes him.

LINDA (*quietly*): Look at me . . . look at me . . . come on . . .
   just look once . . . come on. (*She shakes him.*) Look at me! . . .
   (*She shakes him roughly.*) I said look at me!

CAROL: Linda what y' —

ROBBIE: Come here. (*He starts necking again.*)

CAROL: But she's —

ROBBIE: He can't see anythin' he's well away . . . come here . . .
They begin necking again.

LINDA: Yes . . . that's it . . . that's it . . . (*She holds his brief
gaze, drops him back against the wall. She stands.*)
BERNADETTE *enters, linking arms with* EDDY.
LINDA *begins to walk down the corridor to the toilets.*

BERNADETTE: You all right Linda?

LINDA: Yeh. I'm all right. Stay there. I'm just gonna be sick.

BERNADETTE (*to* EDDY): Wait here. (*She starts to go after*
LINDA.)

LINDA (*turning and pointing; vicious*): I said stay there!

BERNADETTE (*stopped by the force of it*): Linda!
She starts to approach . . . LINDA *backs away.*
I'm only coming to look after you love. You don't wanna be
all on your own when y' sick.

LINDA: Stay there . . . don't come near me . . . I'm warnin' y' . . .

BERNADETTE (*hurrying forward*): Now Linda don't start
this . . .
LINDA *goes to enter the Ladies. Instead, she looks across the
corridor, rushes into the Gents.*
Linda! That's the Gents, Linda . . . Linda come out . . . y'
can't go in the Gents . . . She's gone into the Gents . . . (*To*
EDDY.) I can't go in there . . . you go in, see if she's all
right . . .

EDDY: She'll be all right.

BERNADETTE: Linda! (*She goes to the door, gingerly opens it
and calls through.*) Linda . . .
Throughout the above LINDA *goes into the Gents. She tries
the large window. It is reinforced glass, no way out. She goes
into the WC. She comes out looking for something to break
the window. She sees the towel dispenser and smashes it off
the wall. She goes into the WC, closes the door and bolts it.
There is a crash of glass.* LINDA *exits.*

BERNADETTE *goes in to the Gents. She tries the WC door.*
Eddy . . . Eddy . . . come here . . .
He does so as she is trying to force the lock.
Eddy, Eddy quick . . . get that open.
EDDY *puts his shoulder to it a few times. It flies open.*

BERNADETTE *goes in.*
She's gone . . . she's friggin' gone . . . she's in that van . . .
quick Eddy, quick past the front . . .
Cursing, EDDY *rushes out into the corridor.*
(As he goes.) Fuck . . .
EDDY *exits through the double doors.*
BERNADETTE *looks out of the window.*
Y' won't do it Eddy . . . y' won't . . . she's gone . . . you're
too late Eddy . . .

KAV *(prompted by* EDDY *rushing out):* 'Ey, come on . . . Eddy
must have got a taxi. *(He looks through the doors.)* Come on
there's a couple comin' . . .

CAROL: Quick . . . oogh quick come on . . . someone stop them
. . . come on . . .

MAUREEN: Berni . . . Berni . . . come on . . .
BERNADETTE *slowly walks up the corridor.*

CAROL: Come on Berni we've got taxis . . . we're goin' the club
with the lads, come on . . .

BERNADETTE: Where's Eddy?

CAROL: He must be in the taxi . . . come on . . . get Linda . . .
come on . . .
CAROL *exits with the others.*

BERNADETTE: Carol, Carol hold on . . .
BERNADETTE *exits.*
*Shouting from outside. It's garbled but as it dies away we
hear* EDDY.

EDDY *(off)*: Bastards . . . come back . . . bastards.
He enters, panting for breath.
Bastards. *(He sees* DAVE, *walks down to him, stands getting
his breath back.)* They've bailed out on us Dave. They've left
us. *(Starting to pick him up.)* They've all gone Dave. She's
gone. She's fuckin' gone Dave. The bitch. *(He gets* DAVE
standing.) Well fuck them all. *(He starts to carry* DAVE
towards the doors.) They've gone. She's gone. Well y've got
no baggage weighin' y' down. There's nothin' holdin' us back
now Dave. We can go anywhere.
He carries him through the doors

Black-out.

END

I Want To Write A Musical

For years I'd wanted to write a musical. Not the book of a
musical or even the lyrics and the book. I wanted to write a
musical — book, lyrics *and* the music. Now there's cheek! Book?
Well, yes. Lyrics? Possibly. But the music? I could quite
understand the objections, the pitying looks of disbelief. I'd got
no record of writing music for the theatre and I had to admit that
yes, it's quite true, during my school days a succession of music
teachers had contributed to my annual reports comments such as:
'Shows absolutely no interest', 'If he continues with this subject
next year I will be forced to tender my resignation', 'We will
consider it an achievement if he learns to play the gramophone'.

No wonder that years and years later when asked casually at
parties or in bars what I was working on, the reply, 'A musical',
would invariably provoke the response, 'Ah. And who's writing
the music?'
Feebly, apologetically I'd whisper, 'Me'.
'Pardon?'
'Me', just as feeble, inaudible. A cough and the word repeated,
unintentionally loud, 'ME . . . me'.

And as the other party would nod a sickly, sympathetic nod
and break away with cries of 'Oh, there's Alan, I haven't seen
Alan for weeks', I'd seize his arm and begin my speech about 'But
oh, look, I mean it will be all right. I mean, I can write music,
honest, I wrote music and songs for years and years before I
became a playwright and I mean, I know no-one knows about my
music but if you'd been around in the days of the Green Moose
when I used to write ten, twelve songs a week! Take no notice of
what those daft music teachers said, 'cos they didn't know that
while they were screamin' about my failure to appreciate 'Dashin'
Away With The Smoothin' Iron' or some stupid bloody song
about ripe cherries, I was secretly, secretly goin' round to Roger
Rimmer's house where we had two guitars an' where we'd stand
in front of the mirror for hours pretendin' to be The Shadows!
So there.'

By which time, of course, I was talking to no one but myself.
Which is as it should have been because I really had no one to
convince other than myself. It was true, I had for many years,
before I'd ever put a foot inside a theatre, written and performed
hundreds of songs. I clutched onto this historical fact like a
drowning man clutching at a floating crisp packet. I might have
written hundreds of songs but I couldn't ignore the fact that

every single one of them was quite unknown. Even the few that were recorded passed, quite unnoticed, into the oblivion of instant deletions.

And *I* want to write a musical, am indeed, somewhere in the middle of it when my wise and crazy agent, after listening to my passionate I've-been-writing-songs-for-years speech, fixes me with her fork and says, 'Yes dear boy, but this is the theatre, and in the musical theatre you must, absolutely *must* be hummable. To not be hummable in the musical theatre is nothing less than treason! Well dear?'

'What?'

'Are you? Hummable?'

All the way back on the train, staring glumly into the night, even failing to notice for once that feller who's always trying to get to Glasgow but always ends up on the Liverpool train and always slumps in the seat opposite me, and always tells me he's the ex-Karate champion of Greenock and if I want a fight, he's my man although he's currently one of Glasgow's leading industrialists but could I see my way to buy him a wee can of lager. Or two . . .

I am not hummable!

The woman with the two kids on the seat across the aisle begins to hum a melody to get the baby to sleep. I surreptitiously lean across, discreetly trying to hear what she is humming, in the desperate hope that years ago she might have been in the audience in the Green Moose, that she might be humming one of my . . . I hear the unmistakably hummable strains of 'Memories' and groan audibly as the baby sits bolt upright and accuses me of being its 'dada, dada . . . dada'.

My old friend from Glasgow attempts to fix me with a glare and, addressing a space six inches to the side of my head, tells me I should make a respectable woman out of her. He's distracted by the outraged mother and the kids, who are now both crying, and he offers to sing them to sleep. The mother protests and it's not a spectacle I wish to promote but supposing, I mean you never know, he might have been at the Green Moose . . . Hopes dashed as he launches into a cross between 'Mull of Kintyre' and 'My Way'.

That night, a nightmare consisting of a million snippets from likely reviews, one in particular ringing in my ears as I wake, bathed in sweat:

'It is plain that the composer does not know a crotchet from a hatchet though I would readily concede that armed with a hatchet Mr Russell could do no worse damage than he can with a crotchet.'

In the morning, bog-eyed and trembling, staggering down to the kitchen to find the kids already up, dressed for school, attacking Coco-Pops and each other. Filling the kettle, providing the morning arbitration service, trying to apply futile liberal ideals to the kids' uncomplicated straightforward brutality: 'That's mine', 'No it's not', 'Well I'm not gonna be your friend, ever!', SCREAMS, 'Dad, Dad she's got my Star Wars figure an' I'm gonna take her Cindy Doll 'cos that's fair an' I'm gonna break it!' A normal sort of morning, something like a session at the United Nations, with breakfast cereal. And through it all, inside, I'm composing my defence speech for when I come to stand in the Court Of Musical Crimes, accused of TRYING TO WRITE A MUSICAL, facing a jury which includes the Gershwins, Mr Sondheim, Kern, Porter, Mr Rodgers and Mr Lloyd Webber and all their collaborators. I hardly notice that the kids have signed the day's first cease-fire, that they're ready and on their way out to school, that I've given them the wrong packed lunch or the right dinner money, P.E. pumps, swimming costumes and contributions to the school's Better Housing For Hamsters Fund. Hardly notice anything. Hardly notice that through all this Ruthie has been humming some dimly recognisable melody.

We've kissed goodbye, I've watched them set off on the short walk to school, I've got a cup of tea and a ciggie and I'm slumped in the kitchen chair exhausted. And it's a full ten minutes before I realise what the melody was. I'm out of the door and running wildly towards the school. I catch up with her in the playground and she's surprised and slightly startled and even amused that Dad should be in the playground wearing slippers.

'Quickly,' I say, 'just quickly hum me a few bars of that tune.' And suddenly I'm jumping up and down in the playground, shrieking with delight because from only the briefest of hearings one of my kids has picked up a melody of mine. I'm shouting 'Hummable, hummable', over and over again. Ruthie's beaming at me, asking me if I want to play hop-scotch as well. Other kids are looking at me as though I'm a fully fledged nut and teachers are streaming from all directions to apprehend a man gone mad.

After satisfying the headmaster that I'm a mere parent suffering from nothing more dangerous than Chronic-Desire-to-Write-A-Musical, he instructs the caretaker and the peripatetic music teacher to release their grip on me, lectures me about a playground being no place to behave like a child and has me escorted from the grounds. I walk down Church Road, elated, seeing clearly the green of the trees, the yellow of the sunlight. And I know I can go on — because Ruthie was humming one of my tunes.

About a year later, *Blood Brothers* having opened, audiences and critics having responded more kindly than they had in my dreams, I was driving to Wales with the family. The car radio was playing and a song from *Blood Brothers* was introduced. I reached across to turn up the volume when from the back of the car a small voice said, 'Oh not that bloody song again'. I went to say: 'Ruthie! Don't swear'. But fair's fair. I slipped in a cassette of her favourite nursery rhymes and we carried on to Wales singing 'Lavender's Blue' and 'Cock-A-Doodle-Doo'.

WILLY RUSSELL

BLOOD BROTHERS
A Musical

Blood Brothers was first performed at the Liverpool Playhouse on 8 January, 1983, with the following cast:

MRS JOHNSTONE (*Mother*)	Barbara Dickson
MICKEY	George Costigan
EDDIE	Andrew C. Wadsworth
SAMMY	Peter Christian
LINDA	Amanda York
MRS LYONS	Wendy Murray
MR LYONS	Alan Leith
NARRATOR	Andrew Schofield
CHORUS	Hazel Ellerby
	Eithne Brown
	David Edge

Directed by Chris Bond
Designed by Andy Greenfield
Musical Director Peter Filleul
(Presented by arrangement with Bob Swash)

Blood Brothers was subsequently presented by Bob Swash, by arrangement with Liverpool Playhouse at the Lyric Theatre, London, on 11 April, 1983, with the following cast:

MRS JOHNSTONE (*Mother*)	Barbara Dickson
MICKEY	George Costigan
EDDIE	Andrew C. Wadsworth
SAMMY	Peter Christian
LINDA	Kate Fitzgerald
MRS LYONS	Wendy Murray
MR LYONS	Alan Leith
NARRATOR	Andrew Schofield
CHORUS	Hazel Ellerby
	David Edge
	Ian Burns
	Oliver Beamish

Directed by Chris Bond and Danny Hiller
Designed by Andy Greenfield
Musical Director Richard Spanswick

PRODUCTION NOTE

The setting for *Blood Brothers* is an open stage, with the different settings and time spans being indicated by lighting changes, with the minimum of properties and furniture. The whole play should flow along easily and smoothly, with no cumbersome scene changes. Two areas are semi-permanent — the Lyons house and the Johnstone house. We see the interior of the Lyons' comfortable home but usually only the exterior front door of the Johnstone house, with the 'interior' scenes taking place outside the door. The area between the two houses acts as communal ground for street scenes, park scenes etc.

ACT ONE

The Overture comes to a close.

MRS JOHNSTONE (*singing*): Tell me it's not true
   Say it's just a story.

 The NARRATOR steps forward.

NARRATOR (*speaking*): So did y' hear the story of the
    Johnstone twins?
   As like each other as two new pins,
   Of one womb born, on the self same day,
   How one was kept and one given away?

   An' did you never hear how the Johnstones died,
   Never knowing that they shared one name,
   Till the day they died, when a mother cried
   My own dear sons lie slain.

 *The Lights come up to show a re-enactment of the final
 moments of the play — the deaths of* MICKEY *and* EDWARD.
 The scene fades.

MRS JOHNSTONE *enters with her back to the audience.*
   An' did y' never hear of the mother, so cruel,
   There's a stone in place of her heart?
   Then bring her on and come judge for yourselves
   How she came to play this part.

 The NARRATOR exits.

 Music is heard as MRS JOHNSTONE *turns and walks towards
 us. She is aged thirty but looks more like fifty.*

MRS JOHNSTONE (*singing*): Once I had a husband,
   You know the sort of chap,
   I met him at a dance and how he came on with the chat.
   He said my eyes were deep blue pools,
   My skin as soft as snow,
   He told me I was sexier than Marilyn Monroe.

   And we went dancing,
   We went dancing.

   Then, of course, I found
   That I was six weeks overdue.
   We got married at the registry an' then we had a 'do'.
   We all had curly salmon sandwiches,
   An' how the ale did flow,
   They said the bride was lovelier than Marilyn Monroe.

   And we went dancing,
   Yes, we went dancing.

Then the baby came along,
We called him Darren Wayne,
Then three months on I found that I was in the club again.
An' though I still fancied dancing,
My husband wouldn't go,
With a wife he said was twice the size of Marilyn Monroe.

No more dancing
No more dancing.

By the time I was twenty-five,
I looked like forty-two,
With seven hungry mouths to feed and one more nearly
    due.
Me husband, he'd walked out on me,
A month or two ago,
For a girl they say who looks a bit like Marilyn Monroe.

And they go dancing
They go dancing

Yes they go dancing
They go . . .

An irate MILKMAN *(the* NARRATOR*) rushes in to rudely interrupt the song.*

MILKMAN: Listen love, I'm up to here with hard luck stories; you own me three pounds, seventeen and fourpence an' either you pay up today, like now, or I'll be forced to cut off your deliveries.

MRS JOHNSTONE: I said, I said, look, next week I'll pay y' . . .

MILKMAN: Next week, next week! Next week never arrives around here. I'd be a rich man if next week ever came.

MRS JOHNSTONE: But look, look, I start a job next week. I'll have money comin' in an' I'll be able to pay y'. Y' can't stop the milk. I need the milk. I'm pregnant.

MILKMAN: Well, don't look at me, love. I might be a milkman but it's got nothin' to do with me. Now you've been told, no money, no milk.

The MILKMAN *exits.*

MRS JOHNSTONE *stands alone and we hear some of her kids, off.*

KID ONE (*off*): Mam, Mam the baby's cryin'. He wants his bottle. Where's the milk?

KID TWO (*off*): 'Ey Mam, how come I'm on free dinners? All the other kids laugh at me.

KID THREE (*off*): 'Ey Mother, I'm starvin' an' there's nothin' in. There never bloody well is.

MRS JOHNSTONE (*perfunctorily*): Don't swear, I've told y'.

KID FOUR (*off*): Mum, I can't sleep, I'm hungry, I'm starvin' . . .

KIDS (*off*): An' me, Mam. An' me. An' me.

MRS JOHNSTONE (*singing*): I know it's hard on all you kids,
> But try and get some sleep.
> Next week I'll be earnin',
> We'll have loads of things to eat,
> We'll have ham, an' jam, an' spam an'

(*Speaking.*) Roast Beef, Yorkshire Puddin', Battenberg Cake, Chicken an' Chips, Corned Beef, Sausages, Treacle Tart, Mince an' Spuds, Milk Shake for the Baby:

There is a chorus of groaning ecstasy from the KIDS.

MRS JOHNSTONE *picks up the tune again.*

> When I bring home the dough,
> We'll live like kings, like bright young things,
> Like Marilyn Monroe.

> And we'll go dancing . . .

MRS JOHNSTONE *hums a few bars of the song, and dances a few steps, as she makes her way to her place of work —* MRS LYONS' *house. During the dance she acquires a brush, dusters and a mop bucket.*

MRS LYONS' *house where* MRS JOHNSTONE *is working.*

MRS LYONS *enters, carrying a parcel.*

MRS LYONS: Hello, Mrs Johnstone, how are you? Is the job working out all right for you?

MRS JOHNSTONE: It's, erm, great. Thank you. It's such a lovely house it's a pleasure to clean it.

MRS LYONS: It's a pretty house isn't it? It's a pity it's so big. I'm finding it rather large at present.

MRS JOHNSTONE: Oh. Yeh. With Mr Lyons being away an' that? When does he come back, Mrs Lyons?

MRS LYONS: Oh, it seems such a long time. The Company sent him out there for nine months, so, what's that, he'll be back in about five months' time.

MRS JOHNSTONE: Ah, you'll be glad when he's back won't you? The house won't feel so empty then, will it?

MRS LYONS *begins to unwrap her parcel.*

MRS LYONS: Actually, Mrs J, we bought such a large house for the — for the children — we thought children would come along.

MRS JOHNSTONE: Well y' might still be able to . . .

MRS LYONS: No, I'm afraid . . . We've been trying for such a long time now . . . I wanted to adopt but . . . Mr Lyons is . . well he says he wanted his own son, not someone else's. Myself, I believe that an adopted child can become one's own.

MRS JOHNSTONE: Ah yeh . . . yeh. Ey, it's weird though, isn't it. Here's you can't have kids, an' me, I can't stop havin' them. Me husband used to say that all we had to do was shake hands and I'd be in the club. He must have shook hands with me before he left. I'm havin' another one y' know.

MRS LYONS: Oh, I see . . .

MRS JOHNSTONE: Oh but look, look it's all right, Mrs Lyons, I'll still be able to do me work. Havin' babies, it's like clockwork to me. I'm back on me feet an' workin' the next day y' know. If I have this one at the weekend I won't even need to take one day off. I love this job, y' know. We can just manage to get by now —

She is stopped by MRS LYONS *putting the contents of the package, a pair of new shoes, on to the table.*

Jesus Christ, Mrs Lyons, what are y' trying to do?

MRS LYONS: My God, what's wrong?

MRS JOHNSTONE: The shoes . . . the shoes . . .

MRS LYONS: Pardon?

MRS JOHNSTONE: New shoes on the table, take them off . . .

MRS LYONS *does so.*

(*Relieved*) Oh God, Mrs Lyons, never put new shoes on a table . . . You never know what'll happen.

MRS LYONS (*twigging it; laughing*): Oh . . . you mean you're superstitious?

MRS JOHNSTONE: No, but you never put new shoes on the table.

MRS LYONS: Oh go on with you. Look, if it will make you any happier I'll put them away . . .

MRS LYONS *exits with the shoes.*

Music is heard as MRS JOHNSTONE *warily approaches the table and the* NARRATOR *enters.*

NARRATOR: There's shoes upon the table an' a joker in the pack,
The salt's been spilled and a looking glass cracked,
There's one lone magpie overhead.

MRS JOHNSTONE: I'm not superstitious.

NARRATOR: The Mother said

MRS JOHNSTONE: I'm not superstitious.

NARRATOR: The Mother said.

    The NARRATOR *exits to re-enter as a* GYNAECOLOGIST.

MRS JOHNSTONE: What are you doin' here? The milk bill's not due 'till Thursday.

GYNAECOLOGIST (*producing a listening funnel*): Actually I've given up the milk round and gone into medicine. I'm your gynaecologist. (*He begins to examine her.*) OK, Mummy, let's have a little listen to the baby's ticker, shall we?

MRS JOHNSTONE: I was dead worried about havin' another baby, you know, Doctor. I didn't see how we were gonna manage with another mouth to feed. But now I've got me a little job we'll be OK. If I'm careful we can just scrape by, even with another mouth to feed.

    The GYNAECOLOGIST *completes his examination.*

GYNAECOLOGIST: Mouths, Mummy.

MRS JOHNSTONE: What?

GYNAECOLOGIST: Plural, Mrs Johnstone. Mouths to feed. You're expecting twins. Congratulations. And the next one please, Nurse.

    The GYNAECOLOGIST *exits.*

    MRS JOHNSTONE, *numbed by the news, moves back to her work, dusting the table upon which the shoes had been placed.*

    MRS LYONS *enters.*

MRS LYONS: Hello, Mrs. J. How are you?

    There is no reply.

    (*Registering the silence*) Mrs J? Anything wrong?

MRS JOHNSTONE: I had it all worked out.

MRS LYONS: What's the matter?

MRS JOHNSTONE: We were just getting straight.

MRS LYONS: Why don't you sit down.

MRS JOHNSTONE: With one more baby we could have managed. But not with two. The Welfare have already been on to me. They say I'm incapable of controllin' the kids I've already got. They say I should put some of them into care. But I won't. I love the bones of every one of them. I'll even love these two when they come along. But like they say at the Welfare, kids can't live on love alone.

MRS LYONS: Twins? You're expecting twins?

The NARRATOR *enters.*

NARRATOR: How quickly an idea, planted, can
    Take root and grow into a plan.
    The thought conceived in this very room
    Grew as surely as a seed, in a mother's womb.

The NARRATOR *exits.*

MRS LYONS (*almost inaudibly*): Give one to me.

MRS JOHNSTONE: What?

MRS LYONS (*containing her excitement*): Give one of them
    to me.

MRS JOHNSTONE: Give one to you?

MRS LYONS: Yes . . . yes.

MRS JOHNSTONE (*taking it almost as a joke*): But y' can't
    just . . .

MRS LYONS: When are you due?

MRS JOHNSTONE: Erm, well about . . . Oh, but Mrs . . .

MRS LYONS: Quickly, quickly tell me . . . when are you due?

MRS JOHNSTONE: July he said, the beginning of . . .

MRS LYONS: July . . . and my husband doesn't get back until,
    the middle of July. He need never guess . . .

MRS JOHNSTONE (*amused*): Oh, it's mad . . .

MRS LYONS: I know, it is. It's mad . . . but it's wonderful, it's
    perfect. Look, look, you're what, four months pregnant, but
    you're only just beginning to show . . . so, so I'm four months
    pregnant and I'm only just beginning to show. (*She grabs a
    cushion and arranges it beneath her dress.*) Look, look. I could
    have got pregnant just before he went away. But I didn't tell
    him in case I miscarried, I didn't want to worry him whilst
    he was away. But when he arrives home I tell him we were
    wrong, the doctors were wrong. I have a baby, our baby.
    Mrs Johnstone, it will work, it will if only you'll . . .

MRS JOHNSTONE: Oh, Mrs Lyons, you can't be serious.

MRS LYONS: You said yourself, you said you had too many
    children already.

MRS JOHNSTONE: Yeh, but I don't know if I wanna give one
    away.

MRS LYONS: Already you're being threatened by the Welfare
    people. Mrs Johnstone, with two more children how can you
    possibly avoid some of them being put into care? Surely,

it's better to give one child to me. Look, at least if the child
was with me you'd be able to see him every day, as you came
to work.

MRS LYONS *stares at* MRS JOHNSTONE, *willing her to
agree.*

Please, Mrs Johnstone. Please.

MRS JOHNSTONE: Are y' . . . are y' that desperate to have
a baby?

MRS LYONS (*singing*): Each day I look out from this window,
I see him with his friends, I hear him call,
I rush down but as I fold my arms around him,
He's gone. Was he ever there at all?

I've dreamed of all the places I would take him,
The games we'd play the stories I would tell,
The jokes we'd share, the clothing I would make him,
I reach out. But as I do. He fades away.

The melody shifts into that of MRS JOHNSTONE *who is
looking at* MRS LYONS, *feeling for her.* MRS LYONS *gives
a half smile and a shrug, perhaps slightly embarrassed at what
she has revealed.* MRS JOHNSTONE *turns and looks at the
room she is in. Looking up in awe at the comparative opulence
and ease of the place. Tentatively and wondering she sings*

MRS JOHNSTONE: If my child was raised
In a palace like this one,
(He) wouldn't have to worry where
His next meal was comin' from.
His clothing would be (supplied by)
George Henry Lee.

MRS LYONS *sees that* MRS JOHNSTONE *might be persuaded.*

MRS LYONS (*singing*): He'd have all his own toys
And a garden to play in.

MRS JOHNSTONE: He could make too much noise
Without the neighbours complainin'.

MRS LYONS: Silver trays to take meals on

MRS JOHNSTONE: A bike with *both* wheels on?
MRS LYONS *nods enthusiastically.*

MRS LYONS: And he'd sleep every night
In a bed of his own.

MRS JOHNSTONE: He wouldn't get into fights
He'd leave matches alone.
And you'd never find him
Effin' and blindin'.

And when he grew up
He could never be told
To stand and queue up
For hours on end at the dole
He'd grow up to be

MRS LYONS
MRS JOHNSTONE } (*together*):   A credit to me

MRS JOHNSTONE: To you.

MRS JOHNSTONE: I would still be able to see him every day,
    wouldn't I?

MRS LYONS: Of course.

MRS JOHNSTONE: An' . . . an' you would look after him,
    wouldn't y'?

MRS LYONS (*singing*): I'd keep him warm in the winter
            And cool when it shines.
        I'd pull out his splinters
        Without making him cry.
        I'd always be there
        If his dream was a nightmare.
        My child.
        My child.

There is a pause before MRS JOHNSTONE *nods.* MRS LYONS
goes across and kisses her, hugs her. MRS JOHNSTONE *is
slightly embarrassed.*

Oh. Now you must help me. There's so much . . . I'll have
to . . . (*She takes out the cushion.*) We'll do this properly so
that it's thoroughly convincing, and I'll need to see you walk,
and baby clothes, I'll have to knit and buy bottles and suffer
from piles.

MRS JOHNSTONE: What?

MRS LYONS: Doesn't one get piles when one's pregnant? And
    buy a cot and . . . Oh help me with this, Mrs J. Is it in the right
    place? (*She puts the cushion back again.*) I want it to look
    right before I go shopping.

MRS JOHNSTONE (*helping her with the false pregnancy*): What
    you goin' the shops for? I do the shopping.

MRS LYONS: Oh no, from now on I do the shopping. I want
    everyone to know about my baby. (*She suddenly reaches for
    the Bible.*)
    Music.
    Mrs J. We must make this a, erm, a binding agreement.

MRS LYONS *shows the Bible to* MRS JOHNSTONE, *who is at first reluctant and then lays her hand on it.*

The NARRATOR *enters. A bass note, repeated as a heartbeat.*

NARRATOR: In the name of Jesus, the thing was done,
    Now there's no going back, for anyone.
    It's too late now, for feeling torn
    There's a pact been sealed, there's a deal been born.

MRS LYONS *puts the Bible away.* MRS JOHNSTONE *stands and stares as* MRS LYONS *grabs shopping bags and takes a last satisfied glance at herself in the mirror.*

MRS JOHNSTONE: Why . . . why did we have to do that?

MRS LYONS: Mrs J, nobody must ever know. Therefore we have to have an agreement.

MRS JOHNSTONE *nods but is still uncomfortable.*

Right, I shan't be long. Bye.

MRS LYONS *exits.*

MRS JOHNSTONE *stands alone, afraid.*

The heartbeat grows in intensity.

NARRATOR: How swiftly those who've made a pact,
    Can come to overlook the fact.
    Or wish the reckoning to be delayed
    But a debt is a debt, and must be paid.

The NARRATOR *exits.*

As the heartbeat reaches maximum volume it suddenly stops and is replaced by the sound of crying babies.

Two nurses appear, each carrying a bundle. A pram is wheeled on.

The nurses hand the bundles to MRS JOHNSTONE *who places them smiling, into the pram. Making faces and noises at the babies she stops the crying. The babies settled, she sets off, wheeling the pram towards home.*

Various debt collectors emerge from her house to confront MRS JOHNSTONE.

CATALOGUE MAN: I'm sorry love . . . the kids said you were at the hospital. (*He looks into the pram.*) Ah . . . they're lovely, aren't they? I'm sorry love, especially at a time like this, but, you are twelve weeks behind in your payments. I've got to do this, girl . . .

FINANCE MAN: Y' shouldn't sign for the bloody stuff, missis. If y' know y' can't pay, y' shouldn't bloody well sign.

CATALOGUE MAN: Look, if y' could give me a couple of

weeks' money on this I could leave it.
MRS JOHNSTONE *shakes her head.*

FINANCE MAN: Y' shouldn't have signed for all this stuff, should y'? Y' knew y' wouldn't be able to pay, didn't y'?

MRS JOHNSTONE (*almost to herself*): When I got me job, I thought I would be able to pay. When I went in the showroom I only meant to come out with a couple of things. But when you're standing there, it all looks so nice. When y' look in the catalogue an' there's six months to pay, it seems years away, an' y' need a few things so y' sign.

FINANCE MAN: Yeh, well y' bloody well shouldn't.

MRS JOHNSTONE (*coming out of her trance; angrily*): I know I shouldn't, you soft get. I've spent all me bleedin' life knowin' I *shouldn't*. But I do. Now, take y' soddin' wireless and get off.

CATALOGUE MAN: Honest love, I'm sorry.

MRS JOHNSTONE: It's all right lad . . . we're used to it. We were in the middle of our tea one night when they arrived for the table. (*She gives a wry laugh.*)

CATALOGUE MAN: Ah well as long as y' can laugh about it, eh, that's the main thing isn't it?
The CATALOGUE MAN *exits.*

MRS JOHNSTONE (*not laughing*): Yeh.

Other creditors continue to enter the house and leave with goods.

MRS JOHNSTONE *watches the creditors. The babies begin to cry and she moves to the pram, rocking it gently as she sings, as if to the babies in the pram. (Singing)*

Only mine until
The time comes round
To pay the bill.
Then, I'm afraid,
What can't be paid
Must be returned.
You never, ever learn,
That nothing's yours,
On easy terms.

Only for a time,
I must not learn,
To call you mine.
Familiarize
That face, those eyes

Make future plans
That cannot be confirmed.
On borrowed time,
On easy terms.

Living on the never never,
Constant as the changing weather,
Never sure
Who's at the door
Or the price I'll have to pay.

Should we meet again
I will not recognize your name.
You can be sure
What's gone before
Will be concealed.
Your friends will never learn
That once we were
On easy terms.

Living on the never never,
Constant as the changing weather,
Never sure
Who's at the door
Or the price I'll have to pay . . .

MRS LYONS *enters, still with the pregnancy padding.*

MRS LYONS: They're born, you didn't notify me.

MRS JOHNSTONE: Well I . . . I just . . . it's . . . couldn't I keep
them for a few more days, please, please, they're a pair, they
go together.

MRS LYONS: My husband is due back tomorrow, Mrs Johnstone.
I must have my baby. We made an agreement, a bargain.
You swore on the Bible.

MRS JOHNSTONE: You'd better . . . you'd better see which one
you want.

MRS LYONS: I'll take . . .

MRS JOHNSTONE: No. Don't tell me which one. Just take him,
take him. (*Singing*)
Living on the never never,
Constant as the changing weather,
Never sure
Who's at the door
Or the price I'll have to pay,
Should we meet again . . .

MRS LYONS *rapidly pulls out the padding from beneath her dress. Amongst it is a shawl which she uses to wrap around the baby before picking it up from the pram.*

MRS LYONS: Thank you Mrs Johnstone, thank you. I'll see you next week.

MRS JOHNSTONE: I'm due back tomorrow.

MRS LYONS: I know but why don't you . . . why don't you take the week off, on full pay of course.
MRS LYON *exits.*

MRS JOHNSTONE *turns and enters her house with the remaining twin in the pram.*

KID ONE (*off*): What happened to the other twin, Mother?

KID TWO (*off*): Where's the other twinny, Mam?

MRS JOHNSTONE: He's gone. He's gone up to heaven, love. He's living with Jesus and the angels.

KID THREE (*off*): What's it like there Mam, in heaven?

MRS JOHNSTONE: It's lovely son, he'll be well looked after there. He'll have anything he wants.

KID ONE (*off*): Will he have his own bike?

MRS JOHNSTONE: Yeh. With both wheels on.

KID ONE (*off*): Why can't I have a bike? Eh?

MRS JOHNSTONE: I'll . . . I'll have a look in the catalogue next week. We'll see what the bikes are like in there.

KIDS (*together, off*): Mam, I want a Meccano set.
You said I could have a new dress, Mother.
Why can't I have an air pistol?
Let's look in the catalogue now, Mam.
It's great when we look in the catalogue, Mam.
Go on, let's all look in the catalogue.

MRS JOHNSTONE: I've told y', when I get home, I've got to go to work.

MR and MRS LYONS *enter their house and we see them looking at the child in its cot.*

MRS JOHNSTONE *enters and immediately goes about her work.*

MRS JOHNSTONE *stops work for a moment and glances into the cot, beaming and cooing. MR LYONS is next to her with MRS LYONS in the background, obviously agitated at MRS JOHNSTON's fussing.*

Aw, he's really comin' on now, isn't he, Mr Lyons? I'll bet y' dead proud of him, aren't y', aren't y', eh?

MR LYONS (*good naturedly*): Yes . . . yes I am, aren't I Edward? I'm proud of Jennifer, too.

MR LYONS *beams at his wife who can hardly raise a smile.*

MRS JOHNSTONE: Ah . . . he's lovely. (*She coos into the cot.*) Ah look, he wants to be picked up, I'll just . . .

MRS LYONS: No, no, Mrs Johnstone. He's fine. He doesn't want to be picked up.

MRS JOHNSTONE: Ah, but look he's gonna cry . . .

MRS LYONS: If he needs picking up, *I* shall pick him up. All right?

MRS JOHNSTONE: Well, I just thought, I'm sorry I . . .

MRS LYONS: Yes. Erm, has the bathroom been done? Time is getting on.

MRS JOHNSTONE: Oh. Yeh, yeh . . .

MRS JOHNSTONE *exits.*

MR LYONS: Darling. Don't be hard on the woman. She only wanted to hold the baby. All women like to hold babies, don't they?

MRS LYONS: I don't want her to hold the baby, Richard. She's . . . I don't want the baby to catch anything. Babies catch things very easily, Richard.

MR LYONS: All right, all right, you know best.

MRS LYONS: You don't see her as much as I do. She's always fussing over him; any opportunity and she's cooing and cuddling as if she were his mother. She's always bothering him, Richard, always. Since the baby arrived she ignores most of her work. (*She is about to cry.*)

MR LYONS: Come on, come on . . . It's all right Jennifer. You're just a little . . . it's this depression thing that happens after a woman's had a . . .

MRS LYONS: I'm not depressed Richard; it's just that she makes me feel . . . Richard, I think she should go.

MR LYONS: And what will you do for help in the house?

MRS LYONS: I'll find somebody else. I'll find somebody who doesn't spend all day fussing over the baby.

MR LYONS (*glancing at his watch*): Oh well, I suppose you know best. The house is your domain. Look, Jen, I've got a board meeting. I really must dash.

MRS LYONS: Richard, can you let me have some cash?

MR LYONS: Of course.

MRS LYONS: I need about fifty pounds.

MR LYONS: My God, what for?

MRS LYONS: I've got lots of things to buy for the baby, I've got the nursery to sort out . . .

MR LYONS: All right, all right, here. (*He hands her the money.*) MR LYONS *exits*.

MRS LYONS *considers what she is about to do and then calls*

MRS LYONS: Mrs Johnstone. Mrs Johnstone, would you come out here for a moment, please.
MRS JOHNSTONE *enters*.

MRS JOHNSTONE: Yes?

MRS LYONS. Sit down. Richard and I have been talking it over and, well the thing is, we both think it would be better if you left.

MRS JOHNSTONE: Left where?

MRS LYONS: It's your work. Your work has deteriorated.

MRS JOHNSTONE: But, I work the way I've always worked.

MRS LYONS: Well, I'm sorry, we're not satisfied.

MRS JOHNSTONE: What will I do? How are we gonna live without my job?

MRS LYONS: Yes, well we've thought of that. Here, here's . . . (*She pushes the money into* MRS JOHNSTONE's *hands.*) It's a lot of money . . . but, well . . .

MRS JOHNSTONE (*thinking, desperate. Trying to get it together.*) OK. All right. All right, Mrs Lyons, right. If I'm goin', I'm takin' my son with me, I'm takin' . . .
As MRS JOHNSTONE *moves towards the cot* MRS LYONS *roughly drags her out of the way*.

MRS LYONS: Oh no, you're not. Edward is my son. Mine.

MRS JOHNSTONE: I'll tell someone . . . I'll tell the police . . . I'll bring the police in an' . . .

MRS LYONS: No . . . no you won't. You gave your baby away. Don't you realize what a crime that is. You'll be locked up. You sold your baby.

MRS JOHNSTONE, *horrified, sees the bundle of notes in her hand, and throws it across the room.*

MRS JOHNSTONE: I didn't . . . you told me, you said I could see him every day. Well, I'll tell someone, I'm gonna tell . . .
MRS JOHNSTONE *starts to leave but* MRS LYONS *stops her.*

MRS LYONS: No. You'll tell nobody.
Music.
Because . . . because if you tell anyone . . . and these children
learn of the truth, then you know what will happen, don't
you? You do know what they say about twins, secretly parted,
don't you?

MRS JOHNSTONE (*terrified*): What? What?

MRS LYONS: They say . . . they say that if either twin learns
that he once was a pair, they shall both immediately die.
It means, Mrs Johnstone, that these brothers shall grow up,
unaware of the other's existence. They shall be raised apart
and never, ever told what was once the truth. You won't tell
anyone about this, Mrs Johnstone, because if you do, you will
kill them.

MRS LYONS *picks up the money and thrusts it into* MRS
JOHNSTONE's *hands.* MRS LYONS *turns and walks away.*

The NARRATOR *enters*

NARRATOR (*singing*): Shoes upon the table
An' a spider's been killed.
Someone broke the lookin' glass
A full moon shinin'
An' the salt's been spilled.
You're walkin' on the pavement cracks
Don't know what's gonna come to pass.

Now y' know the devil's got your number,
Y' know he's gonna find y',
Y' know he's right behind y',
He's starin' through your windows
He's creepin' down the hall.

Ain't no point in clutching
At your rosary
You're always gonna know what was done
Even when you shut your eyes you still see
That you sold a son
And you can't tell anyone.

But y' know the devil's got your number,
Y' know he's gonna find y',
Y' know he's right behind y',
He's starin' through your windows
He's creeping down the hall

Yes, y' know the devil's got your number
He's gonna find y',

> Y' know he's right behind y',
> He's standin' on your step
> And he's knocking at your door.
> He's knocking at your door,
> He's knocking at your door.

The NARRATOR exits.

During the song MRS JOHNSTONE has gone to her house and locked herself in.

MICKEY, aged 'seven' is knocking incessantly at the door. He is carrying a toy gun.

MRS JOHNSTONE (*screaming; off*): Go away!

MICKEY: Mother . . . will y' open the bleedin' door or what?

MRS JOHNSTONE (*realizing; with relief; off*): Mickey?
MRS JOHNSTONE *comes to open the door.*

MICKEY: Mam, Mam.
She grabs him and hugs him. He extricates himself.
Why was the door bolted? Did you think it was the rent man?
She laughs and looks at him.
Mam, our Sammy's robbed me other gun an' that was me best one. Why does he rob all me things off me?

MRS JOHNSTONE: Because you're the youngest Mickey. It used to happen to our Sammy when he was the youngest.

MICKEY: Mam, we're playin' mounted police an' Indians. I'm a mountie. Mam, Mam, y' know this mornin', we've wiped out three thousand Indians.

MRS JOHNSTONE: Good.

MICKEY (*aiming the gun at her and firing*): Mam, Mam, you're dead.

MRS JOHNSTONE (*staring at him*): Hmm.

MICKEY: What's up, Mam?

MRS JOHNSTONE: Nothin' son. Go on, you go out an' play, there's a good lad. But, ey, don't you go playin' with those hooligans down at the rough end.

MICKEY (*on his way out*): We're down at the other end, near the big houses in the park.

MRS JOHNSTONE: Mickey! Come here.

MICKEY: What?

MRS JOHNSTONE: What did you say, where have you been playin'?

MICKEY: Mam, I'm sorry, I forgot.

MRS JOHNSTONE: What have I told you about playin' up near
there. Come here. (*She grabs him.*)

MICKEY: It wasn't my fault. Honest.

MRS JOHNSTONE: So whose fault was it then?

MICKEY: The Indians. They rode up that way, they were tryin'
to escape.

MRS JOHNSTONE: Don't you ever go up there. Do you hear me?

MICKEY: Yeh. You let our Sammy go up there.

MRS JOHNSTONE: Our Sammy's older than you.

MICKEY: But why . . .

MRS JOHNSTONE: Just shut up. Never mind why. You don't go
up near there. Now go on, get out an' play. But you stay
outside the front door where I can see y'.

MICKEY: Ah but, Mam, the . . .

MRS JOHNSTONE: Go on!

MRS JOHNSTONE *exits.*

MICKEY *makes his way outside. He is fed up. Desultory.*
Shoots down a few imaginary Indians but somehow the magic
has gone out of genocide.

MICKEY *sits, bored, looking at the ants on the pavement.*

MICKEY (*reciting*): I wish I was our Sammy
Our Sammy's nearly ten.
He's got two worms and a catapult
An' he's built a underground den.
But I'm not allowed to go in there,
I have to stay near the gate,
'Cos me Mam says I'm only seven,
But I'm not, I'm nearly eight!

I sometimes hate our Sammy,
He robbed me toy car y' know,
Now the wheels are missin' an' the top's broke off,
An' the bleedin' thing won't go.
An' he said when he took it, it was just like that,
But it wasn't, it went dead straight,
But y' can't say nott'n when they think y' seven
An' y' not, y' nearly eight.

I wish I was our Sammy,
Y' wanna see him spit,
Straight in y' eye from twenty yards
An' every time a hit.
He's allowed to play with matches,

And he goes to bed dead late,
And I have to go at seven,
Even though I'm nearly eight.

Y' know our Sammy,
He draws nudey women,
Without arms, or legs, or even heads
In the baths, when he goes swimmin'.
But I'm not allowed to go to the baths,
Me Mam says I have to wait,
'Cos I might get drowned, 'cos I'm only seven,
But I'm not, I'm nearly eight.

Y' know our Sammy,
Y' know what he sometimes does?
He wees straight through the letter box
Of the house next door to us.
I tried to do it one night,
But I had to stand on a crate,
'Cos I couldn't reach the letter box
But I will by the time I'm eight.

Bored and petulant, MICKEY *sits and shoots an imaginary Sammy.*

EDWARD, *also aged 'seven' appears. He is bright and forthcoming.*

EDWARD: Hello.

MICKEY (*suspiciously*): Hello.

EDWARD: I've seen you before.

MICKEY: Where?

EDWARD: You were playing with some other boys near my house.

MICKEY: Do you live up in the park?

EDWARD: Yes. Are you going to come and play up there again?

MICKEY: No. I would do but I'm not allowed.

EDWARD: Why?

MICKEY: 'Cos me mam says.

EDWARD: Well, my mummy doesn't allow me to play down here actually.

MICKEY: 'Gis a sweet.

EDWARD: All right. (*He offers a bag from his pocket.*)

MICKEY (*shocked*): What?

EDWARD: Here.

MICKEY (*trying to work out the catch. Suspiciously taking one*):
Can I have another one. For our Sammy?

EDWARD: Yes, of course. Take as many as you want.

MICKEY (*taking a handful*): Are you soft?

EDWARD: I don't think so.

MICKEY: Round here if y' ask for a sweet, y' have to ask about,
about twenty million times. An' y' know what?

EDWARD (*sitting beside MICKEY*): What?

MICKEY: They still don't bleedin' give y' one. Sometimes our
Sammy does but y' have to be dead careful if our Sammy gives
y' a sweet.

EDWARD: Why?

MICKEY: 'Cos, if our Sammy gives y' a sweet he's usually weed
on it first.

EDWARD (*exploding in giggles*): Oh, that sounds like super fun.

MICKEY: It is. If y' our Sammy.

EDWARD: Do you want to come and play?

MICKEY: I might do. But I'm not playin' now 'cos I'm pissed off.

EDWARD (*awed*): Pissed off. You say smashing things don't
you? Do you know any more words like that?

MICKEY: Yeh. Yeh, I know loads of words like that. Y' know,
like the 'F' word.

EDWARD (*clueless*): Pardon?

MICKEY: The 'F' word.
EDWARD *is still puzzled.* MICKEY *looks round to check that
he cannot be overheard, then whispers the word to* EDWARD.
The two of them immediately wriggle and giggle with glee.

EDWARD: What does it mean?

MICKEY: I don't know. It sounds good though, doesn't it?

EDWARD: Fantastic. When I get home I'll look it up in the
dictionary.

MICKEY: In the what?

EDWARD: The dictionary. Don't you know what a dictionary is?

MICKEY: 'Course I do. . . . It's a, it's a thingy innit?

EDWARD: A book which explains the meaning of words.

MICKEY: The meaning of words, yeh. Our Sammy'll be here
soon. I hope he's in a good mood. He's dead mean sometimes.

EDWARD: Why?

MICKEY: It's 'cos he's got a plate in his head.

EDWARD: A plate. In his head?

MICKEY: Yeh. When he was little, me Mam was at work an' our Donna Marie was supposed to be lookin' after him but he fell out the window an' broke his head. So they took him to the hospital an' put a plate in his head.

EDWARD: A plate. A dinner plate?

MICKEY: I don't think so, 'cos our Sammy's head's not really that big. I think it must have been one of them little plates that you have bread off.

EDWARD: A side plate?

MICKEY: No, it's on the top.

EDWARD: And . . . and can you see the shape of it, in his head?

MICKEY: I suppose, I suppose if y' looked under his hair.

EDWARD (*after a reflective pause*): You know the most smashing things. Will you be my best friend?

MICKEY: Yeh. If y' want.

EDWARD: What's your name?

MICKEY: Michael Johnstone. But everyone calls me Mickey. What's yours?

EDWARD: Edward Lyons.

MICKEY: D' they call y' Eddie?

EDWARD: No.

MICKEY: Well, I will.

EDWARD: Will you?

MICKEY: Yeh. How old are y' Eddie?

EDWARD: Seven.

MICKEY: I'm older than you. I'm nearly eight.

EDWARD: Well, I'm nearly eight, really.

MICKEY: What's your birthday?

EDWARD: July the eighteenth.

MICKEY: So is mine.

EDWARD: Is it really?

MICKEY: Ey, we were born on the same day . . . that means we can be blood brothers. Do you wanna be my blood brother, Eddie?

EDWARD: Yes, please.

MICKEY (*producing a penknife*): It hurts y' know. (*He puts a nick in his hand.*) Now, give us yours.

MICKEY *nicks* EDWARD's *hand, then they clamp hands together.*
See this means that we're blood brothers, an' that we always have to stand by each other. Now you say after me: 'I will always defend my brother'.

EDWARD: I will always defend my brother . . .

MICKEY: And stand by him.

EDWARD: And stand by him.

MICKEY: An' share all my sweets with him.

EDWARD: And share . . .

SAMMY *leaps in front of them, gun in hand, pointed at them.*

MICKEY: Hi ya, Sammy.

SAMMY: Give us a sweet.

MICKEY: Haven't got any.

EDWARD: Yes, you have . . .
MICKEY *frantically shakes his head, trying to shut* EDWARD *up.*
Yes, I gave you one for Sammy, remember?
SAMMY *laughs at* EDWARD's *voice and* MICKEY's *misfortune.*

SAMMY: Y' little robbin' get.

MICKEY: No, I'm not. (*He hands over a sweet.*) An' anyway, you pinched my best gun.
MICKEY *tries to snatch the gun from* SAMMY, *but* SAMMY *is too fast.*

SAMMY: It's last anyway. It only fires caps. I'm gonna get a real gun soon, I'm gonna get an air gun.
SAMMY *goes into a fantasy shoot out. He doesn't notice* EDWARD *who has approached him and is craning to get a close look at his head.*
(*Eventually noticing*) What are you lookin' at?

EDWARD: Pardon.

MICKEY: That's Eddie. He lives up by the park.

SAMMY: He's a friggin' poshy.

MICKEY: No, he's not. He's my best friend.

SAMMY (*snorting, deciding it's not worth the bother*): You're soft. Y' just soft little kids. (*In quiet disdain he moves away.*)

MICKEY: Where y' goin'?

SAMMY (*looking at* MICKEY): I'm gonna do another burial. Me worms have died again.

MICKEY (*excitedly; to* EDWARD): Oh, y' comin' the funeral?
   Our Sammy is having a funeral. Can we come, Sammy?
   SAMMY *puts his hand into his pocket and brings forth a*
   handful of soil.

SAMMY: Look, they was alive an wrigglin' this mornin'. But by
   dinner time they was dead.
   MICKEY *and* EDWARD *inspect the deceased worms in*
   SAMMY*'s hand.*
   MRS JOHNSTONE *enters.*

MRS JOHNSTONE: Mickey . . . Mickey . . .

EDWARD: Is that your mummy?

MICKEY: Mam . . . Mam, this is my brother.

MRS JOHNSTONE (*stunned*): What?

MICKEY: My blood brother, Eddie.

MRS JOHNSTONE: Eddie, Eddie who?

EDWARD: Edward Lyons, Mrs Johnstone.
   MRS JOHNSTONE *stands still, staring at him.*

MICKEY: Eddie's my best friend, Mam. He lives up by the park
   an' . . .

MRS JOHNSTONE: Mickey . . . get in the house.

MICKEY: What?

MRS JOHNSTONE: Sammy, you an' all. Both of y' get in.

SAMMY: But I'm older than him, I don't have to . . .

MRS JOHNSTONE: I said get, the pair of y' . . .

MICKEY (*going, almost in tears*): But I haven't done nothin'.
   I'll see y' Eddie. Ta ra, Eddie . . .
   MICKEY *exits.*

MRS JOHNSTONE: Sammy!

SAMMY: Ah. (*To* EDWARD.) I'll get you.

EDWARD: Have I done something wrong, Mrs Johnstone?

MRS JOHNSTONE: Does your mother know that you're down
   here?
   EDWARD *shakes his head.*
   An' what would she say if she did know?

EDWARD: I . . . I think she's be angry?

MRS JOHNSTONE: So don't you think you better get home
   before she finds out?

EDWARD: Yes.

MRS JOHNSTONE: Go on, then.

EDWARD *turns to go, then stops.*

EDWARD: Could I . . . would it be all right if I came to play with Mickey on another day? Or perhaps he could come to play at my house . . .

MRS JOHNSTONE: Don't you ever come round here again. Ever.

EDWARD: But . . .

MRS JOHNSTONE: Ever! Now go on. Beat it, go home before the bogey man gets y'.

> EDWARD *walks towards his home. As he goes* MRS JOHNSTONE *sings*

> Should we meet again,
> I will not recognize your name,
> You can be sure
> What's gone before
> Will be concealed.
> Your friends will never learn
> That once we were
> On easy terms.

MR and MRS LYONS *enter their house as* EDWARD *walks home.*

EDWARD *reaches his home and walks in. His mother hugs him and his father produces a toy gun for him. EDWARD, delighted, seizes it and 'shoots' his father, who spiritedly 'dies' to* EDWARD*'s great amusement. EDWARD and his father romp on the floor. MRS LYONS settles herself in an armchair with a story book, calling EDWARD over to her. EDWARD goes and sits with her, MR LYONS joining them and sitting on the arm of the chair.*

MRS JOHNSTONE *turns and goes into her house at the end of the song.*

MR LYONS *gets up and walks towards the door.*

EDWARD: Daddy . . . we haven't finished the story yet.

MR LYONS: Mummy will read the story, Edward. I've got to go to work for an hour.

> MRS LYONS *gets up and goes to her husband,* EDWARD *goes to the bookshelf and leafs through a dictionary.*

MRS LYONS: Richard you didn't say . . .

MR LYONS: Darling, I'm sorry, but if, if we complete this merger I will, I promise you, have more time. That's why we're doing it, Jen. If we complete this, the firm will run itself and I'll have plenty of time to spend with you both.

MRS LYONS: I just — it's not me, it's Edward. You should spend more time with him. I don't want — I don't want him growing away from you.

EDWARD: Daddy, how do you spell bogey man?

MR LYONS: Ask Mummy. Darling, I'll see you later now. Must dash.
MR LYONS exits.

EDWARD: Mummy, how do you spell bogey man?

MRS LYONS: Mm?

EDWARD: Bogey man?

MRS LYONS (*laughing*): Edward, whever did you hear such a thing?

EDWARD: I'm trying to look it up.

MRS LYONS: There's no such thing as a bogey man. It's a — a superstition. The sort of thing a silly mother might say to her children — 'the bogey man will get you'.

EDWARD: Will he get me?

MRS LYONS: Edward, I've told you, there's no such thing.
A doorbell is heard.
MRS LYONS goes to answer the door.

MICKEY (*off*): Does Eddie live here?

MRS LYONS (*off*): Pardon?

MICKEY (*off*): Does he? Is he comin' out to play, eh?

EDWARD (*shouting*): Mickey!
MICKEY enters, pursued by MRS LYONS.

MICKEY: Hi-ya, Eddie. I've got our Sammy's catapult. Y' comin' out?

EDWARD: Oh! (*He takes the catapult and trys a practice shot.*) Isn't Mickey fantastic, Mum?

MRS LYONS: Do you go to the same school as Edward?

MICKEY: No.

EDWARD: Mickey says smashing things. We're blood brothers, aren't we, Mickey?

MICKEY: Yeh. We were born on the same day.

EDWARD: Come on Mickey, let's go . . .

MRS LYONS: Edward . . . Edward, it's time for bed.

EDWARD: Mummy. It's not.
MRS LYONS takes over and ushers MICKEY out.

MRS LYONS: I'm very sorry, but it's Edward's bedtime.

EDWARD: Mummy. Mummy, it's early.

MRS LYONS *exits with* MICKEY *to show him out. Then she returns.*

Mummy!

MRS LYONS: Edward. Edward where did you meet that boy?

EDWARD: At his house.

MRS LYONS: And . . . and his second name is Johnstone, isn't it?

EDWARD: Yes. And I think you're very, very mean.

MRS LYONS: I've told you never to go where that boy — where boys like that live.

EDWARD: But why?

MRS LYONS: Because, because you're not the same as him. You're not, do you understand?

EDWARD: No, I don't understand. And I hate you!

MRS LYONS (*almost crying*): Edward, Edward, don't. It's . . . what I'm doing is only for your own good. It's only because I love you, Edward.

EDWARD: You don't you don't. If you loved me you'd let me go out with Mickey because he's my best friend. I like him more than you.

MRS LYONS: Edward. Edward don't say that. Don't ever say that.

EDWARD: Well. Well it's true. And I will say it. I know what you are.

MRS LYONS: What? What!

EDWARD: You're . . . you're a fuckoff!

MRS LYONS *hits* EDWARD *hard and instinctively.*

MRS LYONS: You see, you see why I don't want you mixing with boys like that! You learn filth from them and behave like this like a, like a horrible little boy, like them. But you are not like them. You are my son, mine, and you won't, you won't ever . . .

She notices the terror in EDWARD's *face and realizes how heavy she has been. Gently she pulls him to her and cradles him.*

Oh, my son . . . my beautiful, beautiful son.

The scene fades as the next scene begins. We hear cap guns and the sound of children making Indian whoops.

The children rush on into the street playing cowboys and Indians; cops and robbers; goodies and baddies etc.

During the battle MRS LYONS *exits.*

EDWARD *remains on stage, in the background, as though in his garden, watching, unnoticed by the battling children.*
MICKEY *and* LINDA *are in one gang,* SAMMY *in another.*

SAMMY (*singing acapella, kids' rhyme*):
> I got y'
> I shot y'
> An' y' bloody know I did
> I got y'
> I shot y'

LINDA: I stopped it with the bin lid.
There is a mass of derisive jeers from the other side.
Music.

(*Singing*): But you know that if you cross your fingers
> And if you count from one to ten
> You can get up off the ground again
> It doesn't matter
> The whole thing's just a game.

The shooting starts all over again. A KID *raps on the door of a house.* LINDA, *as a 'Moll' appears.*

KID: My name is Elliot Ness,
> And lady, here's my card,
> I'm lookin' for one Al Capone
(*To* LACKEYS):
> Mac, check the back
> Sarge, you check the yard!

LINDA: But pal, I've told y'
> Al ain't home.
We see 'Al' make a break for it. NESS *shoots him like he was eating his breakfast.*

KID: So, lady can I use your telephone.
As NESS *goes to the phone and orders a hearse we see* AL *get up and sing the chorus with the other children*
> But you know that if you cross your fingers,
> And if you count from one to ten,
> You can get up off the ground again,
> It doesn't matter the whole thing's just a game.

The KID *who was playing* AL *becomes a cowboy. He turns to face* SAMMY *and sings*

COWBOY: When I say draw,
> You'd better grab that gun,
> An' maybe say a little prayer

Cos I'm the fastest draw
That man you ever saw.
Call up your woman, say goodbye to her,
Cos y' know you're goin' right down there.

As he draws his gun on SAMMY, SAMMY *produces a bazooka
and blows him off the stage.*

ALL: But you know that if you cross your fingers,
And if you count from one to ten,
You can get up off the ground again,
It doesn't matter,
The whole thing's just a game.

A small group of CHILDREN *become a brigade of US troops.*

SERGEANT: OK men, let's get them
With a hand grenade.

CORPORAL: Let's see them try and get outta this.

REST: He's a hot shot Sergeant
From the Ninth Brigade
He's never been known to miss

SERGEANT (*to grenade*): C'mon give Daddy a kiss. (*He pulls the
pin and lobs it.*)
His BRIGADE *cover their ears and crouch down.* LINDA
*catches the grenade and lobs it back at them. After being
blown to pieces they get up singing the chorus, along with
the 'enemy'.*

ALL: But you know that if you cross your fingers,
And if you count from one to ten.
You can get up off the ground again,
It doesn't matter,
The whole thing's just a game.

SAMMY *comes forward as* PROFESSOR HOWE *carrying a
condom filled with water.*

PROFESSOR: My name's Professor Howe,
An' zees bomb I 'old,
Eet can destroy ze 'emisphere,
I've primed it, I've timed it
To explode,
Unless you let me out of here (NO?)
They don't.
Then I suggest you cover your ears.
*There is an explosion which tops them all. Out of it come all
the children singing the chorus.*

ALL: But you know that if you cross your fingers,
  And if you count from one to ten,
  you can get up off the ground again,
  It doesn't matter,
  The whole thing's just a game
  The whole thing's just a game
  The whole thing's just a . . .

SAMMY (*interrupting; chanting*):
  You're dead
  Y' know y' are
  I got y' standin'
  Near that car.

LINDA: But when y' did
  His hand was hid
  Behind his back
  His fingers crossed
  An' so he's not

MICKEY: So you fuck off!

All the children, apart from MICKEY *and* LINDA, *point and chant the accusing 'Aah!'* MICKEY *is singled out, accused. The rest, led by* SAMMY *suddenly chant at* MICKEY *and point*

ALL (*chanting*): You said the 'F' word
  You're gonna die
  You'll go to hell an' there you'll fry
  Just like a fish in a chip shop fat
  Only twenty five million times hotter than that!

They all laugh at MICKEY.

LINDA *moves in to protect* MICKEY *who is visibly shaken.*

LINDA: Well, well, all youse lot swear, so you'll all go to hell with him.

SAMMY: No, we won't Linda.

LINDA: Why?

SAMMY: 'Cos when we swear . . . we cross our fingers!

MICKEY: Well, my fingers were crossed.

CHILDREN (*variously*): No they were't.
  Liar!
  Come off it.
  I seen them.

LINDA: Leave him alone!

SAMMY: Why? What'll you do about it if we don't?

LINDA (*undaunted; approaching* SAMMY): I'll tell my mother

why all her ciggies always disappear when you're in our house.

SAMMY: What?

LINDA: An' the half crowns.

SAMMY (*suddenly*): Come on gang, let's go. We don't wanna play with these anyway. They're just kids.
The other children fire a barrage of 'shots' at MICKEY and LINDA before they rush off.

LINDA: I hate them!
LINDA notices MICKEY quietly crying.
What's up?

MICKY: I don't wanna die.

LINDA: But y' have to Mickey. Everyone does. (*She starts to dry his tears.*) Like your twinny died, didn't he, when he was a baby. See, look on the bright side of it, Mickey. When you die you'll meet your twinny again, won't y'?

MICKEY: Yeh.

LINDA: An' listen Mickey, if y' dead, there's no school, is there?

MICKEY (*smiling*): An' I don't care about our Sammy, anyway. Look. (*He produces an air pistol.*) He thinks no one knows he's got it. But I know where he hides it.

LINDA (*impressed*): Ooh . . . gis a go.

MICKEY: No . . . come on, let's go get Eddie first.

LINDA: Who?

MICKEY: Come on, I'll show y'.
They go as if to EDWARD's garden.

MICKEY (*loud but conspiratorially*): Eddie . . . Eddie . . . y' comin' out?

EDWARD: I . . . My mum says I haven't got to play with you.

MICKEY: Well, my mum says I haven't got to play with you. But take no notice of mothers. They're soft. Come on, I've got Linda with me. She's a girl but she's all right.
EDWARD decides to risk it and creeps out.

MICKEY: Hi-ya.

EDWARD: Hi-ya, Mickey. Hello, Linda.

LINDA: Hi-ya, Eddie. (*She produces the air pistol.*) Look . . . we've got Sammy's air gun.

MICKEY: Come on, Eddie. You can have a shot at our target in the park.

LINDA: Peter Pan.

MICKEY: We always shoot at that, don't we Linda?

LINDA: Yeh, we try an' shoot his little thingy off, don't we, Mickey?

They all laugh.

Come on gang, let's go.

EDWARD (*standing firm*): But Mickey . . . I mean . . . suppose we get caught . . . by a policeman.

MICKEY: Aah . . . take no notice. We've been caught loads of times by a policeman . . . haven't we, Linda?

LINDA: Oh, my God, yeh. Hundreds of times. More than that.

MICKEY: We say dead funny things to them, don't we, Linda?

EDWARD: What sort of funny things?

LINDA: All sorts, don't we Mickey?

MICKEY: Yeh . . . like y' know when they ask what y' name is, we say things like, like 'Adolph Hitler', don't we Linda?

LINDA: Yeh, an' hey Eddie, y' know when they say, 'What d' y' think you're doin'?' we always say somethin' like like, 'waitin' for the ninety-two bus'.

MICKEY *and* LINDA *crease up with laughter.*

Come on.

EDWARD (*greatly impressed*): Do you . . . do you really? Goodness, that's fantastic.

MICKEY: Come on, bunk under y' fence, y' Ma won't see y'.

MICKEY, LINDA *and* EDWARD *exit.*

MRS LYONS *enters the garden.*

MRS LYONS (*calling*): Edward, Edward, Edward . . .

The NARRATOR *enters.*

Music.

NARRATOR (*singing*): There's gypsies in the wood,
    An' they've been watchin' you,
    They're gonna take your baby away.
    There's gypsies in the wood,
    An' they've been calling you,
    Can Edward please come out and play,
    Please can he come with us and play.

    You know the devil's got your number,
    Y' know he's gonna find y',
    Y' know he's right behind y',
    He's staring through your windows,
    He's creeping down the hall.

MR LYONS *enters the garden.*

MRS LYONS: Oh Richard, Richard.

MR LYONS: For God's sake Jennifer, I told you on the phone, he'll just be out playing somewhere.

MRS LYONS: But where?

MR LYONS: Outside somewhere, with friends. Edward . . .

MRS LYONS: But I don't want him out playing.

MR LYONS: Jennifer, he's not a baby. Edward . . .

MRS LYONS: I don't care, I don't care . . .

MR LYONS: For Christ's sake, you bring me home from work in the middle of the day, just to say you haven't seen him for an hour. Perhaps we should be talking about you getting something for your nerves.

MRS LYONS: There's nothing wrong with my nerves. It's just . . . just this place . . . I hate it. Richard, I don't want to stay here any more. I want to move.

MR LYONS: Jennifer! Jennifer, how many times . . . the factory is here, my work is here . . .

MRS LYONS: It doesn't have to be somewhere far away. But we have got to move, Richard. Because if we stay here I feel that something terrible will happen, something bad.
MR LYONS *sighs and puts his arm round* MRS LYONS.

MR LYONS: Look, Jen. What is this thing you keep talking about getting away from? Mm?

MRS LYONS: It's just . . . it's these people . . . these people that Edward has started mixing with. Can't you see how he's drawn to them? They're . . . they're drawing him away from me.
MR LYONS, *in despair, turns away from her.*

MR LYONS. Oh Christ.
He turns to look at her but she looks away. He sighs and absently bends to pick up a pair of children's shoes from the floor.
I really do think you should see a doctor.

MRS LYONS (*snapping*): I don't need to see a doctor. I just need to move away from this neighbourhood, because I'm frightened. I'm frightened for Edward.
MR LYONS *places the shoes on the table before turning on her.*

MR LYONS: Frightened of what, woman?

MRS LYONS (*wheeling to face him*): Frightened of . . . (*She is stopped by the sight of the shoes on the table. She rushes at the table and sweeps the shoes off.*)

Music.

NARRATOR (*singing*): There's shoes upon the table
    An' a spider's been killed
    Someone broke the lookin' glass
    There's a full moon shinin'
    An' the salt's been spilled
    You're walkin' on pavement cracks
    Don't know what's gonna come to pass

    Now you know the devil's got your number
    He's gonna find y'
    Y' know he's right beyind y'
    He's starin' through your windows
    He's creeping down the hall.

*The song ends with a percussion build to a sudden full stop
and the scene snaps from* MRS LYONS *to the children.*

MICKEY, EDDIE *and* LINDA *are standing in line, taking it in
turns to fire the air pistol.* MICKEY *takes aim and fires.*

LINDA (*with glee*): Missed.

EDWARD *loads and fires.*

Missed!

LINDA *takes the gun and fires. We hear a metallic ping. She
beams a satisfied smile at* MICKEY *who ignores it and reloads,
fires. The routine is repeated with exactly the same outcome until*

MICKEY (*taking the gun*): We're not playin' with the gun no
more. (*He puts it away.*)

LINDA: Ah, why?

MICKEY: It gets broke if y' use it too much.

EDWARD: What are we going to do now, Mickey?

MICKEY: I dunno.

LINDA: I do.

MICKEY: What?

LINDA: Let's throw some stones through them windows.

MICKEY (*brightening*): Ooh, I dare y' Linda, I dare y'.

LINDA (*bending for a stone*): Well, I will. I'm not scared, either.
Are you Eddie?

EDWARD: Erm . . . well . . . erm . . .

LINDA: He is look. Eddie's scared.

MICKEY: No, he isn't! Are y', Eddie?

EDWARD (*stoically*): No . . . I'm not. I'm not scared at all,
actually.

LINDA: Right, when I count to three we all throw together. One, two, three . . .
Unseen by them a POLICEMAN *has approached behind them.*

POLICEMAN: Me mother caught a flea, she put it in the tea pot to make a cup of tea . . . And what do you think you're doing?

LINDA *and* MICKEY *shoot terrified glances at* EDWARD, *almost wetting themselves.*

EDWARD (*mistaking their look for encouragement*): Waiting for the ninety-two bus. (*He explodes with excited laughter.*)

LINDA: He's not with us.

MICKEY: Sir.

LINDA: Sir.

POLICEMAN: No. He's definitely with us. What's your name, son?

EDWARD: Adolph Hitler.

EDWARD *laughs until through the laughter he senses that all is not well. He sees that he alone is laughing. The laughter turns to tears which sets the other two off.*
The three children turn round, crying, bawling, followed by the POLICEMAN.
The three children exit.
MRS JOHNSTONE *enters.*
The POLICEMAN *goes to confront* MRS JOHNSTONE.

POLICEMAN: And he was about to commit a serious crime, love. Now, do you understand that? You don't wanna end up in court again, do y'?
MRS JOHNSTONE *shakes her head.*
Well, that's what's gonna happen if I have any more trouble from one of yours. I warned you last time, didn't I, Mrs Johnstone, about your Sammy?
MRS JOHNSTONE *nods.*
Well, there'll be no more bloody warnings from now on. Either you keep them in order, Missis, or it'll be the courts for you, or worse, won't it?
MRS JOHNSTONE *nods.*
Yes, it will.

As the POLICEMAN *turns and goes towards the* LYON's *house music is heard.*

MRS JOHNSTONE (*singing*): Maybe some day
    We'll move away
    And start all over again
    In some new place

Where they don't know my face
And nobody's heard of my name
Where we can begin again
Feel we can win an' then . . .
Maybe . . .

The music tails off as we see the POLICEMAN *confronting*
MR LYONS. *The* POLICEMAN *has removed his helmet and
holds a glass of scotch.* EDWARD *is there.*

POLICEMAN: An' er, as I say, it was more of a prank, really,
Mr Lyons. I'd just dock his pocket money if I was you. (*Laughs.*)
But, one thing I would say, if y' don't mind me sayin', is well,
I'm not sure I'd let him mix with the likes of them in the future.
Make sure he keeps with his own kind, Mr Lyons. Well, er,
thanks for the drink, sir. All the best now. He's a good lad,
aren't you Adolph? Goodnight, sir. (*He replaces his helmet.*)
The POLICEMAN *leaves.*

MR LYONS: Edward . . . how would you like to move to another
house?

EDWARD: Why, Daddy?

MR LYONS: Erm, well, various reasons really. Erm, actually
Mummy's not been too well lately and we thought a move,
perhaps further out towards the country somewhere, might . . .
Do you think you'd like that?

EDWARD: I want to stay here.

MR LYONS: Well, you think about it, old chap.
EDWARD *leaves his home and goes to the* JOHNSTONE'*s door.*
He knocks at the door.
MRS JOHNSTONE *answers the door.*

EDWARD: Hello, Mrs Johnstone. How are you?

MRS JOHNSTONE: You what?

EDWARD: I'm sorry. Is there something wrong?

MRS JOHNSTONE: No, I just . . . I don't usually have kids
enquiring about my health. I'm er . . . I'm all right. An' how are
you, Master Lyons?

EDWARD: Very well, thank you.
MRS JOHNSTONE *looks at* EDWARD *for a moment.*

MRS JOHNSTONE: Yeh. You look it. Y' look very well. Does
your mother look after you?

EDWARD: Of course.

MRS JOHNSTONE: Now listen, Eddie, I told you not to come
around here again.

EDWARD: I'm sorry but I just wanted to see Mickey.

MRS JOHNSTONE: No. It's best . . . if . . .

EDWARD: I won't be coming here again. Ever. We're moving
    away. To the country.

MRS JOHNSTONE: Lucky you.

EDWARD: But I'd much rather live here.

MRS JOHNSTONE: Would you? When are y' goin'?

EDWARD: Tomorrow.

MRS JOHNSTONE: Oh. So we really won't see you again, eh . . .
    EDWARD *shakes his head and begins to cry.*
    What's up?

EDWARD (*through his tears*): I don't want to go. I want to stay
    here where my friends are . . . where Mickey is.

MRS JOHNSTONE: Come here.
    She takes him, cradling him, letting him cry.
    No listen . . . listen, don't you be soft. You'll probably love it in
    your new house. You'll meet lots of new friends an' in no time
    at all you'll forget Mickey ever existed.

EDWARD: I won't . . . I won't. I'll never forget.

MRS JOHNSTONE: Shush, shush. Listen, listen Eddie, here's you
    wantin' to stay here, an' here's me, I've been tryin' to get out
    for years. We're a right pair, aren't we, you an' me?

EDWARD: Why don't you Mrs Johnstone? Why don't you buy a
    new house near us?

MRS JOHNSTONE: Just like that?

EDWARD: Yes, yes.

MRS JOHNSTONE: Ey.

EDWARD: Yes.

MRS JOHNSTONE: Would you like a picture of Mickey, to take
    with you? So's you could remember him?

EDWARD: Yes, please.
    She removes a locket from around her neck.

MRS JOHNSTONE: See, look . . . there's Mickey, there. He was
    just a young kid when that was taken.

EDWARD: And is that you Mrs Johnstone?
    She nods.
    Can I really have this?

MRS JOHNSTONE: Yeh. But keep it a secret eh, Eddie? Just our
    secret, between you an' me.

EDWARD (*smiling*): All right, Mrs Johnstone. (*He puts the locket*

round his neck)
He looks at her a moment too long.

MRS JOHNSTONE: What y' lookin' at?

EDWARD: I thought you didn't like me. I thought you weren't very nice. But I think you're smashing.

MRS JOHNSTONE (*looking at him*); God help the girls when you start dancing.

EDWARD: Pardon?

MRS JOHNSTON: Nothing. (*Calling into the house.*) Mickey, say goodbye to Eddie — he's moving.
MICKEY *comes out of the house.*

Music is quietly introduced.

EDDIE *moves to* MICKEY *and gives him a small parcel from his pocket.* MICKEY *unwraps a toy gun. The two boys clasp hands and wave goodbye.* MRS JOHNSTONE *and* MICKEY *watch as* EDWARD *joins his parents, dressed in outdoor clothes, on their side of the stage.*

EDWARD: Goodbye.

MR LYONS: Well, Edward . . . do you like it here?

EDWARD (*unenthusiastically*): It's very nice.

MRS LYONS: Oh, look, Edward . . . look at those trees and those cows. Oh Edward you're going to like it so much out here, aren't you?

EDWARD: Yes. Are you feeling better now, Mummy?

MRS LYONS: Much better now, darling. Oh Edward, look, look at those birds . . . Look at that lovely black and white one . . .

EDWARD (*immediately covering his eyes*): Don't Mummy, don't look. It's a magpie, never look at one magpie. It's one for sorrow . . .

MR LYONS: Edward . . . that's just stupid superstition.

EDWARD: It's not, Mickey told me.

MRS LYONS: Edward, I think we can forget the silly things that Mickey said.

EDWARD: I'm going inside. I want to read.
EDWARD *exits.*

MR LYONS (*comforting his wife*): Children take time to adapt to new surroundings. He'll be as right as rain in a few days. He won't even remember he once lived somewhere else.
MRS LYONS *forces a smile and allows herself to be led inside by her husband.*

MICKEY *rings the doorbell of* EDWARD*'s old house.*
A WOMAN *answers the door.*

WOMAN: Yes?

MICKEY: Is er . . . is Eddie in?

WOMAN: Eddie? I'm afraid Eddie doesn't live here now.

MICKEY: Oh, yeh. (*He stands looking at the woman.*)

WOMAN: Goodbye.

MICKEY: Do y' . . . erm, do y' know where he lives now?

WOMAN: Pardon?

MICKEY: See, I've got some money, I was gonna go, on the bus, an' see him. Where does he live now?

WOMAN: I'm afraid I've no idea.

MICKEY: It's somewhere in the country, isn't it?

WOMAN: Look, I honestly don't know and I'm rather busy. Goodbye.

The WOMAN *closes the door on* MICKEY.

MICKEY *wanders away, aimless and bored, deserted and alone.*

Music.

MICKEY (*singing*): No kids out on the street today,
    You could be living on the moon.
    Maybe everybody's packed their bags and moved away,
    Gonna be a long, long, long,
    Sunday Afternoon

    Just killing time and kicking cans around,
    Try to remember jokes I knew,
    I tell them to myself, but they're not funny since I found
    It's gonna be a long, long, long,
    Sunday Afternoon.

EDWARD, *in his garden, equally bored and alone. The scene appears in such a way that we don't know if it is real or in* MICKEY*'s mind.*

    My best friend
    Always had sweets to share, (He)
    Knew every word in the dictionary.
    He was clean, neat and tidy,
    From Monday to Friday,
    I wish that I could be like,
    Wear clean clothes, talk properly like,
    Do sums and history like,

EDWARD
MICKEY } (*together*):   My friend
                        My friend

EDWARD: My best friend
      He could swear like a soldier
      You would laugh till you died
      At the stories he told y'
      He was untidy
      From Monday to Friday
      I wish that I could be like
      Kick a ball and climb a tree like
      Run around with dirty knees like

EDWARD ⎱ (*together*): My friend
MICKEY ⎰ My friend

The Lights fade on EDWARD *as the music shifts back to* 'Long Sunday Afternoon'.

MICKEY: Feels like everybody stayed in bed
      Or maybe I woke up too soon.
      Am I the last survivor
      Is everybody dead?
      On this long long long
      Sunday Afternoon.

MRS JOHNSTONE *appears, clutching a letter.*

MRS JOHNSTONE (*singing*): Oh, bright new day,
      We're movin' away.

MICKEY (*speaking*): Mam? What's up?

MRS JOHNSTONE (*singing*): We're startin' all over again.

DONNA MARIE *enters together with various neighbours.*

DONNA MARIE (*speaking*): Is it a summons, Mother?

MRS JOHNSTONE (*singing*): Oh, bright new day,
      We're goin' away.

MICKEY (*calling*): Sammy!

MRS JOHNSTONE *addresses the various onlookers.*

MRS JOHNSTONE (*singing*): Where nobody's heard of our name.

SAMMY *enters.*

SAMMY (*speaking*): I never robbed nothin', honest, mam.

MRS JOHNSTONE (*singing*): Where we can begin again,
      Feel we can win and then
      Live just like livin' should be
      Got a new situation,
      A new destination,
      And no reputation following me.

MICKEY (*speaking*): What is it, what is it?

MRS JOHNSTONE (*singing*): We're gettin' out,
    We're movin' house,
    We're starting all over again.
    We're leavin' this mess
    For our new address (*pointing it out*)
    'Sixty five Skelmersdale Lane'.

MICKEY (*speaking; worried*): Where's that, mam?

SAMMY (*speaking*): Is that in the country?

DONNA MARIE (*speaking*): What's it like there?

MRS JOHNSTONE (*singing*): The air is so pure,
    You get drunk just by breathing,
    And the washing stays clean on the line.
    Where there's space for the kids,
    'Cos the garden's so big,
    It would take you a week just to reach the far side.
  (*Speaking*): Come on, Sammy, Mickey, now you've all gorra
  help. (*To the* NEIGHBOURS, *in a 'posh' voice.*) Erm would
  youse excuse us, we've gorra pack. We're movin' away.
  MRS JOHNSTONE *and the children go in to pack.*

NEIGHBOUR: What did she say?

MILKMAN: They're movin' away.

ALL: Praise the Lord, he has delivered us at last.

NEIGHBOUR: They're gettin' out,
    They're movin' house,
    Life won't be the same as in the past.

POLICEMAN: I can safely predict
    A sharp drop in the crime rate.

NEIGHBOUR: It'll be calm an' peaceful around here.

MILKMAN: AND now I might even
    Get paid what is mine, mate.

NEIGHBOUR: An' you'll see, grafitti will soon disappear.
  MRS JOHNSTONE *marches out of the house carrying*
  battered suitcases, followed by the children who are struggling
  to get out some of the items mentioned in the verse.

MRS JOHNSTONE: Just pack up the bags,
    We're leavin' the rags,
    The wobbly wardrobe, chest of drawers that never close.
    The two legged chair, the carpet so bare,
    You wouldn't see it if it wasn't for the holes.
    Now that we're movin'
    Now that we're improvin',
    Let's just wash our hands of this lot.

For it's no longer fitting, for me to be sitting
On a sofa, I know for a fact, was knocked off.
Her last line is delivered to SAMMY *who indicates the*
POLICEMAN, *trying to get her to shut up.*
We might get a car,
Be all 'lardie dah',
An' go drivin' out to the sands.
At the weekend,
A gentleman friend,
Might take me dancing
To the local bands.
We'll have a front room,
And then if it should happen,
That His Holiness flies in from Rome,
He can sit there with me, eating toast, drinking tea
In the sort of surroundings that remind him of home.

MICKEY (*speaking*): It's like the country, isn't it, mam?

MRS JOHNSTONE (*speaking*): Ey, we'll be all right out here son,
away from the muck an' the dirt an' the bloody trouble. Eh, I
could dance. Come here.

MICKEY: Get off . . .
MRS JOHNSTONE *picks up a picture of the Pope which is
lying next to one of the suitcases and begins to dance.*

MRS JOHNSTONE (*singing*): Oh, bright new day,
We're movin' away,
We're startin' all over again.
Oh, bright new day,
We're goin' away,
Where nobody's heard of our name.
(*Speaking*): An' what are you laughin' at?

MICKEY: I'm not laughin', I'm smilin'. I haven't seen you happy
like this for ages.

MRS JOHNSTONE: Well, I am happy now. Eh, Jesus where's
the others?

MICKEY: They went into that field, mam.

MRS JOHNSTONE: Sammy. SAMMY! Get off that bleedin' cow
before I kill you. Oh Jesus, what's our Donna Marie stepped
into? Sammy, that cow's a bull. Come here the pair of you.
Now we can begin again,
Feel we can win an' then,
Live just like livin' should be.
Got a new situation,

A new destination,
An' no reputation following me.
ALL: We're gettin' out. We're movin' house
We're goin' away. Gettin' out today.
We're movin' movin' movin' house.
MRS JOHNSTONE: We're goin' away,
Oh, bright new day.

Curtain.

ACT TWO

MRS JOHNSTONE *moves forward to sing.*

MRS JOHNSTONE: The house we got was lovely,
>They neighbours are a treat,
>They sometimes fight on Saturday night,
>But never in the week.

MRS JOHNSTONE *turns and looks 'next door'. Raised voices, and a dog barking, are heard, off.*

NEIGHBOURS (*off, speaking*): What time do you call this then?
>Time I got shot of you, rat bag!
>DOG *barks.*

MRS JOHNSTONE (*singing*): Since I pay me bills on time, the milkman
>Insists I call him Joe.
>He brings me bread and eggs.
>JOE, *the milkman, enters.*
>Says I've got legs
>Like Marilyn Monroe.

MRS JOHNSTONE *and* JOE *dance.*
>Sometimes he takes me dancing
>Even takes me dancing.

JOE *exits, dancing.*
>I know our Sammy burnt the school down
>But it's very easily done.
>If the teacher lets the silly gets
>Play with magnesium.
>Thank God he only got probation,

A JUDGE *is seen, ticking* SAMMY *off.*
>The Judge was old and slow.

MRS JOHNSTONE *sings to the* JUDGE, *laying on a smile for him.*
>Though it was kind of him,
>Said I reminded him of Marilyn Monroe.

JUDGE (*slightly scandalized*): And could I take you dancing?
>Take you dancing.

MRS JOHNSTONE *takes the* JUDGE's *gavel and bangs him on the head.*
The JUDGE *exits, stunned.*

MRS JOHNSTONE: Our Mickey's just turned fourteen
>Y' know he's at *that* age
>MICKEY *is seen in his room.*
>When you mention girls, or courting,

He flies into a rage.

MICKEY (*speaking*): Shut up talking about me, Mother.

MRS JOHNSTONE: He's got a thing for taking blackheads out,
    And he thinks that I don't know,
    That he dreams all night of girls who look like
    Marilyn Monroe. He's even started dancing, secret dancing.
    (*Slower*): And as for the rest, they've flown the nest
    Got married or moved away
    Our Donna Marie's already got three, she's
    A bit like me that way . . .
    (*Slower*): And that other child of mine,
    I haven't seen for years, although
    Each day I pray he'll be OK,
    Not like Marilyn Monroe . . .

On the other side of the stage MRS LYONS *enters, waltzing with a very awkward fourteen-year-old* EDWARD.

MRS LYONS (*speaking*): One, two, three. One, two three.
    (*Singing*): Yes, that's right, you're dancing.
    That's right, you're dancing.
    (*Speaking*): You see, Edward, it is easy.

EDWARD: It is if you have someone to practice with. Girls. But in term time we hardly ever see a girl, let alone dance with one.

MRS LYONS: I'll give you some more lessons when you're home for half term. Now come on, come on, you're going to be late. Daddy's at the door with the car. Now, are you sure you've got all your bags?

EDWARD: Yes, they're in the boot.

MRS LYONS (*looking at him*): I'll see you at half term then, darling. (*She kisses him, a light kiss, but holds on to him.*) Look after yourself my love.

EDWARD: Oh Mummy . . . stop fussing . . . I'm going to be late.

MRS LYONS: We have had a very good time this holiday though, haven't we?

EDWARD: We always do.

MRS LYONS: Yes. We're safe here, aren't we?

EDWARD: Mummy what are you on about? Sometimes . . .
    A car horn is heard.

MRS LYONS (*hustling him out, good naturedly*): Go on, go on . . . There's Daddy getting impatient. Bye, bye, Edward.

EDWARD: Bye, Ma.
    EDWARD *exits.*

We see MRS JOHNSTONE *hustling* MICKEY *to school.*

MRS JOHNSTONE: You're gonna be late y' know. Y' late already.

MICKEY: I'm not.

MRS JOHNSTONE: You're gonna miss the bus.

MICKEY: I won't.

MRS JOHNSTONE: Well, you'll miss Linda, she'll be waitin' for y'.

MICKEY: Well, I don't wanna see her. What do I wanna see her for?

MRS JOHNSTONE (*laughing at his transparency*): You've only been talkin' about her in your sleep for the past week . . .

MICKEY (*outraged*): You liar . . .

MRS JOHNSTONE: 'Oh, my sweet darling . . .'

MICKEY: I never. That was — a line out the school play!

MRS JOHNSTONE (*her laughter turning to a smile*): All right. I believe y'. Now go before you miss the bus. Are y' goin'.
We see LINDA *at the bus stop.*

LINDA: Hi-ya, Mickey.

MRS JOHNSTONE: Ogh, did I forget? Is that what you're waitin' for? Y' waitin' for y' mum to give y' a big sloppy kiss, come here . . .

MICKEY: I'm goin', I'm goin' . . .
SAMMY *runs through the house, pulling on a jacket as he does so.*

SAMMY: Wait for me, YOU.

MRS JOHNSTONE: Where you goin' Sammy?

SAMMY (*on his way out*): The dole.
MICKEY *and* SAMMY *exit.*

MRS JOHNSTONE *stands watching them as they approach the bus stop. She smiles at* MICKEY's *failure to cope with* LINDA's *smile of welcome.*

The 'bus' appears, with the NARRATOR *as the conductor.*

CONDUCTOR: Come on, if y' gettin' on. We've not got all day.
SAMMY, MICKEY *and* LINDA *get on the 'bus'.*

MRS JOHNSTONE (*calling to her kids*): Tarrah, lads. Be good, both of y' now. I'll cook a nice surprise for y' tea.

CONDUCTOR (*noticing her as he goes to ring the bell*): Gettin' on, Missis?
MRS JOHNSTONE *shakes her head, still smiling.*

(*Speaking*): Happy are y'. Content at last?
   Wiped out what happened, forgotten the past?
She looks at him, puzzled.
   But you've got to have an endin', if a start's been made.
   No one gets off without the price bein' paid.
The 'bus' pulls away as the conductor begins to collect fares.
   No one can embark without the price bein' paid.
(*To* MICKEY): Yeh?

MICKEY (*handing over his money*): A fourpenny scholar.

CONDUCTOR: How old are y'?

LINDA: He's fourteen. Both of us are. A fourpenny scholar for
   me as well.
   The CONDUCTOR *gives out the ticket as* SAMMY *offers
   his money.*

SAMMY: Same for me.

CONDUCTOR: No son.

SAMMY: What?

CONDUCTOR: You're older than fourteen.

MICKEY (*worried*): Sammy . . .

SAMMY: Shut it. (*To the* CONDUCTOR.) I'm fourteen. I wanna
   fourpenny scholar.

CONDUCTOR: Do you know the penalty for tryin' to defraud . . .

SAMMY: I'm not defraudin' no one.

CONDUCTOR (*shouting to the* DRIVER): 'Ey, Billy, take the
   next left will y'. We've got one for the cop shop here.

SAMMY: What? (*He stands.*)

MICKEY: He didn't mean it, Mister. Don't be soft. He, he was
   jokin'. Sammy tell him, tell him you're really sixteen. I'll lend
   you the rest of the fare . . .

SAMMY (*considers; then*): Fuck off. (*He produces a knife. To
   the* CONDUCTOR.) Now move, you. Move! Give me the bag.
   Music.

MICKEY: Sammy . . . Sammy . . .

SAMMY (*to the* CONDUCTOR): I said give. Stop the bus.
   The CONDUCTOR *rings the bell to stop the 'bus'.*
   Come on, Mickey.

LINDA: You stay where y' are, Mickey. You've done nothin'.

MICKEY: Sammy, Sammy put that away . . . it's still not too
   late. (*To the* CONDUCTOR.) Is it Mister?

SAMMY: Mickey.

LINDA: He's stayin' here.

SAMMY: No-mark!

   SAMMY *leaps from the 'bus' and is pursued by two policemen.*
   The 'bus' pulls away leaving MICKEY *and* LINDA *alone on*
   the pavement.

LINDA: He'll get put away for this, y' know, Mickey.

MICKEY: I know.

LINDA: He's always been a soft get, your Sammy.

MICKEY: I know.

LINDA: You better hadn't do anything soft, like him.

MICKEY: I wouldn't.

LINDA: Y' better hadn't or I won't be in love with y' anymore!

MICKEY: Shut up! Y' always sayin' that.

LINDA: I'm not.

MICKEY: Yis y' are. Y' bloody well said it in assembly yesterday.

LINDA: Well. I was only tellin' y'.

MICKEY: Yeh, an' five hundred others as well.

LINDA: I don't care who knows. I just love you. I love you!

MICKEY: Come on . . . we're half an hour late as it is.

   MICKEY *hurries off, followed by* LINDA.

   EDWARD's *school where* EDWARD *is confronted by a*
   teacher (the NARRATOR*) looking down his nose at*
   EDWARD.

TEACHER: You're doing very well here, aren't you, Lyons?

EDWARD: Yes, sir. I believe so.

TEACHER: Talk of Oxbridge.

EDWARD: Yes, sir.

TEACHER: Getting rather big for your boots, aren't you?

EDWARD: No, sir.

TEACHER: No, sir? Yes, sir. I think you're a tyke, Lyons. The
   boys in your dorm say you wear a locket around your neck.
   Is that so?
   Pause.

EDWARD: Yes, sir.

TEACHER: A locket? A locket. This is a boys' school, Lyons.

EDWARD: I am a boy, sir.

TEACHER: They you must behave like one. Now give this locket
   to me.

EDWARD: No, sir.

TEACHER: No sir? Am I to punish you Lyons? Am I to have you flogged?

EDWARD: You can do exactly as you choose Sir. You can take a flying fuck at a rolling doughnut! But you shall not take my locket!

TEACHER (*thunderstruck*): I'm going to . . . I'm going to have you suspended, Lyons.

EDWARD: Yes, sir.
EDWARD *exits.*

As EDWARD *exits a class in a Secondary Modern school is formed – all boredom and futility. The school bell rings. The teacher becomes the teacher of this class in which we see* LINDA *and* MICKEY.

TEACHER: And so, we know then, don't we, that the Boro Indian of the Amazon Basin lives on a diet of . . .

PERKINS: Sir, sir . . .

TEACHER: A diet of . . .

PERKINS: Sir, sir . . .

TEACHER: A diet of what, Johnstone? The Boro Indian of the Amazon Basin lives on a diet of what?

MICKEY: What?

TEACHER: Exactly lad, exactly. What?

MICKEY: I don't know.

TEACHER (*his patience gone*): Y' don't know. (*Mimicking.*) You don't know. I told y' two minutes ago, lad.

LINDA: Leave him alone will y'.

TEACHER: You just stay out of this, Miss. It's got nothing to do with you. It's Johnstone, not you . . .

PERKINS: Sir!

TEACHER: Oh, shut up Perkins, y' borin' little turd. But you don't listen do you, Johnstone?

MICKEY (*shrugging*): Yeh.

TEACHER: Oh, y' do? Right, come out here in front of the class. Now then, what is the staple diet of the Boro Indian of the Amazon Basin?
MICKEY *looks about for help. There is none.*

MICKEY (*defiantly*): Fish Fingers!

TEACHER: Just how the hell do you hope to get a job when you never listen to anythin'?

MICKEY: It's borin'.

TEACHER: Yes, yes, you might think it's boring but you won't be sayin' that when you can't get a job.

MICKEY: Yeh. Yeh an' it'll really help me to get a job if I know what some soddin' pygmies in Africa have for their dinner! *The class erupts into laughter.*

TEACHER (*to class*): Shut up. Shut up.

MICKEY: Or maybe y' were thinkin' I was lookin' for a job in an African restaurant.

TEACHER: Out!

LINDA: Take no notice Mickey. I love you.

TEACHER: Johnstone, get out!

LINDA: Oh, leave him alone you. Y' big worm!

TEACHER: Right you as well . . . out . . . out . . .

LINDA: I'm goin' . . . I'm goin' . . .

TEACHER: You're both suspended.
LINDA *and* MICKEY *leave the class.*

The classroom sequence breaks up as we see MRS LYONS *staring at a piece of paper.* EDWARD *is standing before her.*

MRS LYONS (*incredulously*): Suspended? Suspended? (*She looks at the paper.*) Because of a locket?

EDWARD: Because I wouldn't let them have my locket.

MRS LYONS: But what's so . . . Can I see this locket?
There is a pause.

EDWARD: I suppose so . . . if you want to.
EDWARD *takes off the locket from around his neck and hands it to his mother. She looks at it without opening it.*

MRS LYONS: Where did you get this?

EDWARD: I can't tell you that. It's a secret.

MRS LYONS (*finally smiling in relief*): I know it's from a girlfriend, isn't it? (*She laughs.*) Is there a picture in here?

EDWARD: Yes, Mummy. Can I have it back now?

MRS LYONS: You won't let Mummy see your girl friend. Oh, Edward, don't be so . . . (*She playfully moves away.*) Is she beautiful?

EDWARD: Mummy can . . .

MRS LYONS: Oh, let me look, let me look. (*She beams a smile at him and then opens the locket.*)
Music.

EDWARD: Mummy . . . Mummy what's wrong . . . (*He goes to her and holds her steady.*) Mummy!
MRS LYONS *takes his arms away from her.*
What is it?

MRS LYONS: When . . . when were you photographed with this woman?

EDWARD: Pardon!

MRS LYONS: When! Tell me, Edward.
EDWARD *begins to laugh.*
Edward!

EDWARD: Mummy . . . you silly old thing. That's not me. That's Mickey.

MRS LYONS: What?

EDWARD: Mickey . . . you remember my friend when I was little. (*He takes the locket and shows it to her.*) Look. That's Mickey . . . and his mother. Why did you think it was me? (*He looks at it.*) I never looked a bit like Mickey.
EDWARD *replaces the locket around his neck.* MRS LYONS *watches him.*

MRS LYONS: No it's just . . . (*She stares, deep in thought.*)

EDWARD (*looking at her*): Are you feeling all right Mummy? You're not ill again, like you used to be . . . are you?

MRS LYONS: Where did you get that . . . locket from, Edward? Why do you wear it?

EDWARD: I can't tell you that, Ma. I've explained, it's a secret, I can't tell you.

MRS LYONS: But . . . but I'm your mother.

EDWARD: I know but I still can't tell you. It's not important, I'm going up to my room. It's just a secret, everybody has secrets, don't you have secrets?
EDWARD *exits to his room.*
The NARRATOR *enters.*
Music (continues).

NARRATOR (*singing*): Did you really feel that you'd become secure
That time had brushed away the past
That there's no one by the window, no one knocking on your door
Did you believe that you were free at last
Free from the broken looking glass.
Oh y' know the devil's got your number

He's never far behind you
He always knows where to find you
And someone said they'd seen him walking past your door.
NARRATOR *exits*.

We see MICKEY *and* LINDA *making their way up the hill.*
LINDA *having some difficulty in high heeled shoes.*

LINDA: Tch . . . you didn't tell me it was gonna be over a load of fields.

MICKEY: I didn't tell y' nothin'. I didn't ask y' to come, y' followed me. (*He walks away from her.*)

LINDA (*watching him walk away*): Mickey, Mickey . . . I'm stuck . . . (*Holding out her helpless arms.*) Me foot's stuck. Honest.
MICKEY *goes back, timidly takes a wrist and ineffectually pulls.*
Mickey, I think y' might be more successful if you were to sort of put your arms around here. (*She puts her hands on her waist.*) Oh Mickey, be gentle, be gentle . . .

MICKEY (*managing to pull her free*): Will you stop takin' the piss out of me!

LINDA: I'm not, I'm not.
MICKEY *points down in the direction they have come from.*

MICKEY: Look . . . y' can see the estate from up here.

LINDA: Have we come all this way just to look at the bleedin' estate? Mickey we're fourteen.
She beams at him. He can't take it and looks the other way.

MICKEY: Look.

LINDA: What?

MICKEY: There's that lad lookin' out the window. I see him sometimes when I'm up here.

LINDA: Oh him . . . he's gorgeous, isn't he?

MICKEY: What?

LINDA: He's lovely lookin', isn't he?

MICKEY: All right, all right! You've told me once.

LINDA: Well, he is. An' what do you care if I think another feller's gorgeous eh?

MICKEY: I don't.

LINDA: You . . . I give up with you, Mickey Johnstone. I'm off. You get on my bleedin' nerves.
LINDA *exits*.

MICKEY: What . . . Linda . . . Linda . . . Don't . . . Linda, I

wanna kiss y', an' put me arms around y' an' kiss y' and kiss y'
an even fornicate with y' but I don't know how to tell y',
because I've got pimples an' me feet are too big an' me bum
sticks out an' . . .

He becomes conscious of EDWARD *approaching, and affects
nonchalance.*

(*Speaking*): If I was like him
    I'd know (*singing*) all the right words
EDWARD: If I was like . . . him
    I'd know some real birds
    Apart from those in my dreams
    And in magazines.
MICKEY: Just look at his hair
EDWARD: His hair's dark and wavy
    Mine's mousey to fair
MICKEY: Mine's the colour of gravy

EDWARD   }
MICKEY   } (*together*):   Each part of his face
    Is in just the right place
    He laughing at me
    At my nose, did he notice
MICKEY: I should wear a brace
EDWARD: That I've got halitosis

MICKEY   }
EDWARD   } (*together*):   When nature picked on me
    She chose to stick on me
EDWARD: Eyes that don't match
MICKEY: And ears that stand out

EDWARD   }
MICKEY   } (*together*):   She picked the wrong batch
    When she handed mine out
    And then she attacked me
    With permanent acne
EDWARD: I wish I was a bit like
    Wish that I could score a hit like
    And be just a little bit like
    That guy
    That guy
MICKEY: I wish that I could be like
    Just a little less like me
    Like the sort of guy I see, like
    That guy
    That guy.
EDWARD: Hi.
MICKEY: Hi. Gis a ciggie?
EDWARD: Oh, I don't smoke actually. But I can go and get

you some.

MICKEY: Are you soft? (*He suddenly realizes.*) A blood brother.

EDWARD: Mickey? Well, shag the vicar.

MICKEY *laughs.*

What's wrong?

MICKEY: You, it sounds dead funny swearin' in that posh voice.

EDWARD: What posh voice?

MICKEY: That one.

EDWARD: Well, where do you live?

MICKEY: The estate, look. (*He points.*)

EDWARD: My God, I only live . . .

MICKEY: I know.

EDWARD: That girl I saw you with, was that . . .

MICKEY: Linda. Do you remember Linda?

EDWARD: Wow, was that Linda? And is she your girl friend?

MICKEY: Yeh. She's one of them.

EDWARD: One of them.

MICKEY: Have you got a girl friend?

EDWARD: Me? Me? No!

MICKEY: Haven't y'?

EDWARD: Look, you seem to have rather a lot of them, erm . . . perhaps you'd share one with me.

MICKEY: Share one. Eddie I haven't even got one girl friend.

EDWARD: But Linda . . . you said . . .

MICKEY: I know, but she's not. I mean, I mean she would be me girl friend, she even says she loves me all over the place, but it's just like dead difficult.

EDWARD: What?

MICKEY: Like knowing what to say.

EDWARD: But you must, you must . . .

MICKEY: I know that. But every time I see her I promise meself I'll ask her but, but the words just disappear.

EDWARD: But you mustn't let them.

MICKEY: What do I say, though?

EDWARD: Mickey, it's easy, I've read about it. Look the next time you see Linda, you stare straight into her eyes and you say, 'Linda, I love you, I want you, the very core of my being is longing for you, my loins are burning for you. Let me lay my weary head between your warm breasts'! And then,

Mickey, her eyes will be half closed and her voice may appear somewhat husky as she pleads with you, 'be gentle with me, be gentle'. It would work, you know. Listen, we can see how it's done; look the Essoldo for one week only, *Nymphomaniac Nights* and *Swedish Au Pairs*. Whoa . . .

MICKEY: I'll have to go home and get some money . . .

As the boys are going, we see MRS LYONS *appear. She has seen* EDWARD *and* MICKEY *and she stares after them. Making up her mind she quickly goes and fetches a coat, then follows the two boys.*

The NARRATOR *enters.*

Music.

EDWARD: I've got plenty, I'll lend . . .

MICKEY: No, it's all right, me Mam'll give it me . . .

EDWARD: Come on then, before my Ma sees me. She's off her beam, my Ma . . .

The boys exit, followed by MRS LYONS.

NARRATOR (*singing*): Did you really feel that you'd become secure,
 And that the past was tightly locked away,
 Did you really feel that you would never be found,
 Did you forget you've got some debts to pay,
 Did you forget about the reckoning day.

 Yes, the devil he's still got your number,
 He's moved in down the street from you,
 Someone said he wants to speak to you,
 Someone said they'd seen him leanin' on your door.

The NARRATOR *exits.*

We see MRS JOHNSTONE *in her kitchen as* MICKEY *bursts in followed by* EDWARD.

MICKEY: Mother, mam, look, look it's Eddie . . . Eddie . . .

MRS JOHNSTONE *stands looking at* EDWARD *and smiling.*

EDWARD: Hi-ya, Mrs Johnstone. Isn't it fantastic. We're neighbours again.

MICKEY: Mum, mum, mum, Eddie lives in that house, y' know that big house on the hill. Mam, can y' lend us a quid to go to the pictures . . .

MRS JOHNSTONE: Yes, it's, erm . . . it's in the sideboard . . .

MICKEY: Oh thanks, mam. I love y'.

MICKEY *exits to the next room.*

EDWARD: You're looking very well, Mrs Johnstone.

MRS JOHNSTONE: Am I? Do you . . . Do you still keep that locket I gave y'?

EDWARD: Of course . . . Look . . .
MICKEY enters.

MICKEY: Mam, Mam, can I bring Eddie back afterwards, for coffee?

MRS JOHNSTONE: Yeh. Go on . . . go an' enjoy yourselves but don't be too late will y'?

MICKEY: See y', Mam . . .

EDWARD: Bye Mrs Johnstone.
The boys prepare to leave.

MRS JOHNSTONE: 'Ey. What's the film you're gonna see?

EDWARD: Erm what?

MRS JOHNSTONE: What film . . .

EDWARD } *(together)*: *Dr Zhivago*
MICKEY }   *Magnificent Seven*

MRS JOHNSTONE: Dr Zhivago's Magnificent Seven.

EDWARD: It's a double bill.

MRS JOHNSTONE: I see. An' where's it on?

MICKEY } *(together)*: WHAT?
EDWARD }   The Essoldo

MRS JOHNSTONE: Oh . . . the Essoldo eh? When I passed the Essoldo this mornin' they were showin' *Nymphomaniac Nights* and *Swedish Au Pairs.*

EDWARD: Ah yes, Mrs Johnstone, yes, yes they're just the trailers: a documentary and and . . .

MICKEY: An' a travelogue. About Sweden!

MRS JOHNSTONE: Do the pair of you really think I was born yesterday?
EDWARD can't hold it any longer and breaks into embarrassed laughter.

MICKEY *(trying to hold on)*: It is, it is . . . it's just a travelogue . . .

MRS JOHNSTONE: Showing the spectacular bends and curves of Sweden . . . Go on y' randy little sods . . .

MICKEY *(scandalized)*: Mother!

MRS JOHNSTONE: Go on before I throw a bucket of water over the pair of y' . . .
MICKEY drags EDWARD out.
I don't know about coffee . . . you'd be better off with bromide. *(She gets on with her work.)*

EDWARD (*outside the house but looking back*): She's fabulous your ma, isn't she?

MICKEY: She's a fuckin' head case. Come on . . .

As they run off we see MRS LYONS *appear from where she has been concealed in the alley.*

MRS JOHNSTONE *is lilting the 'We Go Dancing' line as* MRS LYONS *appears in the kitchen.* MRS JOHNSTONE *gets a shock as she looks up and sees* MRS LYONS *there. The two women stare at each other.*

MRS JOHNSTONE (*eventually nodding*): Hello.

MRS LYONS: How long have you lived here?
Pause.

MRS JOHNSTONE: A few years.
Pause.

MRS LYONS: Are you always going to follow me?

MRS JOHNSTONE: We were rehoused here . . . I didn't follow . . .

MRS LYONS: Don't lie! I know what you're doing to me! You gave him that locket didn't you? Mm?
MRS JOHNSTONE *nods.*
He never takes it off you know. You're very clever aren't you?

MRS JOHNSTONE: I . . . I thought I'd never see him again. I wanted him to have . . . a picture of me . . . even though he'd never know.

MRS LYONS: Afraid he might eventually have forgotten you? Oh no. There's no chance of that. He'll always remember you. After we'd moved he talked less and less of you and your family. I started . . . just for a while I came to believe that he was actually mine.

MRS JOHNSTONE: He is yours.

MRS LYONS: No. I took him. But I never made him mine. Does he know? Have you told . . .

MRS JOHNSTONE: Of course not!

MRS LYONS: Even when — when he was a tiny baby I'd see him looking straight at me and I'd think, he knows . . . he knows. (*Pause.*) You have ruined me. (*Pause.*) But you won't ruin Edward! Is it money you want?

MRS JOHNSTONE: What?

MRS LYONS: I'll get it for you. If you move away from here. How much?

MRS JOHNSTONE: Look . . .

MRS LYONS: How much?

MRS JOHNSTONE: Nothin'! Nothing. (*Pause.*) You bought me off once before . . .

MRS LYONS: Thousands . . . I'm talking about thousands if you want it. And think what you could do with money like that.

MRS JOHNSTONE: I'd spend it. I'd buy more junk and trash; that's all. I don't want your money. I've made a life out here. It's not much of one maybe, but I made it. I'm stayin' here. You move if you want to.

MRS LYONS: I would. But there's no point. You'd just follow me again wouldn't you?

MRS JOHNSTONE: Look I'm not followin' anybody.

MRS LYONS: Wherever I go you'll be just behind me. I know that now . . . always and forever and ever like, like a shadow . . . unless I can . . . make . . . you go . . . But you won't so . . .

We see that throughout the above MRS LYONS *has opened the knife drawer and has a lethal-looking kitchen knife in her hand.* MRS JOHNSTONE, *unaware, has her back to her. On impulse, and punctuated by a note,* MRS JOHNSTONE *wheels. On a punctuated note* MRS LYONS *lunges.*
MRS JOHNSTONE *moves and avoids it.* MRS LYONS *lunges again but* MRS JOHNSTONE *manages to get hold of her wrist, rendering the knife hand helpless.* MRS JOHNSTONE *takes the knife from* MRS LYON*'s grasp and moves away.*

MRS JOHNSTONE (*staring at her; knowing*): YOU'RE MAD. MAD.

MRS LYONS (*quietly*): I curse the day I met you. You ruined me.

MRS JOHNSTONE: Go. Just go!

MRS LYONS: Witch. (*Suddenly pointing.*) I curse you. Witch!

MRS JOHNSTONE (*screaming*): Go!
    MRS LYONS *exits to the street.*
    KIDS *voices are heard, chanting, off.*

KIDS (*off*): High upon the hill the mad woman lives,
        Never ever eat the sweets she gives,
        Just throw them away and tell your Dad,
        High upon a hill there's a woman gone mad.

        Mad woman, mad woman living on the hill,
        If she catches your eye then you never will

> Grow any further, your teeth will go bad
> High upon a hill there's a woman gone mad.

*EDDIE and MICKEY emerge from the cinema, blinking as
they try to adjust to the glare of the light in the street.*

*They are both quite overcome with their celluloid/erotic
encounter. As they pause and light up cigarettes by a corner
lamp post they groan in their ecstatic agony. Each is in an
aroused trance.*

MICKEY: Ooh . . . !

EDWARD: Naked knockers, ooh . . . !

MICKEY: Naked knockers with nipples . . .

EDWARD: Playing tennis. Ooh. Tennis with tits. Will Wimbledon
ever be the same?

MICKEY: Tits!

EDWARD: Tits, tits, tits . . . (*He begins a frustrated chant of the
word, oblivious to everything.*)

LINDA and a mate enter.

*Finally MICKEY realizes LINDA's presence and knocks
EDWARD, who becomes aware of the girls' presence. He goes
into a song without missing a beat.*

> Tits, tits, tits a lovely way,
> To spend an evening . . .

*EDWARD grabs LINDA's mate and begins to waltz her around
the street.*

> Can't think of anything
> I'd rather do . . .

MATE (*simultaneously with the above*): Gerroff. Put me down,
get y' friggin' paws off me you. Linda. Y' bloody lunatic,
gettoff.

EDWARD finally releases her and bows.

Linda, come on. I'm goin' . . .

*The MATE begins to walk away. LINDA makes no attempt
to follow.*

LINDA: What y' doin' in town, Mick?

MICKEY: We've erm, we've . . .

EDWARD: We have been undergoing a remarkable celluloid
experience!

MATE: We'll miss the bus, Linda.

MICKEY: We've been the pictures.

LINDA: So have we. What did y' go see?

EDWARD: *Nympho ...*

MICKEY: *Bridge Over the River Kwai.*

LINDA: Ah, we've seen that. We went to see *Nymphomaniac Nights* instead. An' *Swedish Au Pairs.*

MICKEY: You what!
EDWARD begins to laugh.

MATE: Oh, sod y' then. I'm goin'.
The MATE exits.

MICKEY (*to* EDWARD): What are you laughin' at? Take no notice. Remember Eddie? He's still a head case. Shurrup.

EDWARD (*shouting*): Tits. Tits, tits, tits, tits, tits.
EDWARD leaps around and hopefully ends up sitting at the top of the lamp post. LINDA *and* MICKEY *laugh at him, while* EDWARD *chants.*

A POLICEMAN enters.

The three do not see the arrival of the POLICEMAN.

POLICEMAN: An' what the bloody hell do you think you're doin'?

EDWARD: Adolph Hitler?

POLICEMAN: Get down.
EDWARD gets down from the lamp post.

POLICEMAN (*getting out his black book*): Right. I want your names. What's your name?

LINDA:
MICKEY: (*together*):   Waitin' for the ninety-two bus!
EDWARD:

LINDA (*pointing upwards*): Oh my God, look ...

POLICEMAN: Now listen ...
The POLICEMAN falls for it and looks up.
The three make their exit.
The POLICEMAN realizes and gives chase.
MICKEY, LINDA *and* EDWARD *enter, laughing and exhausted.*
The NARRATOR enters.

NARRATOR: There's a few bob in your pocket and you've got
          good friends,
          And it seems that Summer's never coming to an end,
          Young, free and innocent, you haven't got a care,
          Apart from decidin' on the clothes you're gonna wear.
          The street's turned into Paradise, the radio's singing dreams
          You're innocent, immortal, you're just fifteen.

The NARRATOR *becomes the rifle range man at the fairground.*

LINDA, MICKEY *and* EDWARD *rush on.*

LINDA, MICKEY *and* EDWARD *pool their money and hand it to the rifle range man. He gives the gun to* MICKEY, *who smiles, shakes his head and points to* LINDA. *The man offers the gun to* EDWARD *but* LINDA *takes it. The boys indicate to the rifle range man that he has had it now* LINDA *has the gun. They eagerly watch the target but their smiles fade as* LINDA *misses all three shots.* MICKEY *and* EDWARD *turn on* LINDA *in mock anger. They are stopped by the rifle range man throwing them a coconut which is used as a ball for a game of piggy-in-the-middle. When* LINDA *is caught in the middle the game freezes.*

> And who'd dare tell the lambs in Spring,
> What fate the later seasons bring.
> Who'd tell the girl in the middle of the pair
> The price she'll pay for just being there.

Throughout the following we see LINDA, MICKEY *and* EDWARD *suiting their action to the words – coming out of the chip shop, talking, lighting a cigarette by the lamp post.*

> But leave them alone, let them go and play
> They care not for what's at the end of the day.
> For what is to come, for what might have been,
> Life has no ending when you're sweet sixteen
> And your friends are with you to talk away the night,
> Or until Mrs Wong switches off the chippy light.
> Then there's always the corner and the street lamp's glare
> An' another hour to spend, with your friends, with her,
> To share your last cigarette and your secret dream
> At the midnight hour, at seventeen.

Throughout the following we see LINDA, MICKEY *and* EDWARD, *as if at the beach,* LINDA *taking a picture of* MICKEY *and* EDWARD, *arms around each other camping it for the camera but eventually giving good and open smiles.* MICKEY *taking a picture of* EDWARD *and* LINDA. EDWARD *down on one knee and kissing her hand* EDWARD *taking a picture of* MICKEY *and* LINDA. MICKEY *pulling a distorted face,* LINDA *wagging a finger at him.* MICKEY *chastened.* LINDA *raising her eyebrows and putting one of his arms round her.* LINDA *moving forward and taking the camera.* LINDA *waving the* NARRATOR *to snap them. He goes.* LINDA *showing the* NARRATOR *how to operate the camera.* LINDA, MICKEY *and* EDWARD, *grouped together, arms around each other as the* NARRATOR *takes the picture. They get the camera and wave their thanks to the* NARRATOR.

It's just another ferry boat, a trip to the beach
But everything is possible, the world's within your reach
An' you don't even notice broken bottles in the sand
The oil in the water and you can't understand
How living could be anything other than a dream
When you're young, free and innocent and just eighteen.

LINDA, MICKEY *and* EDWARD *exit.*

And only if the three of them could stay like that forever,
And only if we could predict no changes in the weather,
And only if we didn't live in life, as well as dreams
And only if we could stop and be forever, just eighteen.

We see EDWARD, *waiting by a street lamp.*
LINDA *approaches, sees him, and goes into a street walk.*

LINDA: Well, hallo, sweetie pie; looking for a good time? Ten to seven (*She laughs.*) Good time . . . ten to seven . . . it was a joke . . . I mean I know it was a lousy joke but y' could at least go into hysterics!
EDWARD *smiles.*
That's hysterics?

EDWARD: Where's Mickey?

LINDA: He must be workin' overtime.

EDWARD: Oh.

LINDA: What's wrong with you, misery?

EDWARD (*after a pause*): I go away to university tomorrow.

LINDA: Tomorrow! You didn't say.

EDWARD: I know. I think I've been pretending that if I didn't mention it the day would never come. I love it when we're together, the three of us, don't you?
LINDA *nods.*
Can I write to you?

LINDA: Yeh . . . yeh, if you want.

EDWARD: Would Mickey mind?

LINDA: Why should he?

EDWARD: Come on . . . because you're his girl friend.

LINDA: No, I'm not.

EDWARD: You are, Linda.

LINDA: I'm not, he hasn't asked me.

EDWARD (*laughing*): You mean he still hasn't?

LINDA (*laughing*): No.

EDWARD: But it's ridiculous.

LINDA: I know. I hope for his sake he never has to ask me to
marry him. He'll be a pensioner before he gets around to it.

EDWARD (*after a pause*): He's mad. If I was Mickey I would
have asked you years ago.

LINDA: I know *you* would. Cos y soft you are.

EDWARD (*singing*): If I could stand inside his shoes I'd say,
How can I compare thee to a summer's day

LINDA (*speaking*): Oh go away . . .

EDWARD: I'd take a page in all the papers, I'd announce it on
the news
If I was the guy, if I
Was in his shoes.

If I was him I'd bring you flowers
And ask you to dance
We'd while away the hours making future plans
For rainy days in country lanes
And trips to the sea
I'd just tell you that I love you
If it was me.

But I'm not saying a word,
I'm not saying I care,
Though I would like you to know,
That I'm not saying a word,
I'm not saying I care,
Though I would like you to know.

If I was him I'd have to tell you,
What I've kept in my heart,
That even if we had to live
Some worlds apart
There would not be a day
In which I'd not think of you
If I was him, if I was him
That's what I'd do.

But I'm not saying a word
I'm not saying I care
Though I would like you to know
That I'm not saying a word
I'm not saying I care
Though I would like you to know.

EDWARD: But I'm not.

LINDA: What?

EDWARD: Mickey.
  MICKEY *enters.*
  Mickey!

MICKEY: Hi-ya, Ed. Lind.

LINDA: Where've y' been?

MICKEY: I had to do overtime. I hate that soddin' place.

EDWARD: Mickey. I'm going away tomorrow . . . to University.

MICKEY: What? Y' didn't say.

EDWARD: I know . . . but the thing is I won't be back until
  Christmas. Three months. Now you wouldn't want me to
  continue in suspense for all that time would you?

LINDA: What are you on about?

EDDIE: Will you talk to Linda.

LINDA: Oh Eddie . . .

EDWARD: Go on . . . go on.
  MICKEY *turns and goes to her.* LINDA *tries to keep a straight*
  face.

MICKEY: Erm . . . well, the er thing is . . . Linda, I've erm . . .
  (*Quickly.*) Linda for Christ's sake will you go out with me?

LINDA (*just as quickly*): Yeh.

MICKEY: Oh . . . erm . . . Good. Well, I suppose I better . . . well
  er . . . come here . . . (*He quickly embraces and kisses* LINDA.)

LINDA (*fighting for air*): My God. Y' take y' time gettin' goin'
  but then there's no stoppin' y'.

MICKEY: I know . . . come here . . .
  They kiss again. EDWARD *turns and begins to leave.*
  Eddie . . . Eddie where y' goin'? I though we were all goin'
  the club. There's a dance.

EDWARD: No . . . I've got to, erm, I've got to pack for tomorrow.

MICKEY: Are y' sure?
  EDWARD *nods.*
  See y' at Christmas then, Eddie? Listen, I'm gonna do loads of
  overtime between now and then, so the Christmas party's
  gonna be on me . . . right?

EDWARD: Right. It's a deal, Mick. See you.
  LINDA *rushes across and kisses* EDWARD *lightly.*

LINDA: Thanks Eddie.

MICKEY: Yeh, Eddie . . . thanks.

LINDA *and* MICKEY, *arms around each other, watch him go.*
They turn and look at each other.

MICKEY *and* LINDA *exit.*

The Lights crossfade to the JOHNSTONE *house.*

MICKEY *enters and prepares to go to work.*

MRS JOHNSTONE *enters with* MICKEY's *lunch bag.*

The NARRATOR *enters.*

> It was one day in October when the sun began to fade,
> And Winter broke the promise that Summer had just made,
> It was one day in October when the rain came falling down,
> And someone said the bogey man was seen around the
>   town.

The NARRATOR *exits.*

MRS JOHNSTONE: Y' gonna be late Mick. I don't want you
gettin' the sack an' spendin' your days idlin' round like our
Sammy. Come on.

MICKEY *instead of making an effort to go, stands looking*
at her.

MICKEY: Mam!

MRS JOHNSTONE: What?

MICKEY: What!

MRS JOHNSTONE: Come on.

MICKEY: Mam. Linda's pregnant!
A moment.

MRS JOHNSTONE: Do you love her?

MICKEY: Yeh!

MRS JOHNSTONE: When's the weddin'?

MICKEY: We thought, about a month . . . before Christmas
anyway. Mam, could we live here for a bit?
She looks at him and nods.
Are you mad?

MRS JOHNSTONE: At you? Some hypocrite I'd be. No . . . I'm
not mad son. I'm just thinkin' . . . you've not had much of a
life with me, have y'?

MICKEY: Don't be stupid, course I have. You're great, you are,
Mam. (*He gives her a quick kiss.*) Tar-ra I'd better get a move
on. They've started layin' people off in the other factory
y' know. Tarrah, Mam. Thanks.

MICKEY *exits.*

Music.

MRS JOHNSTONE *watches him go. As 'Miss Jones' begins she whips off her overall and a wedding suit is underneath. She acquires a hat.*

A wedding party assembles. MICKEY *remains in his working clothes.* LINDA *is in white. Other guests are suitably attired. A* MANAGING DIRECTOR *enters and sings as his secretary,* MISS JONES, *takes notes.*

MR LYONS (*singing*): Take a letter, Miss Jones (quote)
    I regret to inform you,
    That owing to circumstances
    Quite beyond our control.
    It's a premature retirement
    For those surplus to requirement,
    I'm afraid it's a sign of the times,
    Miss Jones,
    An unfortunate sign of the times.

Throughout the next verse we see the wedding party wave goodbye to MICKEY *who goes to work, only to have his cards given to him when he gets there.*

    Take a letter, Miss Jones,
    Due to the world situation
    The shrinking pound, the global slump,
    And the price of oil
    I'm afraid we must fire you,
    We no longer require you,
    It's just another
    Sign of the times,
    Miss Jones,
    A most miserable sign of the times.

The GUESTS *at the wedding become a line of men looking for work.* MICKEY *joins them as* LINDA *watches. They are constantly met with shaking heads and by the end of the following verse have assembled in the dole office.*

    Take a letter Miss Jones, of course we'll
    Let the workforce know when
    Inflation's been defeated
    And recession is no more.
    And for the moment we suggest
    You don't become too depressed
    As it's only a sign
    Of the times,
    Miss Jones,
    A peculiar sign of the times.

Take a letter Miss Jones:
My dear Miss Jones, we'd like to thank you
Many years of splendid service,
Etcetara blah blah blah
You've been a perfect poppet
Yes that's right Miss Jones, you've got it
It's just another sign
Of the times,
Miss Jones, it's
Just another sign of the times.

*He shows her the door. Crying she approaches the dole queue
but then hesitates. The men in the queue take up the song.*

DOLEITES: Dry your eyes, Miss Jones
It's not as bad as it seems (you)
Get used to being idle
In a year or two.
Unemployment's such a pleasure
These days, we call it leisure
It's just another sign
Of the times,
Miss Jones, it's
Just another sign of the times.

MICKEY *leaves the group and stands apart.* MISS JONES
takes his place. Behind MICKEY *we can see* LINDA *and his*
MOTHER.

There's a young man on the street, Miss Jones,
He's walkin' round in circles,
He's old before his time,
But still too young to know.
Don't look at him, don't cry though
This living on the Giro
Is only a sign of the times,
Miss Jones, it's
Just another sign of the times.
As they exit.
Miss Jones,
It's just another sign of the times . . .

CROWD *exits.*

MICKEY *is left alone, sitting dejected. We hear Christmas Bells.*

EDWARD *enters in a duffle coat and college scarf, unseen by*
MICKEY. EDWARD *creeps up behind* MICKEY *and puts his
hands over his eyes.*

EDWARD: Guess who?

MICKEY: Father Christmas.

EDWARD (*leaping out in front of them*): Mickey . . . (*Laughing.*)
Merry Christmas.
MICKEY, *unamused, looks at* EDWARD *and then looks away.*
Come on then . . . I'm back, where's the action, the booze, the
Christmas parties, the music and the birds.
No reaction.
What's wrong, Mickey?

MICKEY: Nothin'. How's University?

EDWARD: Mickey, it's fantastic. I haven't been to so many
parties in my life. And there's just so many tremendous
people, but you'll meet them Mick, some of them, Baz,
Ronnie and Clare and oh, lots of them. They're coming over
to stay for the New Year, for the party. Ooh it's just . . . it's
great, Mickey.

MICKEY: Good.

EDWARD: Come on, what's wrong? It's nearly Christmas, we
were going to do everything. How's Linda?

MICKEY: She's OK.

EDWARD (*trying again to rally him*): Well, come on then, let's
go then . . . come on.

MICKEY: Come on where?

EDWARD: Mickey, what's wrong?

MICKEY: You. You're a dick head!
EDWARD *is slightly unsure but laughs anyway.*
There are no parties arranged. There is no booze or music.
Christmas? I'm sick to the teeth of Christmas an' it isn't even
here yet. See, there's very little to celebrate, Eddie. Since you
left I've been walking around all day, every day, lookin' for
a job.

EDWARD: What about the job you had?

MICKEY: It disappeared. (*Pause.*) Y' know somethin', I bleedin'
hated that job, standin' there all day never doin' nothin' but
put cardboard boxes together. I used to get . . . used to get
terrified that I'd have to do it for the rest of me life. But, but
after three months of nothin', the same answer everywhere,
nothin', nothin' down for y', I'd crawl back to that job for
half the pay and double the hours. Just . . . just makin' up
boxes it was. But after bein' fucked off from everywhere, it
seems like it was paradise.

Pause.

EDWARD: Why . . . why is a job so important? If I couldn't get a job I'd just say, sod it and draw the dole, live like a bohemian, tilt my hat to the world and say 'screw you'. So you're not working. Why is it so important?

MICKEY (*looking at him*): You don't understand anythin' do y'? I don't wear a hat that I could tilt at the world.

EDWARD: Look . . . come on . . . I've got money, plenty of it. I'm back, let's forget about bloody jobs, let's go and get Linda and celebrate. Look, look, money, lots of it, have some . . . (*He tries to thrust some notes into* MICKEY's *hands.*)

MICKEY: No. I don't want your money, stuff it.
He throws the notes to the ground. EDWARD *picks them up and stands looking at* MICKEY.
Eddie, just do me a favour an' piss off, will y'?
Pause.

EDWARD: I thought, I thought we always stuck together. I thought we were . . . were blood brothers.

MICKEY: That was kids' stuff, Eddie. Didn't anyone tell y'? (*He looks at* EDWARD.) But I suppose you still are a kid, aren't y'?

EDWARD: I'm exactly the same age as you, Mickey.

MICKEY: Yeh. But you're still a kid. An' I wish I could be as well Eddie, I wish I could still believe in all that blood brother stuff. But I can't, because while no one was looking I grew up. An' you didn't, because you didn't need to; an' I don't blame y' for it Eddie. In your shoes I'd be the same, I'd still be able to be a kid. But I'm not in your shoes, I'm in these, lookin' at you. An' you make me sick, right? That was all just kids' stuff, Eddie, an' I don't want to be reminded of it. Right? So just, just take yourself away. Go an' see your friends an' celebrate with them.
Pause.
Go on . . . beat it before I hit y'.

EDWARD *looks at* MICKEY *and then slowly backs away.*

SAMMY *approaches* MICKEY *as, on the other side, we see* LINDA *hurrying on passing* EDWARD *who stops and calls.*

EDWARD: Linda!

SAMMY: Mickey.

EDWARD: Linda.
Reluctantly she stops, goes back a few paces.

Hello, Linda.

LINDA: Hello, Eddie.

EDWARD: Why haven't you called to see me?

LINDA: I heard you had friends, I didn't like butting in.

EDWARD: You'd never be butting in and you know it. It wouldn't matter if I never saw those friends again, if I could be with you.

LINDA: Eddie . . .

SAMMY: Look, I'm offerin' . . . all we need is someone to keep the eye for us. Look at y' Mickey. What have y' got? Nothin', like me Mam. Where y' takin' y' tart for New Year? Nowhere.

EDWARD: You might as well know, if I'm not going to, see you again. I've always loved you, you must have known that.

SAMMY: We don't *use* the shooters. They're just frighteners. Y' don' need to use them. Everyone behaves when they see a shooter. You won't even be where the action is. Just keep the eye out for us.

EDWARD: I'm sorry.

SAMMY: Fifty quid Mickey. Fifty quid for an hour's work. Just think where y' could take Linda if you had cash like that.

EDWARD: I'm sorry, Linda.

LINDA: It's all right. I suppose, I suppose I always . . . loved you, in a way.

EDWARD: Then marry me.

LINDA: Didn't Mickey tell y'? We got married two weeks before you came home and I'm expecting a baby.

MICKEY: Fifty notes?
SAMMY *nods*.
All right.

SAMMY: Great.
MICKEY *nods*.
Cheer up, will y'? It's New Year.
SAMMY *exits*.

EDWARD'S FRIENDS (*variously; off*): Where's Lyo? Come on Lyons, you pillock, you're supposed to be helping us with the booze. Come on Lyonese. Edward, come on.

LINDA: I'll see y' Eddie. Happy New Year. (*She moves away.*)
EDWARD *exits*.

MICKEY: Linda . . . Linda . . .

LINDA: Are you comin' in?

MICKEY: Look . . . I'll be back about eight o'clock. An' listen, get dressed up. I'm takin' y' out.

LINDA: What?

MICKEY: We're goin' dancin'. Right? Then we're goin' for a slap-up meal an' tomorrow you can go into town an' get some new clothes.

LINDA: Oh yeh? Where's the money comin' from?

MICKEY: I'm . . . doin' some work . . .

LINDA: What?

MICKEY: Look, stop arguin', will y'? I'm doin' some work and then I'm takin' you out.

SAMMY (*off*): Mickey!

LINDA: Is that your Sammy?

MICKEY: Now shut up, Linda. Right, right? Just make sure you're ready at eight . . . (*He starts to leave.*)

LINDA (*as he goes*): Mickey . . . Mickey . . . No!
    LINDA *exits.*
    MICKEY *moves away.*
    The NARRATOR *enters.*
    SAMMY *enters.*

NARRATOR: There's a full moon shining and a joker in the pack,
        The dealers dealt the cards, and he won't take them back,
        There's a black cat stalking and a woman who's afraid,
        That there's no getting off without the price being paid.

We see MICKEY, *nervously keeping look-out as behind him, as if inside a filling station office, we see* SAMMY, *his back to us, talking to an off-stage character.*

SAMMY: Don't piss about with me, pal . . . I said give! (*Pause.*) Listen, it's not a toy y' know . . . We're not playin' games. Y' don't get up again if one of these hits y' . . . What are you doin'? I said listen to me, I said . . . don't you fuckin' touch that . . . Listen.
    An alarm bell is heard, followed by an explosion from the gun. SAMMY *reels backwards. He and* MICKEY *run and enter their house.*

NARRATOR: There's a man lies bleeding on a garage floor,

SAMMY: Quick, get in the house an' bolt the fuckin' door.
    MICKEY *stands unable to move, tears streaming down his face.*

NARRATOR: And maybe, if you counted ten and kept your
        fingers crossed

It would all be just a game and then no one would have
   lost.

MICKEY: You shot him, you shot him.

SAMMY: I know I bloody did.

MICKEY: You shot him, you shot him.

SAMMY: Move, I've got to get this hid.

LINDA (*off*): Mickey . . . Mickey, is that you?

SAMMY: Ooh, fuck . . . (*He quickly pulls back a mat, pulls up a
   floorboard and puts the gun beneath it.*)
   LINDA *enters.*
   Two POLICEMEN *arrive at the house.*
   SAMMY *splits out the back.* MICKEY *remains silently crying.*
   LINDA *goes to him and puts her arms around him. As*
   SAMMY *is being apprehended at the back, the other*
   POLICEMAN *enters and gently removes* LINDA *from*
   MICKEY *and leads him out and into the police station.*

LINDA: But I've ironed him a shirt.

   Music.

   MICKEY, *placed in a prison cell, stands quietly crying.*
   MRS JOHNSTON *enters.*

MRS JOHNSTONE (*singing*): The jury found him guilty
   Sent him down for seven years,
   Though he acted like they gave him life,
   He couldn't stop the tears.
   And when we went to visit him,
   He didn't want to know,
   It seems like jail's sent him off the rails,
   Just like Marilyn Monroe
   His mind's gone dancing
   Can't stop dancing
   A DOCTOR *enters the cell and examines* MICKEY.
   They showed him to a doctor,
   And after routine test,
   A prescription note the doctor wrote,
   For the chronically depressed.
   And now the tears have stopped
   He sits and counts the days to go
   And treats his ills with daily pills
   Just like Marilyn Monroe.
   The DOCTOR *exits.*
   They stop his mind from dancing
   Stop it dancing.

A prison warder leads LINDA *into the cell. He indicates a seat opposite* MICKEY.

LINDA: What are y' doin'?

MICKEY: What? I'm takin' me tablet.

LINDA: Listen, Mickey. I've told y'. They're just junk. You'll be home soon, Mickey, and you should come off them.

MICKEY: Why? I need . . . I need to take them.

LINDA: Listen, Mickey, you've . . .

MICKEY: No! See, he says, the doctor, he said . . .

LINDA: What did he say?

MICKEY: He said, about me nerves. An' how I get depressed an' I need to take these cos they make me better . . .

LINDA: I get depressed but I don't take those. You don't need those, Mickey.

MICKEY: Leave me alone, will y'? I can't cope with this. I'm not well. The doctor said, didn't he, I'm not well . . . I can't do things . . . leave me alone . . .

The WARDER *escorts* LINDA *from the cell.*

Throughout the following verse MICKEY *leaves the prison and goes home.*

MRS JOHNSTONE (*singing*): With grace for good behaviour
        He got out before his time
        The family and the neighbours told him
        He was lookin' fine.
        But he's feelin' fifteen years older
        And his speech is rather slow
        And the neighbours said
        You'd think he was dead
        Like Marilyn Monroe
        No cause for dancing
        No more dancing . . .

    LINDA *approaches* MRS JOHNSTONE. LINDA *is weighed down with shopping bags and is weary.*

MRS JOHNSTONE: Linda, where've y' been? We've gorra do somethin' about him. He's been out for months and he's still takin' those pills. Linda, he needs a job, you two need a place of your own an' . . .

LINDA: Mam . . . Mam that's why I'm late, I've been to see . . . We're movin' at the end of the month. We've got our own place an' I think I've got Mickey a job . . .

MRS JOHNSTONE: Oh, Jesus, thank God. But how . . .

LINDA: It's all right . . . I . . someone I know . . .

MRS JOHNSTONE: But who . . .

LINDA: It's all right Mam. Did y' get our Sarah from school?

MRS JOHNSTONE: Yeh, she's in bed, but listen how did y' manage to . . .

LINDA: Never mind, Mam. Mam, isn't it great; if he's workin' an' we've got our own place he'll be able to get himself together an' stop takin' those friggin' things . . .
They start to leave.

MRS JOHNSTONE: But, listen Linda, who . . .

LINDA: Oh just some . . . some feller I know. He's . . . he's on the housin' committee. You don't know him, Mam . . .
MRS JOHNSTONE *exits.*

MICKEY *and* LINDA *are in their new house. In the lounge* LINDA *is preparing* MICKEY*'s working things.*
(*Shouting*): Mickey, Mickey, come on, you'll be late . . .
MICKEY *enters his house.*

MICKEY: Where's me . . .

LINDA: Here . . . here's y' bag. Y' sandwiches are in there . . .
He ignores the bag and begins looking through a cupboard drawer.
Mickey, what y' lookin' for?

MICKEY: Y' know what I'm lookin' for.

LINDA: Mickey, Mickey listen to me . . .

MICKEY: Where's me tablets gone, Linda?

LINDA: Mickey you don't need your tablets!

MICKEY: Linda!

LINDA: Mickey. You're workin' now, we're livin' on our own — you've got to start makin' an effort.

MICKEY: Give them to me, Linda.

LINDA: You promised.

MICKEY: I know I promised but I can't do without them.
I tried. Last week I tried to do without them. By dinner time I was shakin' an' sweating so much I couldn't even work.
I need them. That's all there is to it. Now give.
Pause.

LINDA: Is that it then? Are y' gonna stay on them forever?

MICKEY: Linda.

LINDA: Look. We've . . . we've managed to sort ourselves out this far but what's the use if . . .

MICKEY: *We* have sorted ourselves out? Do you think I'm really stupid?

LINDA: What?

MICKEY: I didn't sort anythin' out Linda. Not a job, not a house, nothin'. It used to be just sweets an' ciggies he gave me, because I had none of me own. Now it's a job and a house. I'm not stupid, Linda. You sorted it out. You an' Councillor Eddie Lyons.
LINDA doesn't deny it.
Now give me the tablets . . . I need them.

LINDA: An' what about what I need? I need you. I love you. But, Mickey, not when you've got them inside you. When you take those things, Mickey, I can't even see you.

MICKEY: That's why I take them. So I can be invisible. (*Pause.*) Now give me them.
Music. We see LINDA mutely hand MICKEY her bag.
MICKEY quickly grabs the tablets.
MICKEY exits.
The NARRATOR enters.
The NARRATOR watches LINDA. She moves to telephone, but hesitates.

NARRATOR: There's a girl inside the woman
    Who's waiting to get free
    She's washed a million dishes
    She's always making tea.

LINDA (*speaking on the 'phone*): Could I talk to Councillor Lyons, please?

NARRATOR: There's a girl inside the woman
    And the mother she became
    And a half remembered song
    Comes to her lips again.

LINDA (*on the 'phone*): Eddie, could I talk to you? Yeh, I remember.

NARRATOR: The girl would sing the melody
    But the woman stands in doubt
    And wonders what the price would be
    For letting the young girl out.
MRS JOHNSTONE enters.

MRS JOHNSTONE (*singing*): It's just a light romance,
    It's nothing cruel,
    They laid no plans,

How it came,
Who can explain?

LINDA *approaches* EDWARD *who is waiting at the park fence.*

They just said 'hello',
And foolishly they gazed,
They should have gone
Their separate ways.

The music continues.

EDWARD: Hey. (*He mimes firing a gun.*)

LINDA: Missed.

EDWARD *laughs, grabbing* LINDA *jokingly. Their smiles fade as they look at each other. Suddenly they kiss. They walk together, hand in hand. All this through the following verse.*

MRS JOHNSTONE (*singing*): It's just the same old song,
Nothing cruel,
Nothing wrong.
It's just two fools,
Who know the rules,
But break them all,
And grasp at half a chance
To play their part
In a light romance.

Throughout the following chorus we see MICKEY *at work. We see him go to take his pills. We see him make the effort of not taking them. We see the strain of this upon him but see that he is determined.*

Living on the never never,
Constant as the changing weather,
Never sure
Who's at the door,
Or the price
You're gonna have to pay.

We see LINDA *and* EDWARD *kicking up the leaves before parting.*

It's just a secret glance,
Across a room.
A touch of hands
That part too soon.
That same old tune
That always plays,
And lets them dance as friends,

> Then stand apart,
> As the music ends.

During the next chorus EDWARD *and* LINDA *wave goodbye,
as* EDWARD *and* MICKEY *once did.*

MRS LYONS *enters and goes to* MICKEY.

She turns MICKEY *round and points out* EDWARD *and*
LINDA *to him. By the end of the chorus* MICKEY *is
hammering on his own door.*

> Living on the never never,
> Constant as the changing weather,
> Never sure
> Who's at the door
> Or the price you're gonna have to pay.

As the music abruptly segues MICKEY *is heard hammering on
his door and calling for* LINDA, *as he once did for his mother.
The music pulsates and builds as he runs to his mothers's
house. He enters and flings back the floorboard to reveal the
gun hidden by* SAMMY.

MRS JOHNSTONE *enters just as* MICKEY *disappears with
the gun.*

MRS JOHNSTONE (*screaming*): Mickey . . . Mickey . . .

We see MICKEY *comb the town, breaking through groups of
people, looking, searching, desperate, not even knowing what
he's looking for or what he is going to do. His mother is
frantically trying to catch him but not succeeding.*

NARRATOR: There's a man gone mad in the town tonight,
> He's gonna shoot somebody down,
> There's a man gone mad, lost his mind tonight
> There's a mad man
> There's a mad man
> There's a mad man running round and round.

> Now you know the devil's got your number,
> He's runnin' right beside you,
> He's screamin' deep inside you,
> And someone said he's callin' your number up today.

As MRS JOHNSTONE *makes her way to* LINDA's *house.*
> There's a mad man/There's a mad man/There's a mad man.

MRS JOHNSTONE *hammers on* LINDA's *door, shouting her
name.* LINDA, *just returning home, comes up behind her.*

LINDA: Mam . . . Mam . . . what's . . .

MRS JOHNSTONE (*out of breath*) He's . . . Mickey . . . Mickey's got a gun . . .

LINDA: Mickey? . . . Eddie? . . . The Town Hall . . .

MRS JOHNSTONE: What?

LINDA (*beginning to run*): Eddie Lyons!

NARRATOR: There's a mad man running round and round
You know the devil's got your number
You know he's right beside you
He's screamin' deep inside you
And someone said he's callin' your number up today
Today
Today
TODAY!

On the last three words of the chorus MRS JOHNSON *runs off. On the last 'Today' the music stops abruptly.*

We see EDWARD, *standing behind a table, on a platform. He is in the middle of addressing his audience. Two Councillors stand either side.*

EDWARD: And if, for once, I agree with Councillor Smith, you mustn't hold that against me. But in this particular instance, yes, I do agree with him. You're right, Bob, there is a light at the end of the tunnel. Quite right. None of us would argue with you on that score. But what we would question is this, how many of us . . .

From his audience a commotion beginning. He thinks he is being heckled and so tries to carry on. In fact his audience is reacting to the sight of MICKEY *appearing from the stalls, a gun held two-handed, to steady his shaking hands, and pointed directly at* EDWARD. EDWARD *turns and sees* MICKEY *as someone on the platform next to him realizes the reality of the situation and screams.*

MICKEY: Stay where you are!
MICKY *stops a couple of yards from* EDWARD. *He is unsteady and breathing awkwardly.*

EDWARD (*eventually*): Hello, Mickey.

MICKEY: I stopped takin' the pills.

EDWARD (*pause*): Oh.

MICKEY (*eventually*): I began thinkin' again. Y' see. (*To the* COUNCILLOR.) Just get her out of here, mister, now!
The COUNCILLORS *hurry off.*
EDWARD *and* MICKEY *are now alone on the platform.*
I had to start thinkin' again. Because there was one thing left in my life. (*Pause.*) Just one thing I had left, Eddie — Linda —

an' I wanted to keep her. So, so I stopped takin' the pills. But
it was too late. D'y' know who told me about . . . you . . . an'
Linda . . . Your mother . . . she came to the factory and told
me.

EDWARD: Mickey, I don't know what she told you but Linda
and I are just friends . . .

MICKEY (*shouting for the first time*): Friends! I could kill you.
We were friends weren't we? Blood brothers, wasn't it?
Remember?

EDWARD: Yes, Mickey, I remember.

MICKEY: Well, how come you got everything . . . an' I got
nothin'? (*Pause.*) Friends. I've been thinkin' again Eddie. You
an' Linda were friends when she first got pregnant, weren't y'?

EDWARD: Mickey!

MICKEY: Does my child belong to you as well as everythin' else?
Does she, Eddie, does she?

EDWARD (*shouting*): No, for God's sake!
Pause.
From the back of the auditorium we hear a POLICEMAN
through a loudhailer.

POLICEMAN 1: Now listen, son, listen to me; I've got armed
marksmen with me. But if you do exactly as I say we won't
need to use them, will we? Now look, Michael, put down
the gun, just put the gun down, son.

MICKEY (*dismissing their presence*): What am I doin' here
Eddie? I thought I was gonna shoot y'. But I can't even do
that. I don't even know if the thing's loaded.
*MRS JOHNSTONE slowly walks down the centre aisle
towards the platform.*

POLICEMAN 2: What's that woman doin'?

POLICEMAN 1: Get that woman away . . .

POLICEMAN 2: Oh Christ.

MRS JOHNSTONE: Mickey. Mickey. Don't shoot him
Mickey . . .
MICKEY continues to hold the gun in position.

MICKEY: Go away Mam . . . Mam you go away from here.

MRS JOHNSTONE: No, son. (*She walks on to the platform.*)

MICKEY (*shouting*): Mam!

MRS JOHNSTONE: Mickey. Don't shoot Eddie. He's your
brother. You had a twin brother. I couldn't afford to keep

both of you. His mother couldn't have kids. I agreed to give one of you away!

MICKEY (*something that begins deep down inside him*): You! (*Screaming.*) You! Why didn't you give me away! (*He stands glaring at her, almost uncontrollable with rage.*) I could have been ... I could have been him!

On the word 'him' MICKEY waves at EDWARD with his gun hand. The gun explodes and blows EDWARD apart. MICKEY turns to the POLICE screaming the word 'No'. They open fire and four guns explode, blowing MICKEY away.

LINDA *runs down the aisle.*

The POLICE *are heard through the loudhailer.*

Nobody move, please. It's all right, it's all over, just stay where you are.

Music.

As the Light on the scene begins to dim we see the NARRATOR, *watching.*

NARRATOR: And do we blame superstition for what came to pass?
    Or could it be what we, the English, have come to know as
        class?
    Did you ever hear the story of the Johnstone twins,
    As like each other as two new pins,
    How one was kept and one given away,
    How they were born, and they died, on the self same day?

MRS JOHNSTONE (*singing*): Tell me it's not true,
    Say it's just a story.
    Something on the news
    Tell me it's not true.
    Though it's here before me,
    Say it's just a dream,
    Say it's just a scene
    From an old movie of years ago,
    From an old movie of Marilyn Monroe.

    Say it's just some clowns,
    Two players in the limelight,
    And bring the curtain down.
    Say it's just two clowns,
    Who couldn't get their lines right,
    Say it's just a show
    On the radio,
    That we can turn over and start again,
    That we can turn over; it's only a game.

COMPANY: Tell me it's not true,
    Say I only dreamed it,
    And morning will come soon,
    Tell me it's not true,
    Say you didn't mean it,
    Say it's just pretend,
    Say it's just the end,
    Of an old movie from years ago
    Of an old movie with Marilyn Monroe.

Curtain.

Educating The Author

I was born in Whiston, which is just outside Liverpool. They talk funny in Whiston. To a Liverpudlian everyone else talks funny. Fortunately, when I was five my mum and dad moved to Knowsley, into an estate full of Liverpudlians who taught me how to talk correctly.

My dad worked in a factory (later, having come to hate factory life, he got out and bought a chip shop) and my mother worked in a warehouse; in those days there was a common ritual called employment. I went to school just down the road from my grandma's mobile grocer's (it was in an old charabanc which had long since lost any chance of going anywhere but everyone called it the mobile).

In school I learned how to read very early. Apart from reading books I played football and kick-the-can and quite enjoyed the twice-weekly gardening lessons. We each had a plot and at the end of the summer term we could take home our turnips and lettuces and radish and stuff. We used to eat it on the way. Our headmaster (Pop Chandler) had a war wound in his leg and everyone said it was 'cause of the shrapnel. When we went to the baths (if he was in a good mood) he'd show us this hold in his leg. It was horrible. It was blue. We loved looking at it.

Other than reading books, gardening, playing football and looking at shrapnel wounds I didn't care much for school. I watched the telly a lot. Never went to any theatres or anything like that. Saw a show at the village hall once but it was all false. They talked funny and got married at the end. I only remember it 'cause I won the raffle, a box of fruit, with a coconut right in the middle. When we opened it the coconut stunk. It was bad.

When I was eleven they sent me to a secondary school in Huyton. Like all the other Knowsley kids I was frightened of Huyton. There were millions of new houses there and flats, and everyone said there were gangs with bike chains and broken bottles and truck spanners. What everyone said was right; playtime was nothing to do with play, it was about survival. Thugs roamed the concrete and casually destroyed anything that couldn't move fast enough. Dinner time was the same only four times as long.

If you were lucky enough to survive the food itself you then had to get out into the playground world of protection rackets, tobacco hustlers, trainee contract killers and plain no-nonsense sadists. And that's without the teachers!

Anders his name was, the metalwork teacher. All the other

kids loved metalwork. First thing we had to do was file a small
rectangle of metal so that all the sides were straight; this would
then be name-stamped and used as a nameplate to identify each
kid's work. I never completed mine. After a matter of weeks
other kids had moved from making nameplates to producing
anything from guns and daggers to boiler-room engines while it
was obvious that I was never going to be able to get the sides of
my piece of metal straight. Eventually it was just a sliver, a
near-perfect needle, though not straight. I showed it to him,
Anders; I couldn't hide it from him any longer. He chucked it in
the bin and wordlessly handed me another chunk of metal and
indicated that I had to do it again and again and again until I
did it *right*! And I did, for a whole school year, every metalwork
lesson, tried and failed and with every failure there came a chunk
of metal and the instruction to do it again. I started to have
terrible nightmares about Anders. It's the only time I can
remember feeling real hatred for another human being.

After another year I moved schools, to Rainford where it used
to be countryside, where they all talked funny, where the thugs
were rather old-fashioned, charming even. Whereas in Huyton you
could be bike-chained to bits without warning, in Rainford the
thugs observed some sort of manners: 'Ey you, does t' want t'
fight wi me?' You could still get hurt, of course, and some of
the teachers were headcases; but there were no sadists, metalwork
was not on the curriculum, there were fields and lawns in place
of concrete playgrounds and compared to Huyton it was paradise.
We even had a long lesson every week called 'silent reading'; just
enter the classroom and pick up a book, start reading and as long
as you made no noise you were left completely alone with your
book. I remember clearly, during one of these lessons, locked into
a novel, the sun streaming through the windows, experiencing
the feeling of total peace and security and thinking what a great
thing it must be to write books and create in people the sort of
feeling the author had created in me. I wanted to be a writer!

It was a wonderful and terrible thought — wonderful because
I sensed, I knew, it was the only thing for me. Terrible because
how could I, a kid from the 'D' stream, a piece of factory fodder,
ever change the course that my life was already set upon? How
the hell could I ever be the sort of person who could become a
writer? It was a shocking and ludicrous thought, one that I hid
deep in myself for years, but one that would not go away.

During my last year at school they took us to a bottle-making
factory in St Helens, me and all the other kids who were
obviously factory types. I could feel the brutality of the place

even before I entered its windowless walls. Inside, the din and the
smell were overpowering. Human beings worked in there but the
figures I saw, feeding huge and relentlessly hungry machines,
seemed not to be a part of humanity but a part of the machinery
itself. Those men who were fortunate enough to not have to work
directly with the machinery, the supervisors, foremen I suppose,
glared, prodded, occasionally shouted. Each one of them looked
like Anders from the metalwork class.

Most of the kids with whom I visited that place accepted that
it was their lot to end up in that place. Some even talked of the
money they would earn and made out that they couldn't wait
to get inside those walls.

But in truth, I think they all dreaded it as much as I. Back in
school I stared at the geography books I hadn't read, the history
pages and science I hadn't studied, the maths books (which would
still be a mystery today, even if I'd studied them from birth), and
I realized that with only six months' schooling to go, I'd left it
all hopelessly too late. Like it or not I'd end up in a factory.
There was no point in trying to catch up with years of schoolwork
in a mere six months. And so I didn't. The months I had left
were spent sagging school and going to a dark underground club
every lunchtime. It was called the Cavern and the smell of sweat
in there was as pungent as any in a factory, the din was louder
than any made by machines. But the sweat was mingled with
cheap perfume and was produced by dancing and the noise was
music, made by a group called the Beatles.

One afternoon in summer I left the Cavern after the lunchtime
session and had to go to the Bluecoat Chambers to sit an
examination, the result of which would determine how suited
I was to become an apprentice printer. I didn't want to be an
apprentice printer; I wanted to be back in the Cavern. I did the
exam because my dad thought it would be a good thing. I
answered the questions on how many men it would take to lift
three tons of coal in seven hours if it took one man two minutes
to lift a sack of coal on a rainy day etc. And I wrote the essay of
my choice (titled 'A Group Called The Beatles'). And I failed.

At home there were conferences, discussions, rows and slanging
matches all on the same subject — me and the job I'd get.
Eventually my mother resolved it all. She suggested I become a
ladies' hairdresser! I can only think that a desire to have her hair
done free must have clouded her normally reasonable mind. It
was such a bizzare suggestion that I went along with it. I went
to a college for a year or so and pretended to learn all about
hairdressing. In reality most of my time was spent at parties or

arranging parties. It was a good year but when it ended I had to go to work. Someone was actually prepared to hire me as a hairdresser, to let me loose on the heads of innocent and unsuspecting customers. There were heads scalded during shampooing, heads which should have become blonde but turned out green, heads of Afro frizz (before Afro frizz had been invented) and heads rendered temporarily bald. Somehow, probably from moving from one shop to another before my legendary abilities were known, I survived. For six years I did a job I didn't understand and didn't like. Eventually I even had my own small salon and it was there that on slack days I would retire to the back room and try to do the one and only thing I felt I understood, felt that I could do: write.

I wrote songs mostly but tried, as well, to write sketches and poetry, even a book. But I kept getting interrupted by women who, reasonably enough on their part, wanted their hair done. It dawned upon me that if ever I was to become a writer I had first to get myself into the sort of world which allowed for, possibly even encouraged such aspiration. But that would mean a drastic change of course. Could I do it? Could I do something which those around me didn't understand? I would have to break away. People would be puzzled and hurt. I compromised. I sensed that the world in which I would be able to write would be the academic world. Students have long holidays. I'd be able to spend a good part of the year writing and the other part learning to do a job, teaching perhaps, which would pay the rent. I wasn't qualified to train as a teacher but I decided to dip my toe in the water and test the temperature. I enrolled in a night class for O level English Literature and passed it. To go to a college though, I'd need at least five O levels. Taking them at night school would take too long. I had to find a college which would let me take a full-time course, pack everything into one year. I found a college but no authority was prepared to give me a maintenance grant or even pay my fees. I knew I couldn't let the course go, knew I could survive from day to day — but how was I going to find the money to pay the fees? The hairdressing paid nothing worth talking of.

I heard of a job, a contract job in Fords, cleaning oil from the girders high above the machinery. With no safety equipment whatsoever and with oil on every girder the danger was obvious. But the money was big.

I packed up the hairdresser's and joined the night-shift girder cleaners. Some of them fell and were injured, some of them took just one look at the job and walked away. Eventually there were just a few of us desperate or daft enough to take a chance.

I stayed in that factory just long enough to earn the fees I needed; no extras, nothing. Once I'd earned enough for the fees, I came down from the girders, collected my money and walked away. I enrolled at the college and one day in September made my way along the stone-walled drive. The obvious difference in age between me and the sixteen-year-olds pouring down the drive made me feel exposed and nervous but as I entered the glass doors of Childwall College I felt as if I'd made it back to the beginning. I could start again. I felt at home.

WILLY RUSSELL

EDUCATING RITA

Educating Rita was first performed on 10 June 1980 at the Royal Shakespeare Company Warehouse, London with the following cast:

FRANK   Mark Kingston
RITA   Julie Walters

Directed by Mike Ockrent
Designed by Poppy Mitchell

Educating Rita subsequently transferred to the Piccadilly Theatre, London, and the cast changed several times during a long run. It was also filmed with Michael Caine as Frank and Julie Walters as Rita directed by Lewis Gilbert.

ACT ONE

Scene One

A room on the first floor of a Victorian-built university in the north of England.

There is a large bay window with a desk placed in front of it and another desk covered with various papers and books. The walls are lined with books and on one wall hangs a good print of a nude religious scene.

FRANK, who is in his early fifties, is standing holding an empty mug. He goes to the bookcases and starts taking books from the shelves, hurriedly replacing them before moving on to another section.

FRANK (*looking along the shelves*): Where the hell . . . ? Eliot? (*He pulls out some books and looks into the bookshelf.*) No. (*He replaces the books.*) 'E' (*He thinks for a moment.*) 'E', 'e', 'e' . . . (*Suddenly he remembers.*) Dickens. (*Jubilantly he moves to the Dickens section and pulls out a pile of books to reveal a bottle of whisky. He takes the bottle from the shelf and goes to the small table by the door and pours himself a large slug into the mug in his hand.*)

The telephone rings and startles him slightly. He manages a gulp at the whisky before he picks up the receiver and although his speech is not slurred, we should recognize the voice of a man who shifts a lot of booze.

Yes? . . . Of course I'm still here . . . Because I've got this Open University woman coming, haven't I? . . . Tch. . . . Of course I told you. . . . But darling, you shouldn't have prepared dinner should you? Because I said, I distinctly remember saying that I would be late. . . . Yes. Yes, I probably shall go to the pub afterwards, I shall need to go to the pub afterwards, I shall need to wash away the memory of some silly woman's attempts to get into the mind of Henry James or whoever it is we're supposed to study on this course. . . . Oh God, why did I take this on? . . . Yes. . . . Yes I suppose I did take it on to pay for the drink. . . . Oh, for God's sake, what is it? . . . Yes, well — erm — leave it in the oven. . . . Look if you're trying to induce some feeling of guilt in me over the prospect of a burnt dinner you should have prepared something other than lamb and ratatouille. . . . Because, darling, I like my lamb done to the point of abuse and even I know that ratatouille cannot be burned. . . . Darling, you could incinerate ratatouille and still it wouldn't burn. . . . What

do you mean am I determined to go to the pub? I don't need
determination to get me into a pub . . .
There is a knock at the door.
Look, I'll have to go. . . . There's someone at the door. . . .
Yes, yes I promise. . . . Just a couple of pints. . . . Four. . . .
There is another knock at the door.
(*Calling in the direction of the door.*) Come in! (*He continues
on the telephone.*) Yes. . . . All right . . . yes. . . . Bye, bye. . . .
(*He replaces the receiver.*) Yes, that's it, you just pop off and
put your head in the oven. (*Shouting:*) Come in! Come in!
The door swings open revealing RITA.

RITA (*from the doorway*): I'm comin' in, aren't I? It's that
stupid bleedin' handle on the door. You wanna get it fixed!
(*She comes into the room.*)

FRANK (*staring, slightly confused*): Erm — yes, I suppose I
always mean to . . .

RITA (*going to the chair by the desk and dumping her bag*): Well
that's no good always meanin' to, is it? Y' should get on with
it; one of these days you'll be shoutin' 'Come in' an' it'll go
on forever because the poor sod on the other side won't be
able to get in. An' you won't be able to get out.

FRANK *stares at* RITA *who stands by the desk.*

FRANK: You are?

RITA: What am I?

FRANK: Pardon?

RITA: What?

FRANK (*looking for the admission papers*): Now you are?

RITA: I'm a what?

FRANK *looks up and then returns to the papers as* RITA
goes to hang her coat on the door hooks.

RITA (*noticing the picture*): That's a nice picture, isn't it? (*She
goes up to it.*)

FRANK: Erm — yes, I suppose it is — nice . . .

RITA (*studying the picture*): It's very erotic.

FRANK (*looking up*): Actually I don't think I've looked at it
for about ten years, but yes, I suppose it is.

RITA: There's no suppose about it. Look at those tits.
He coughs and goes back to looking for the admission paper.
Is it supposed to be erotic? I mean when he painted it do y'
think he wanted to turn people on?

FRANK: Erm — probably.

RITA: I'll bet he did y' know. Y' don't paint pictures like that just so that people can admire the brush strokes, do y'?

FRANK (*giving a short laugh*): No — no — you're probably right.

RITA: This was the pornography of its day, wasn't it? It's sort of like *Men Only*, isn't it? But in those days they had to pretend it wasn't erotic so they made it religious, didn't they? Do *you* think it's erotic?

FRANK (*taking a look*): I think it's very beautiful.

RITA: I didn't ask y' if it was beautiful.

FRANK: But the term 'beautiful' covers the many feelings I have about that picture, including the feeling that, yes, it is erotic.

RITA (*coming back to the desk*): D' y' get a lot like me?

FRANK: Pardon?

RITA: Do you get a lot of students like me?

FRANK: Not exactly, no . . .

RITA: I was dead surprised when they took me. I don't suppose they would have done if it'd been a proper university. The Open University's different though, isn't it?

FRANK: I've — erm — not had much more experience of it than you. This is the first O.U. work I've done.

RITA: D' y' need the money?

FRANK: I do as a matter of fact.

RITA: It's terrible these days, the money, isn't it? With the inflation an' that. You work for the ordinary university, don't y'? With the real students. The Open University's different, isn't it?

FRANK: It's supposed to embrace a more comprehensive studentship, yes.

RITA (*inspecting a bookcase*): Degrees for dishwashers.

FRANK: Would you — erm — would you like to sit down?

RITA: No! Can I smoke? (*She goes to her bag and rummages in it.*)

FRANK: Tobacco?

RITA: Yeh. (*She half-laughs.*) Was that a joke? (*She takes out a packet of cigarettes and a lighter.*) Here — d' y' want one? (*She takes out two cigarettes and dumps the packet on the desk.*)

FRANK (*after a pause*): Ah — I'd love one.

RITA: Well, have one.

FRANK (*after a pause*): I — don't smoke — I made a promise
    not to smoke.

RITA: Well, I won't tell anyone.

FRANK: Promise?

As FRANK *goes to take the cigarette* RITA *whips it from his
reach.*

RITA (*doing a Brownie salute*): On my oath as an ex Brownie.
    (*She gives him the cigarette.*) I hate smokin' on me own. An'
    everyone seems to have packed up these days. (*She lights the
    cigarettes.*) They're all afraid of gettin' cancer.
    FRANK *looks dubiously at his cigarette.*
    But they're all cowards.

FRANK: Are they?

RITA: You've got to challenge death an' disease. I read this poem
    about fightin' death . . .

FRANK: Ah — Dylan Thomas . . .

RITA: No. Roger McGough. It was about this old man who runs
    away from hospital an' goes out on the ale. He gets pissed an'
    stands in the street shoutin' an' challengin' death to come out
    an' fight. It's dead good.

FRANK: Yes. I don't think I know the actual piece you mean . . .

RITA: I'll bring y' the book — it's great.

FRANK: Thank you.

RITA: You probably won't think it's any good.

FRANK: Why?

RITA: It's the sort of poetry you can understand.

FRANK: Ah. I see.

    RITA *begins looking idly round the room.*

FRANK: Can I offer you a drink?

RITA: What of?

FRANK: Scotch?

RITA (*going to the bookcase*): Y' wanna be careful with that
    stuff, it kills y' brain cells.

FRANK: But you'll have one? (*He gets up and goes to the small
    table.*)

RITA: All right. It'll probably have a job findin' my brain.

FRANK (*pouring the drinks*): Water?

RITA (*looking at the bookcase*): Yeh, all right. (*She takes a copy
    of* Howards End *from the shelf.*) What's this like?

FRANK *goes over to* RITA, *looks at the title of the book and then goes back to the drinks.*

FRANK: *Howards End?*

RITA: Yeh. It sounds filthy, doesn't it? E.M. Foster.

FRANK: Forster.

RITA: Oh yeh. What's it like?

FRANK: Borrow it. Read it.

RITA: Ta. I'll look after it. (*She moves back towards the desk.*) If I pack the course in I'll post it to y'.

FRANK *comes back to the desk with drinks.*

FRANK (*handing her the mug*): Pack it in? Why should you do that?

RITA *puts her drink down on the desk and puts the copy of* Howards End *in her bag.*

RITA: I just might. I might decide it was a soft idea.

FRANK (*looking at her*): Mm. Cheers. If — erm — if you're already contemplating 'packing it in', why did you enrol in the first place?

RITA: Because I wanna know.

FRANK: What do you want to know?

RITA: Everything.

FRANK: Everything? That's rather a lot, isn't it? Where would you like to start?

RITA: Well, I'm a student now, aren't I? I'll have to do exams, won't I?

FRANK: Yes, eventually.

RITA: I'll have to learn about it all, won' I? Yeh. It's like y' sit there, don't y', watchin' the ballet or the opera on the telly an' — an' y' call it rubbish cos that's what it looks like? Cos y' don't understand. So y' switch it off an' say, that's fuckin' rubbish.

FRANK: Do you?

RITA: I do. But I don't want to. I wanna see. Y' don't mind me swearin', do y'?

FRANK: Not at all.

RITA: Do you swear?

FRANK: Never stop.

RITA: See, the educated classes know it's only words, don't they? It's only the masses who don't understand. I do it to

shock them sometimes. Y' know when I'm in the hairdresser's
— that's where I work — I'll say somethin' like, 'Oh, I'm really
fucked', y' know, dead loud. It doesn't half cause a fuss.

FRANK: Yes — I'm sure . . .

RITA: But it doesn't cause any sort of fuss with educated people,
does it? Cos they know it's only words and they don't worry.
But these stuck-up idiots I meet, they think they're royalty
just cos they don't swear; an' I wouldn't mind but it's the
aristocracy that swears more than anyone, isn't it? They're
effin' an' blindin' all day long. It's all 'Pass me the fackin'
grouse' with them, isn't it? But y' can't tell them that round
our way. It's not their fault; they can't help it. (*She goes to
the window and looks out.*) But sometimes I hate them. God,
what's it like to be free?

FRANK: Ah. Now there's a question. Will you have another
drink? (*He goes to the small table.*)

RITA (*shaking her head*): If I'd got some other tutor I wouldn't
have stayed.

FRANK (*pouring himself a drink*): What sort of other tutor?

RITA: Y' know, someone who objected to swearin'.

FRANK: How did you know I wouldn't object?

RITA: I didn't. I was just testin' y'.

FRANK (*coming back to the desk and looking at her*): Yes.
You're doing rather a lot of that, aren't you?

RITA: That's what I do. Y' know, when I'm nervous.

FRANK (*sitting in the swivel chair*): And how am I scoring so
far?

RITA: Very good, ten out of ten go to the top of the class an'
collect a gold star. I love this room. I love that window. Do
you like it?

FRANK: What?

RITA: The window.

FRANK: I don't often consider it actually. I sometimes get an
urge to throw something through it.

RITA: What?

FRANK: A student usually.

RITA (*smiling*): You're bleedin' mad you, aren't y'?

FRANK: Probably.
Pause.

RITA: Aren't you supposed to be interviewin' me?

FRANK (*looking at the drink*): Do I need to?

RITA: I talk too much, don't I? I know I talk a lot. I don't at home. I hardly ever talk when I'm there. But I don't often get the chance to talk to someone like you; to talk at you. D' y' mind?

FRANK: Would you be at all bothered if I did?
She shakes her head and then turns it into a nod.
I don't mind. (*He takes a sip of his drink.*)

RITA: What does assonance mean?

FRANK (*half-spluttering*): What? (*He gives a short laugh.*)

RITA: Don't laugh at me.

FRANK: No. Erm — assonance. Well, it's a form of rhyme. What's a — what's an example — erm — ? Do you know Yeats?

RITA: The wine lodge?

FRANK: Yeats the poet.

RITA: No.

FRANK: Oh. Well — there's a Yeats poem, called 'The Wild Swans at Coole'. In it he rhymes the word 'swan' with the word 'stone'. There, you see, an example of assonance.

RITA: Oh. It means gettin' the rhyme wrong.

FRANK (*looking at her and laughing*): I've never really looked at it like that. But yes, yes you could say it means getting the rhyme wrong; but purposefully, in order to achieve a certain effect.

RITA: Oh. (*There is a pause and she wanders round.*) There's loads I don't know.

FRANK: And you want to know everything?

RITA: Yeh.
FRANK nods and then takes her admission paper from his desk and looks at it.

FRANK: What's your name?

RITA (*moving towards the bookcase*): Rita.

FRANK (*looking at the paper*): Rita. Mm. It says here Mrs S. White.
RITA goes to the right of FRANK, takes a pencil, leans over and scratches out the initial 'S'.

RITA: That's 'S' for Susan. It's just me real name. I've changed it to Rita, though. I'm not a Susan any more. I've called meself Rita — y' know, after Rita Mae Brown.

FRANK: Who?

RITA: Y' know, Rita Mae Brown who wrote *Rubyfruit Jungle*?
   Haven't y' read it? It's a fantastic book. D' y' wanna lend it?

FRANK: I'd — erm — I'd be very interested.

RITA: All right.
   RITA *gets a copy of* Rubyfruit Jungle *from her bag and gives
   it to* FRANK. *He turns it over and reads the blurb on the
   back cover.*
   What's your name?

FRANK: Frank.

RITA: Oh. Not after Frank Harris?

FRANK: Not after Frank anyone.

RITA: Maybe y' parents named y' after the quality. (*She sits in
   the chair by the desk.*)
   FRANK *puts down* Rubyfruit Jungle.
   Y' know Frank, Frank Ness, Elliot's brother.

FRANK: What?

RITA: I'm sorry — it was a joke. Y' know, Frank Ness, Elliot's
   brother.

FRANK (*bemused*): Ah.

RITA: You've still not got it, have y'? Elliot Ness — y' know, the
   famous Chicago copper who caught Al Capone.

FRANK: Ah. When you said Elliot I assumed you meant
   T.S. Eliot.

RITA: Have you read his stuff?

FRANK: Yes.

RITA: All of it?

FRANK: Every last syllable.

RITA (*impressed*): Honest? I couldn't even get through one
   poem. I tried to read this thing he wrote called 'J. Arthur
   Prufrock'; I couldn't finish it.

FRANK: 'J. Alfred'.

RITA: What?

FRANK: I think you'll find it was 'J. Alfred Prufrock', Rita.
   J. Arthur is something else altogether.

RITA: Oh yeh. I never thought of that. I've not half got a lot to
   learn, haven't I?

FRANK (*looking at her paper*): You're a ladies' hairdresser?

RITA: Yeh.

FRANK: Are you good at it?

RITA (*getting up and wandering around*): I am when I wanna be. Most of the time I don't want to though. They get on me nerves.

FRANK: Who?

RITA: The women. They never tell y' things that matter. Like, y' know, doin' a perm, well y' can't use a strong perm lotion on a head that's been bleached with certain sorts of cheap bleach. It makes all the hair break off. But at least once a month I'll get a customer in for a perm who'll swear to God that she's not had any bleach on; an' I can tell, I mean I can see it. So y' go ahead an' do the perm an' she comes out the drier with half an inch of stubble.

FRANK: And what do you do about it?

RITA: Try and sell them a wig.

FRANK: My God.

RITA: Women who want their hair doin', they won't stop at anythin', y' know. Even the pensioners are like that, y' know; a pensioner'll come in an' she won't tell y' that she's got a hearin' aid: so y' start cuttin' don't y'? Next thing – snip – another granny deaf for a fortnight. I'm always cuttin' hearin' aid cords. An' ear lobes.

FRANK: You sound like something of a liability.

RITA: I am. But they expect too much. They walk in the hairdresser's an' an hour later they wanna walk out a different person. I tell them I'm a hairdresser, not a plastic surgeon. It's worse when there's a fad on, y' know like Farrah Fawcett Majors.

FRANK: Who?

RITA: Far-rah Fawcett Majors. Y' know, she used to be with *Charlie's Angels*.
FRANK *remains blank*.

RITA: It's a telly programme on ITV.

FRANK: Ah.

RITA (*wandering towards the door*): You wouldn't watch ITV though, would y'? It's all BBC with you, isn't it?

FRANK: Well, I must confess . . .

RITA: It's all right, I know. Soon as I walked in here I said to meself, 'Y' can tell he's a Flora man'.

FRANK: A what?

RITA: A Flora man.

FRANK: Flora? Flowers?

RITA (*coming back to the desk*): No, Flora, the bleedin'
    margarine, no cholesterol; it's for people like you who eat
    pebble-dashed bread, y' know the bread, with little hard bits
    in it, just like pebble-dashin'.

FRANK (*realizing and smiling*): Ah — pebble-dashed bread.

RITA: Quick? He's like lightnin'. But these women, you see, they
    come to the hairdresser's cos they wanna be changed. But if
    you want to change y' have to do it from the inside, don't y'?
    Know like I'm doin'. Do y' think I'll be able to do it?

FRANK: Well, it really depends on you, on how committed you
    are. Are you sure that you're absolutely serious about wanting
    to learn?

RITA: I'm dead serious. Look, I know I take the piss an' that but
    I'm dead serious really. I take the piss because I'm not, y'
    know, confident like, but I wanna be, honest.
    *He nods and looks at her. She becomes uncomfortable and
    moves away a little.*
    Tch. What y' lookin' at me for?

FRANK: Because — I think you're marvellous. Do you know,
    I think you're the first breath of air that's been in this room
    for years.

RITA (*wandering around*): Tch. Now who's taking the piss?

FRANK: Don't you recognize a compliment?

RITA: Go way . . .

FRANK: Where to?

RITA: Don't be soft. Y' know what I mean.

FRANK: What I want to know is what is it that's suddenly led
    you to this?

RITA: What? Comin' here?

FRANK: Yes.

RITA: It's not sudden.

FRANK: Ah.

RITA: I've been realizin' for ages that I was, y' know, slightly out
    of step. I'm twenty-six. I should have had a baby by now;
    everyone expects it. I'm sure me husband thinks I'm sterile.
    He was moanin' all the time, y' know, 'Come off the pill, let's
    have a baby'. I told him I'd come off it, just to shut him up.
    But I'm still on it. (*She moves round to* FRANK.) See, I don't
    wanna baby yet. See, I wanna discover meself first. Do you
    understand that?

FRANK: Yes.

RITA: Yeh. They wouldn't round our way. They'd think I was mental. I've tried to explain it to me husband but between you an' me I think he's thick. No, he's not thick, he's blind, he doesn't want to see. You know if I'm readin', or watchin' somethin' different on the telly he gets dead narked. I used to just tell him to piss off but then I realized that it was no good doin' that, that I had to explain to him. I tried to explain that I wanted a better way of livin' me life. An' he listened to me. But he didn't understand because when I'd finished he said he agreed with me and that we should start savin' the money to move off our estate an' get a house out in Formby. Even if it was a new house I wanted I wouldn't go an' live in Formby. I hate that hole, don't you?

FRANK: Yes.

RITA: Where do you live?

FRANK: Formby.

RITA (*sitting*): Oh.

FRANK (*getting up and going to the small table*): Another drink?
She shakes her head.
You don't mind if I do? (*He pours himself a drink.*)

RITA: No. It's your brain cells y' killin'.

FRANK (*smiling*): All dead long ago I'm afraid. (*He drinks.*)
RITA *gets up and goes to* FRANK*'s chair. She plays with the swivel and then leans on it.*

RITA: When d' y' actually, y' know, start teaching me?

FRANK (*looking at her*): What can I teach you?

RITA: Everything.
FRANK *leans on the filing cabinet, drinks, shakes his head and looks at her.*

FRANK: I'll make a bargain with you. Yes? I'll tell you everything I know — but if I do that you must promise never to come back here . . . You see I never — I didn't actually want to take this course in the first place. I allowed myself to be talked into it. I knew it was wrong. Seeing you only confirms my suspicion. My dear, it's not your fault, just the luck of the draw that you got me; but get me you did. And the thing is, between you, me and the walls, I'm actually an appalling teacher. (*After a pause.*) Most of the time, you see, it doesn't actually matter — appalling teaching is quite in order for most of my appalling students. And the others manage to get by despite me. But you're different. You want a lot, and I can't give it. (*He moves towards her.*) Everything I know — and you must listen to this — is that I know absolutely nothing. I don't like the hours, you know. (*He goes to the swivel chair and sits.*) Strange hours for this Open University thing. They expect us to teach when the pubs are open. I can be a good teacher when I'm in the pub, you know. Four pints of weak Guinness and I can be as witty as Wilde. I'm sorry — there are other tutors — I'll arrange it for you . . . post it on . . . (*He looks at her.*)

RITA *slowly turns and goes towards the door. She goes out and quietly closes the door behind her. Suddenly the door bursts open and* RITA *flies in.*

RITA (*going up to him*): Wait a minute, listen to me. Listen: I'm on this course, you are my teacher — an' you're gonna bleedin' well teach me.

FRANK: There are other tutors — I've told you . . .

RITA: You're my tutor. I don't want another tutor.

FRANK: For God's sake, woman — I've told you . . .

RITA: You're my tutor.

FRANK: But I've told you — I don't want to do it. Why come to me?

RITA (*looking at him*): Because you're a crazy mad piss artist who wants to throw his students through the window, an' I like you. (*After a pause.*) Don't you recognize a compliment?

FRANK: Do you think I could have a cigarette?

RITA (*offering the packet of cigarettes*): I'll bring me scissors next week and give y' a haircut.

FRANK: You're not coming here next week.

RITA (*lighting his cigarette*): I am. And you're gettin' y' hair cut.

FRANK: I am not getting my hair cut.

RITA (*getting her bag*): I suppose y' wanna walk round like that, do y'? (*She goes towards the door.*)

FRANK: Like what?

RITA (*getting her coat*): Like a geriatric hippie.

Blackout.

RITA *exits.*

Scene Two

FRANK *is standing in the centre of the room. He glances at his watch, moves to the window, looks out, glances at his watch again and then moves across to the books. He glances at his watch and then his attention is caught by the door handle being turned. He looks at the door but no one enters although the handle keeps being turned. Eventually he goes to the door and pulls it open.*

RITA *is standing in the doorway, holding a small can of oil.*

FRANK: Oh.

RITA: Hello. I was just oilin' it for y'. (*She comes into the room.*) I knew you wouldn't get round to it. Y' can have that. *She gives the oil can to* FRANK.

FRANK: Erm — thanks. (*He puts the can on the filing cabinet and then goes and sits in the swivel chair.*)

Slightly amused, he watches her as she wanders round the room.

RITA (*turning to him*): What y' lookin' at?

FRANK: Don't you ever just walk into a room and sit down?

RITA: Not when I've got the chair with its back to the door.

FRANK (*getting up*): Well — if it'd make you happier you take my chair.

RITA: No. You're the teacher, you sit there.

FRANK: But it doesn't matter where I sit. If you'd be happier with that chair then you sit there.

RITA: Tch. Is that what y' call democracy at work? I don't wanna sit down anyway. I like walkin' around this room. (*After a pause.*) How d' y' make a room like this?

FRANK: I didn't make it. I just moved in. The rest sort of happened.

RITA (*looking round*): Yeh. That's cos you've got taste. I'm gonna have a room like this one day. There's nothing phoney about it. Everything's in its right place. (*After a pause.*) It's a mess. But it's a perfect mess. (*She wanders round.*) It's like wherever you've put something down it's grown to fit there.

FRANK (*sitting down*): You mean that over the years it's acquired a certain patina.

RITA: Do I?

FRANK: I think so.

RITA: Yeh. 'It's acquired a certain patina.' It's like somethin' from a romantic film, isn't it? 'Over the years your face has acquired a certain patina.'

FRANK *smiles.*

RITA (*sniffing*): You've not been drinking, have y'?

FRANK: No.

RITA: Is that because of me, because of what I said last week?

FRANK (*laughing*): My God. You think you've reformed me?

RITA (*going to the window*): I don't wanna reform y'. Y' can do what y' like. (*Quickly.*) I love that lawn down there. When it's summer do they sit on it?

FRANK (*going to the window*): Who?

RITA (*going back to the desk*): The ones who come here all the time. The proper students.

FRANK: Yes. First glimmer of sun and they're all out there.

RITA: Readin' an' studyin'?

FRANK: Reading and studying? What do you think they are, human? Proper students don't read and study.

RITA: Y' what?

FRANK: A joke, a joke. Yes. They read and study, sometimes. *Pause.* RITA *dumps her bag on the chair and then goes and hangs up her coat on the door.*

RITA: It looks the way I always imagined a public school to look, y' know a boardin' school. When I was a kid I always wanted to go to a boardin' school.

FRANK: God forbid it; why?

RITA (*going to her chair at the desk*): I always thought they sounded great, schools like that, y' know with a tuck-shop an' a matron an' prep. An' a pair of kids called Jones minor an' Jones major. I told me mother once. (*She opens her bag and takes out the copy of* Howards End, *ring bound file, note-pad, ruler and pencil-case, placing them methodically on the desk in front of her.*) She said I was off me cake.

FRANK (*with an exaggerated look at her*): What in the name of God is being off one's cake?

RITA: Soft. Y' know, mental.

FRANK: Aha. I must remember that. The next student to ask me if Isabel Archer was guilty of protestant masochism shall be told that one is obviously very off one's cake!

RITA: Don't be soft. You can't say that.

FRANK: Why ever not?

RITA: You can't. If you do it, it's slummin' it. Comin' from you it'd sound dead affected, wouldn't it?

FRANK: Dead affected?

RITA: Yeh. You say that to your proper students they'll think you're off your — y' know . . .

FRANK: Cake, yes. Erm — Rita, why didn't you ever become what you call a proper student?

RITA: What? After goin' to the school I went to?

FRANK: Was it bad?

RITA *starts sharpening the pencils one by one into perfect spikes, leaving the shavings on the desk.*

RITA: Nah, just normal, y' know; borin', ripped-up books, broken glass everywhere, knives an' fights. An' that was just in the staffroom. Nah, they tried their best I suppose, always tellin' us we stood more of a chance if we studied. But studyin' was just for the whimps, wasn't it? See, if I'd started takin' school seriously I would have had to become different from me mates, an' that's not allowed.

FRANK: By whom?

RITA: By your mates, by your family, by everyone. So y' never admit that school could be anythin' other than useless.
FRANK *passes her the ashtray but she ignores it and continues sharpening the pencils on to the table.*

RITA: Like what you've got to be into is music an' clothes an' lookin' for a feller, y' know the real qualities of life. Not that I went along with it so reluctantly. I mean, there was always somethin' in me head, tappin' away, tellin' me I might have got it all wrong. But I'd just play another record or buy another dress an' stop worryin'. There's always somethin' to make you forget about it. So y' do, y' keep goin', tellin' yourself life's great. There's always another club to go to, a new feller to be chasin', a laugh an' a joke with the girls. Till, one day, y' own up to yourself an' y' say, is this it? Is this the absolute maximum I can expect from this livin' lark? An' that's the big moment that one, that's the point when y' have to decide whether it's gonna be another change of dress or a change in yourself. An' it's really temptin' to go out an' get another dress y' know, it is. Cos it's easy, it doesn't cost anythin', it doesn't upset anyone around y'. Like cos they don't want y' to change.

FRANK: But you — erm — you managed to resist another new dress?

RITA: Can't y' tell? Look at the state of this; I haven't had a new dress in twelve months. An' I'm not gonna get one either, not till – till I pass me first exam. Then I'll get a proper dress, the sort of dress you'd only see on an educated woman, on the sort of woman who knows the difference between Jane Austen an' Tracy Austin. (*She finishes sharpening the last pencil, and arranges it in line with the others. She gathers the pencil shavings into her hand and chucks them in the waste-bin.*) Let's start.

FRANK: Now the piece you wrote for me on – what was it called . . . ?

RITA (*getting out her cigarettes and lighter*): *Rubyfruit Jungle*.

FRANK: Yes, it was – erm . . .

RITA: Crap?

FRANK: No. Erm – the thing is, it was an appreciation, a descriptive piece. What you have to learn is criticism.

RITA: What's the difference? (*She lights a cigarette.*)

FRANK: Well. You must try to remember that criticism is purely objective. It should be approached almost as a science. It must be supported by reference to established literary critique. Criticism is never subjective and should not be confused with partisan interpretation. In criticism sentiment has no place. (*He picks up the copy of* Howards End.) Tell me, what did you think of *Howards End*?

RITA: It was crap.

FRANK: What?

RITA: I thought it was crap!

FRANK: Crap? And who are you citing in support of your thesis, F.R. Leavis?

RITA: No. Me!

FRANK: What have I just said? 'Me' is subjective.

RITA: Well it's what I think.

FRANK: You think *Howards End* is crap? Well would you kindly tell me why you think it's quote, 'Crap', unquote.

RITA: Yeh, I will tell y'. It's crap because the feller who wrote it was a louse. Because halfway through that book I couldn't go on readin' it because he, Mr Bleedin' E.M. Forster says, quote 'We are not concerned with the poor' unquote. That's why it's crap. An' that's why I didn't go on readin' it, that's why.

FRANK (*astounded*): Because he said we are not concerned with the poor?

RITA: Yeh, that's it!

FRANK: But he wasn't writing about the poor.

RITA: When he wrote that book the conditions of the poor in this country were appalling. An' he's sayin' he couldn't care less. Mr E.M. Bleedin' Foster.

FRANK: Forster.

RITA: I don't care what his name was, he was sittin' up there in his ivory tower an' sayin' he couldn't care less.
FRANK *laughs.*

RITA: Don't laugh at me.

FRANK (*getting up*): But you cannot interpret E.M. Forster from a Marxist viewpoint.

RITA: Why?

FRANK: Look before discussing this I said no subjectivity, no sentimentality.

RITA: I wasn't bein' sentimental.

FRANK: Of course you were. You stopped reading the book because you wanted Forster to concern himself with the poor. Literature can ignore the poor.

RITA: Well, it's immoral.

FRANK (*wandering around*): Amoral. But you wanted to know. You see what sort of mark you'd get if you approached Forster in this way during an examination?

RITA: What sort?

FRANK: Well, you might manage one or two per cent if the examiner was sympathetic to the one dubious quality your criticism displays.

RITA: What's that?

FRANK: Brevity.

RITA: All right. But I hated that book. Can't we do somethin' else? Can't we do somethin' I like?

FRANK: But the sort of stuff you like is not necessarily the sort of thing that will form the basis of your examination next Christmas. Now if you're going to pass any sort of exam you have to begin to discipline that mind of yours.

RITA: Are you married?

FRANK (*moving back to the swivel chair*): It's — ogh . . .

RITA: Are y'? What's y' wife like?

FRANK: Is my wife at all relevant?

RITA: What? You should know, you married her.

FRANK: Well, she's not relevant. I haven't seen her for a long time. We split up. All right?

RITA: I'm sorry.

FRANK: Why are you sorry?

RITA: I'm sorry for askin'. For bein' nosey.

FRANK (*sitting in his swivel chair*): The thing about *Howards End* is that . . .

RITA: Why did y' split up?

FRANK (*taking off his glasses and looking at her*): Perhaps you'd like to take notes! When you have to answer a question on Forster you can treat the examiner to an essay called Frank's marriage!

RITA: Oh go way. I'm only interested.

FRANK (*leaning towards her; conspiratorially.*) We split up, Rita, because of poetry.

RITA: Y' what?

FRANK: One day my wife pointed out to me that for fifteen years my output as a poet had dealt exclusively with the period in which we — discovered each other.

RITA: Are you a poet?

FRANK: Was. And so, to give me something new to write about she left. A very noble woman my wife. She left me for the good of literature.

RITA: An' what happened?

FRANK: She was right. Her leaving was an enormous benefit to literature.

RITA: What, y' wrote a load of good stuff?

FRANK: No. I stopped writing altogether.

RITA (*slightly puzzled*): Are you takin' the piss?
    FRANK *gives a short laugh and leans back in his chair.*

FRANK: No.

RITA: People don't split up because of things like that. Because of literature.

FRANK: Maybe you're right. But that's how I remember it.

RITA: Were you a famous poet?

FRANK: No. I sold a few books, all out of print now.

RITA: Can I read some of your stuff?

FRANK: You wouldn't like it.

RITA: How d' y' know?

FRANK: It's the sort of poetry you can't understand — unless you happen to have a detailed knowledge of the literary references.

RITA: Oh. (*After a pause.*) Do you live on y' own then?

FRANK: Rita! Tch.

RITA: I was only askin'.

FRANK: I live with a girl. Ex student. She's very caring, very tolerant, admires me tremendously and spends a great deal of time putting her head in the oven.

RITA: Does she try an' do herself in?

FRANK: Mm? No, she just likes to watch the ratatouille cook.

RITA: The what?

FRANK: Ratatouille. Though Julia has renamed it the 'stopouts dish'. It can simmer in an oven for days. In our house it often has no choice.

RITA: D' you stop out for days?

FRANK: Occasionally. And that is the end of . . .

RITA: Why do y'?

FRANK: And that is the end of that.

RITA: If y' were mine an' y' stopped out for days y' wouldn't get back in.

FRANK: Ah, but Rita, if I was yours would I stop out for days?

RITA: Don't y' like Julia?

FRANK: I like her enormously; it's myself I'm not too fond of.

RITA: Tch. Y' great . . .

FRANK: A vote of confidence; thank you. But, I'm afraid, Rita, that you'll find there's less of me than meets the eye.

RITA: See — look — y' can say dead clever things like that, can't y'? I wish I could talk like that. It's brilliant.

FRANK: Staggering. Now look, *Howards* . . . (*He swivels the chair round so that he faces away from* RITA).

RITA: Oh ey . . . leave that. I just like talkin' to y'. It's great. That's what they do wrong in schools y' know — (*She gets up and warms her legs by the fire.*) — they get y' talkin' an' that, an' y' all havin' a great time talkin' about somethin' an' the next thing they wanna do is turn it into a lesson. We was out with the teacher once, y' know outside school, an' I'm right at the back with these other kids an' I saw this fantastic bird, all coloured it was, like dead out of place round our way. I was just gonna shout an' tell Miss but this kid next to me said,

'Keep your mouth shut or she'll make us write an essay on it.'

FRANK (*sighing*): Yes, that's what we do, Rita; we call it education.

RITA: Tch. Y'd think there was somethin' wrong with education to hear you talk.

FRANK: Perhaps there is.

RITA: So why are y' givin' me an education?

FRANK: Because it's what you want, isn't it? What I'd actually like to do is take you by the hand and run out of this room forever.

RITA (*going back to her chair*): Tch — be serious . . .

FRANK: I am. Right now there's a thousand things I'd rather do than teach; most of them with you, young lady . . .

RITA (*smiling gently*): Tch. Oh sod off . . . You just like saying things like that. (*She sits down.*)

FRANK: Do I?

RITA: Yeh. Y' know y' do.

FRANK: Rita — why didn't you walk in here twenty years ago?

RITA: Cos I don't think they would have accepted me at the age of six.

FRANK: You know what I mean.

RITA: I know. But it's not twenty years ago, Frank. It's now. You're there an' I'm here.

FRANK: Yes. And you're here for an education. (*He waves his finger.*) You must keep reminding me of that. Come on, Forster!

RITA: Tch. Forget him.

FRANK: Listen to me; you said that I was going to teach you. You want to learn. Well that, I'm afraid, means a lot of work. You've barely had a basic schooling, you've never passed an examination in your life. Possessing a hungry mind is not, in itself, a guarantee of success.

RITA: All right. But I just don't like *Howards* bleedin' *End*.

FRANK: Then go back to what you do like and stop wasting my time. You go out and buy yourself a new dress and I'll go to the pub.

RITA (*after a pause*): Is that you putting your foot down?

FRANK: It is actually.

RITA: Oh. Aren't you impressive when y' angry?

FRANK: Forster!

RITA: All right, all right, Forster. Does Forster's repeated use of the phrase 'only connect' suggest that he was really a frustrated electrician?

FRANK: Rita.

RITA: In considering Forster it helps if we examine the thirteen amp plug . . .

Blackout.

RITA *goes out.*

Scene Three

FRANK *working at his desk.*

RITA *flounces into the room and goes to the desk.*

RITA: God, I've had enough of this. It's borin', that's what it is, bloody borin'. This Forster, honest to God he doesn't half get on my tits.
She dumps her bag on the chair and makes towards the hook by the door, taking off her coat as she goes. She hangs the coat on the hook.

FRANK: Good. You must show me the evidence.

RITA: Y' dirty sod.

FRANK (*wagging his finger at her*): True, true . . . it's cutting down on the booze that's done it. Now. (*He waves a sheet of paper at her.*) What's this?

RITA (*sitting by the desk*): It's a bleedin' piece of paper, isn't it?

FRANK: It's your essay. Is it a joke? Is it?

RITA: No. It's not a joke.

FRANK: Rita, how the hell can you write an essay on E.M. Forster with almost total reference to Harold Robbins.

RITA: Well? You said bring in other authors.

FRANK: Tch.

RITA: Don't go on at me. You said; y' said, 'Reference to other authors will impress the examiners'.

FRANK: I said refer to other works but I don't think the examiner, God bless him, will have read, (*he consults the paper.*) A Stone For Danny Fisher.

RITA: Well, that's his hard luck, isn't it?

FRANK: It'll be your hard luck when he fails your paper.

RITA: Oh that's prime, isn't it? That's justice for y'. I get failed just cos I'm more well read than the friggin' examiner!

FRANK: Devouring pulp fiction is not being well read.

RITA: I thought reading was supposed to be good for one. (*She gets out her cigarettes.*)

FRANK: It is, but you've got to be selective. In your favour you do mention *Sons and Lovers* somewhere in here. When did you read that?

RITA: This week. I read that an' the Harold Robbins an' this dead fantastic book, what was it called? Erm — ogh what was it? It sounded like somethin' dead perverted, it was by that English feller . . .

FRANK: Which English feller?

RITA: You know, the one who was like Noël Coward — erm. Oh, I know — Somerset Maughan?

FRANK: A perverted book by Somerset Maugham?

RITA: No, it wasn't perverted it was great — the title sounds perverted . . .
He starts to laugh.
Don't laugh.

FRANK: Do you mean *Of Human Bondage*?

RITA: Yeh — that's it. Well it does sound perverted doesn't it?

FRANK: Well! (*After a pause.*) You read three novels this week?

RITA (*taking a cigarette from the pack*): Yeh. It was dead quiet in the shop.

FRANK: And if I asked you to make a comparison between those books, what would you say?

RITA: Well, they were all good in their own way.

FRANK: But surely you can see the difference between the Harold Robbins and the other two?

RITA: Apart from that one bein' American like?

FRANK: Yes.

RITA: Yeh. I mean the other two were sort of posher. But they're all books, aren't they?

FRANK: Yes. Yes. But you seem to be under the impression that all books are literature.

RITA: Aren't they?

FRANK: No.

RITA: Well — well how d' y' tell?

FRANK: I — erm — erm — one's always known really.

RITA: But how d' y' work it out if y' don't know? See that's what I've got to learn, isn't it? I'm dead ignorant y' know.

FRANK: No. You're not ignorant. It's merely a question of becoming more discerning in your choice of reading material.

RITA: I've got no taste. Is that what you're saying?

FRANK: No.

RITA: It is. Don't worry. I won't get upset. I'm here to learn. My mind's full of junk, isn't it? It needs a good clearin' out. Right, that's it, I'll never read a Robbins novel again.

FRANK: Read it, by all means read it. But don't mention it in an exam.

RITA: Aha. You mean, it's all right to go out an' have a bit of slap an' tickle with the lads as long as you don't go home an' tell your mum?

FRANK: Erm — well, yes, that's probably what I do mean.

Blackout.

RITA *exits.*

Scene Four

FRANK *is standing by the window.*

RITA *enters and shuts the door behind her, standing just inside the room.*

FRANK *goes to his briefcase on the window-desk and starts looking for* RITA*'s* Peer Gynt *essay.*

RITA: I can't do it. Honest, I just can't understand what he's on about. (*She goes to her chair at the desk, dumps her bag and then goes and hangs up her coat.*) He's got me licked, I don't know what he's on about, 'Only connect, only connect', it's just bleedin' borin'. It's no good, I just can't understand.

FRANK: You will. You will.

RITA: It's all right for you sayin' that. You know what it's about. (*She goes to her chair by the desk.*) But I just can't figure it.

FRANK: Do you think we could forget about Forster for a moment?

RITA: With pleasure.

FRANK *takes the* Peer Gynt *essay and stands over her for a moment. Then he perches on the corner of the desk.*

FRANK: I want to talk about this that you sent me. (*He holds up a sheet of A4 paper.*)

RITA: That? Oh.

FRANK: Yes. In response to the question, 'Suggest how you would resolve the staging difficulties inherent in a production of Ibsen's *Peer Gynt*', you have written, quote, 'Do it on the radio', unquote.

RITA: Precisely.

FRANK: Well?

RITA: Well what?

FRANK: Well I know it's probably quite naïve of me but I did think you might let me have a considered essay.

RITA *sits down by the desk and unpacks the student's pad, pencil case, ruler, copy of* Peer Gynt *and eight reference books from her bag.*

RITA: That's all I could do in the time. We were dead busy in the shop this week.

FRANK: You write your essays at work?

RITA: Yeh.

FRANK: Why?

RITA: Denny gets dead narked if I work at home. He doesn't like me doin' this. I can't be bothered arguin' with him.

FRANK: But you can't go on producing work as thin as this.

RITA: Is it wrong?

FRANK: No, it's not wrong, it's just . . .

RITA: See, I know it's short. But I thought it was the right answer.

FRANK: It's the basis for an argument, Rita, but one line is hardly an essay.

RITA: I know, but I didn't have much time this week, so I sort of, y' know, encapsulated all me ideas in one line.

FRANK: But it's not enough.

RITA: Why not?

FRANK: It just isn't.

RITA: But that's bleedin' stupid, cos you say — you say, don't y' — that one line of exquisite poetry says more than a thousand pages of second-rate prose.

FRANK: But you're not writing poetry. What I'm trying to make
you see is that whoever was marking this would want more
than, 'Do it on the radio'. (*He gets up and moves around to
the other side of* RITA's *chair.*) There is a way of answering
examination questions that is expected. It's a sort of accepted
ritual, it's a game, with rules. And you must observe those
rules. (*He leans with one hand on the back of* RITA's *chair.*)
When I was at university there was a student taking his final
theology exam. He walked into the examination hall, took out
his pen and wrote 'God knows all the answers', then he handed
in his paper and left.

RITA (*impressed*): Did he?

FRANK: When his paper was returned to him, his professor had
written on it, 'And God gives out the marks'.

RITA: Did he fail?

FRANK (*breaking away slightly*): Of course he failed. You see,
a clever answer is not necessarily the correct answer.

RITA (*getting out her cigarettes*): I wasn't tryin' to be clever;
I didn't have much time an' I . . .

FRANK: All right, but look, you've got some time now. (*He
leans on her chair, bending over her.*) Just give it a quarter of
an hour or so adding some considered argument to this: 'In
attempting to resolve the staging difficulties in *Peer Gynt*
I would present it on the radio because . . .' and outline your
reasons supporting them, as much as possible, with quotes
from accepted authorities. All right?

RITA: Yeh. All right. (*She picks up the essay, pen, copy of* Peer
Gynt, *eight reference books, sticks the cigarette in her mouth,
and starts to move towards the window desk.*)

FRANK: Now, are you sure you understand?
RITA *stops and speaks over her shoulder with the cigarette
still in her mouth.*

RITA: Yeh. What d' y' think I am, thick? (*She takes her usual
chair and puts it in front of the window desk. She sits down
and puts her belongings on the desk, moving* FRANK's
briefcase out of the way.)
FRANK *moves the swivel chair to the end of his desk and
settles down to marking essays.*
RITA *leans back in the chair and tries to blow smoke-rings.*
Y' know Peer Gynt? He was searchin' for the meaning of life
wasn't he?

FRANK: Erm — put at its briefest, yes.

RITA: Yeh. (*She pauses.*) I was doin' this woman's hair on
Wednesday . . .

FRANK: Tch . . .

RITA (*facing* FRANK): I'm gonna do this, don't worry. I'll do it.
But I just wanna tell y'; I was doin' her hair an' I was dead
bored with what the others in the shop were talkin' about. So
I just said to this woman, I said, 'Do you know about *Peer
Gynt*?' She thought it was a new perm lotion. So I told her all
about it, y' know the play. An' y' know somethin', she was
dead interested, she was y' know.

FRANK: Was she?

RITA: Yeh. She said, 'I wish I could go off searchin' for the
meanin' of life.' There's loads of them round by us who feel
like that. Cos by us there is no meanin' to life. (*She thinks.*)
Frank, y' know culture, y' know the word culture? Well it
doesn't just mean goin' to the opera an' that, does it?

FRANK: No.

RITA: It means a way of livin', doesn't it? Well we've got no
culture.

FRANK: Of course you have.

RITA: What? Do you mean like that working-class culture thing?

FRANK: Mm.

RITA: Yeh. I've read about that. I've never seen it though.

FRANK: Well, look around you.

RITA: I do. But I don't see any, y' know, culture. I just see
everyone pissed, or on the Valium, tryin' to get from one day
to the next. Y' daren't say that round our way like, cos they're
proud. They'll tell y' they've got culture as they sit there
drinkin' their keg beer out of plastic glasses.

FRANK: Yes, but there's nothing wrong with that, if they're
content with it.

During the following FRANK*'s attention is caught gradually
and he stops marking and starts listening.*

RITA: But they're not. Cos there's no meanin'. They tell y'
stories about the past, y' know, the war, or when they were
fightin' for food an' clothin' an' houses. Their eyes light up as
they tell y', because there was some meanin' to it. But the
thing is that now, I mean now that most of them have got
some sort of house an' there's food an' money around, they
know they're better off but, honest, they know they've got
nothin' as well. There's like this sort of disease, but no one

mentions it; everyone behaves as though it's normal, y' know
inevitable that there's vandalism an' violence an' houses burnt
out an' wrecked by the people they were built for. There's
somethin' wrong. An' like the worst thing is that y' know the
people who are supposed to like represent the people on our
estate, y' know the *Daily Mirror* an' the *Sun*, an' ITV an' the
Unions, what are they tellin' people to do? They just tell them
to go out an' get more money, don't they? But they don't
want more money; it's like me, isn't it? Y' know, buyin' new
dresses all the time, isn't it? The Unions tell them to go out
an' get more money an' ITV an' the papers tell them what to
spend it on so the disease is always covered up.

FRANK *swivels round in his chair to face* RITA.

FRANK (*after a pause*): Why didn't you take a course in politics?

RITA: Politics? Go way, I hate politics. I'm just tellin' y' about
round our way. I wanna be on this course findin' out. You
know what I learn from you, about art an' literature, it feeds
me, inside. I can get through the rest of the week if I know
I've got comin' here to look forward to. Denny tried to stop
me comin' tonight. He tried to get me to go out to the pub
with him an' his mates. He hates me comin' here. It's like drug
addicts, isn't it? They hate it when one of them tries to
break away. It makes me stronger comin' here. That's what
Denny's frightened of.

FRANK: 'Only connect.'

RITA: Oh, not friggin' Forster again.

FRANK: 'Only connect.' You see what you've been doing?

RITA: Just tellin' y' about home.

FRANK: Yes, and connecting, your dresses/ITV and the *Daily
Mirror*. Addicts/you and your husband.

RITA: Ogh!

FRANK: You see?

RITA: An' — an' in that book — no one does connect.

FRANK: Irony.

RITA: Is that it? Is that all it means?

FRANK: Yes.

RITA: Why didn't y' just tell me, right from the start?

FRANK: I could have told you; but you'll have a much better
understanding of something if you discover it in your own
terms.

RITA (*sincerely*): Aren't you clever?

FRANK: Brilliant. Now. *Peer Gynt.*

RITA: All right, all right, hold on. (*She opens a couple of books and starts writing.*)
   FRANK *continues his marking and does not notice as* RITA *finishes writing. She picks up her chair, essay, pen and books, and moves across in front of his desk. She replaces the chair by the desk and stands watching him.*

FRANK (*looking up*): What?

RITA: I've done it.

FRANK: You've done it?
   She hands him the essay.
   (*Reading aloud.*) 'In attempting to resolve the staging difficulties in a production of Ibsen's *Peer Gynt* I would present it on the radio because as Ibsen himself says, he wrote the play as a play for voices, never intending it to go on in a theatre. If they had the radio in his day that's where he would have done it.'
   He looks up as she beams him a satisfied smile.

Blackout.

Scene Five

FRANK *is sitting in the swivel chair and* RITA *stands by the filing cabinet.*

FRANK: What's wrong? (*After a pause.*) You know this is getting to be a bit wearisome. When you come to this room you'll do anything except start work immediately. Couldn't you just come in prepared to start work? Where's your essay?

RITA (*staring out of the window*): I haven't got it.

FRANK: You haven't done it?

RITA: I said I haven't got it.

FRANK: You've lost it?

RITA: It's burnt.

FRANK: Burnt?

RITA: So are all the Chekhov books you lent me. Denny found out I was on the pill again; it was my fault, I left me prescription out. He burnt all me books.

FRANK: Oh Christ!

RITA: I'm sorry. I'll buy y' some more.

FRANK: I wasn't referring to the books. Sod the books.

RITA: Why can't he just let me get on with me learnin'? You'd think I was havin' a bloody affair the way he behaves.

FRANK: And aren't you?

RITA *wanders. She fiddles with the library steps, smoothing the top step.*

RITA (*looking at him*): No. What time have I got for an affair? I'm busy enough findin' meself, let alone findin' someone else. I don't want anyone else. I've begun to find me — an' it's great y' know, it is Frank. It might sound selfish but all I want for the time bein' is what I'm findin' inside me. I certainly don't wanna be rushin' off with some feller, cos the first thing I'll have to do is forget about meself for the sake of him.

FRANK: Perhaps, perhaps your husband thinks you're having an affair with me.

RITA: Oh go way. You're me teacher. I've told him.

FRANK: You've told him about me? What?

RITA (*sitting down*): I've — tch — I've tried to explain to him how you give me room to breathe. Y' just, like feed me without expectin' anythin' in return.

FRANK: What did he say?

RITA: He didn't. I was out for a while. When I come back he'd burnt me books an' papers, most of them. I said to him, y' soft get, even if I was havin' an affair there's no point burnin' me books. I'm not havin' it off with Anton Chekhov. He said, 'I wouldn't put it past you to shack up with a foreigner'.

FRANK (*after a pause*): What are you going to do?

RITA: I'll order some new copies for y' an' do the essay again.

FRANK: I mean about your husband.

RITA (*standing up*): I've told him, I said, 'There's no point cryin' over spilt milk, most of the books are gone, but if you touch my *Peer Gynt* I'll kill y'.'

FRANK: Tch. Be serious.

RITA: I was!

FRANK: Do you love him?

RITA (*after a pause*): I see him lookin' at me sometimes, an' I know what he's thinkin', I do y' know, he's wonderin' where the girl he married has gone to. He even brings me presents sometimes, hopin' that the presents'll make her come back. But she can't, because she's gone, an' I've taken her place.

FRANK: Do you want to abandon this course?

RITA: No. No!

FRANK: When art and literature begin to take the place of life itself, perhaps it's time to . . .

RITA (*emphatically*): But it's not takin' the place of life, it's providin' me with life itself. He wants to take life away from me; he wants me to stop rockin' the coffin, that's all. Comin' here, doin' this, it's given me more life than I've had in years, an' he should be able to see that. Well, if he doesn't want me when I'm alive I'm certainly not just gonna lie down an' die for him. I told him I'd only have a baby when I had a choice. But he doesn't understand. He thinks we've got choice because we can go into a pub that sells eight different kinds of lager. He thinks we've got choice already: choice between Everton an' Liverpool, choosin' which washin' powder, choosin' between one lousy school an' the next, between lousy jobs or the dole, choosin' between Stork an' butter.

FRANK: Yes. Well, perhaps your husband . . .

RITA: No. I don't wanna talk about him. (*She comes to the front of the desk.*) Why was Chekhov a comic genius?

FRANK: Rita. Don't you think that for tonight we could give the class a miss?

RITA: No. I wanna know. I've got to do this. He can burn me books an' me papers but if it's all in me head he can't touch it. It's like that with you, isn't it? You've got it all inside.

FRANK: Let's leave it for tonight. Let's go to the pub and drink pots of Guinness and talk.

RITA: I've got to do this, Frank. I've got to. I want to talk about Chekhov.

FRANK: We really should talk about you and Denny, my dear.

RITA: I don't want to.

FRANK (*after a pause*): All right. Chekhov.
'C' for Chekhov.
He gets up and moves towards the bookcase, taking RITA*'s chair with him. He stands on the chair and begins rummaging on the top shelf, dropping some of the books on the floor.* RITA *turns to sit down and notices her chair has gone. She sees* FRANK *and watches him as he finds a bottle of whisky hidden behind some books. He gets down and takes the whisky to the small table.*
We'll talk about Chekhov and pretend this is the pub.

RITA: Why d' y' keep it stashed behind there?

FRANK (*pouring the drinks*): A little arrangement I have with my immediate employers. It's called discretion. They didn't tell me to stop drinking, they told me to stop displaying the signs.

RITA (*climbing on to the chair to replace the books*): Do you actually like drinking?

FRANK: Oh yes. I love it. Absolutely no guilt at all about it.

RITA: Know when you were a poet, Frank, did y' drink then?

FRANK: Some. Not as much as now. (*He takes a drink.*) You see, the great thing about the booze is that it makes one believe that under all the talk one is actually saying something.

RITA: Why did you stop being a poet?

FRANK (*wagging his finger at her*): That is a pub question.

RITA: Well. I thought we were pretendin' this was the pub. (*She gets down from the chair.*)

FRANK: In which we would discuss Chekhov.

RITA: Well he's second on the bill. You're on first. Go on, why did y' stop?

FRANK: I didn't stop, so much as realize I never was. I'd simply got it wrong, Rita. (*After a pause.*) Instead of creating poetry I spent — oh — years and years trying to create literature. You see?

RITA: Well I thought that's what poets did.

FRANK: What? (*He gives RITA her drink.*)

RITA: Y' know, make literature. (*She perches on the small table.*)

FRANK (*shaking his head*): Poets shouldn't believe in literature.

RITA (*puzzled*): I don't understand that.

FRANK: You will. You will.

RITA: Sometimes I wonder if I'll ever understand any of it. It's like startin' all over again, y' know with a different language. Know I read that Chekhov play an' I thought it was dead sad, it was tragic; people committin' suicide an' that Constantin kid's tryin' to produce his masterpiece an' they're all laughin' at him? It's tragic. Then I read the blurb on it an' everyone's goin' on about Checkhov bein' a comic genius.

FRANK: Well, it's not comedy like — erm — well it's not stand-up comedy. Have you ever seen Chekhov in the theatre?

RITA: No. Does he go?

FRANK: Have you ever been to the theatre?

RITA: No.

FRANK: You should go.

RITA (*standing up*): Hey! Why don't we go tonight?

FRANK: Me? Go to the theatre? God no, I hate the theatre.

RITA: Why the hell are y' sendin' me?

FRANK: Because you want to know.

RITA (*packing her things into her bag*): Well, you come with me.

FRANK: And how would I explain that to Julia?

RITA: Just tell her y' comin' to the theatre with me.

FRANK: 'Julia, I shall not be in for dinner as I am going to the
    theatre with ravishing Rita.'

RITA: Oh sod off.

FRANK: I'm being quite serious.

RITA: Would she really be jealous?

FRANK: If she knew I was at the theatre with an irresistible
    thing like you? Rita, it would be deaf and dumb brekafasts
    for a week.

RITA: Why?

FRANK: Why not?

RITA: I dunno — I just thought . . .

FRANK (*pouring himself another drink*): Rita, ludicrous as it
    may seem to you, even a woman who possesses an M.A. is not
    above common jealousy.

RITA: Well, what's she got to be jealous of me for? I'm not
    gonna try an' rape y' in the middle of *The Seagull*.

FRANK: What an awful pity. You could have made theatre
    exciting for me again.

RITA: Come on, Frank. Come with me. Y' never tell the truth
    you, do y'?

FRANK: What d' y' mean?

RITA: Y' don't; y' like evade it with jokes an' that, don't y'?
    Come on, come to the theatre with me. We'll have a laugh . . .

FRANK: Will we?

RITA: Yeh. C'mon we'll ring Julia. (*She goes to the telephone
    and picks up the receiver.*)

FRANK: What?

RITA: C'mon, what's your number?

FRANK (*taking the receiver from her and replacing it*): We will
    not ring Julia. Anyway Julia's out tonight.

RITA: So what will you do, spend the night in the pub?

FRANK: Yes.

RITA: Come with me, Frank, y'll have a better time than y' will in the pub.

FRANK: Will I?

RITA: Course y' will. (*She goes and gets both coats from the hook by the door, comes back and throws her coat over the back of the chair.*)

FRANK (*putting down his mug on the bookcase*): What is it you want to see?
  RITA *helps* FRANK *into his coat.*

RITA: *The Importance of Bein' Thingy* . . .

FRANK: But The Importance isn't playing at the moment . . .

RITA: It is — I passed the church hall on the bus an' there was a poster . . .
  FRANK *breaks loose, turns to her and throws off his coat.*

FRANK (*aghast*): An amateur production?

RITA: What?

FRANK: Are you suggesting I miss a night at the pub to watch *The Importance* played by amateurs in a church hall?
  RITA *picks his coat up and puts it round his shoulders.*

RITA: Yeh. It doesn't matter who's doin' it, does it? It's the same play, isn't it?

FRANK: Possibly, Rita . . . (*He switches off the desk lamp.*)

RITA (*putting on her coat and picking up her bag*): Well come on — hurry up — I'm dead excited. I've never seen a live play before.
  FRANK *goes round switching off the electric fire and desk lamp and then picks up his briefcase.*

FRANK: And there's no guarantee you'll see a 'live' play tonight.

RITA: Why? Just cos they're amateurs? Y've gorra give them a chance. They have to learn somewhere. An' they might be good.

FRANK (*doubtfully*): Yes . . .

RITA: Oh y' an awful snob, aren't y'?

FRANK (*smiling acknowledgement*): All right — come on.
  They go towards the door.

RITA: Have you seen it before?

FRANK: Of course.

RITA: Well, don't go tellin' me what happens will y'? Don't

go spoilin' it for me.

FRANK *switches off the light switch. Blackout.*

FRANK *and* RITA *exit.*

Scene Six

FRANK *enters carrying a briefcase and a pile of essays. He goes to the filing cabinet, takes his lecture notes from the briefcase and puts them in a drawer. He takes the sandwiches and apple from his briefcase and puts them on his desk and then goes to the window desk and dumps the essays and briefcase. He switches on the radio and then sits in the swivel chair. He opens the packet of sandwiches, takes a bite and then picks up a book and starts reading.*

RITA *bursts through the door out of breath.*

FRANK: What are you doing here? (*He looks at his watch.*) It's Thursday, you . . .

RITA (*moving over to the desk; quickly*): I know I shouldn't be here, it's me dinner hour, but listen, I've gorra tell someone, have y' got a few minutes, can y' spare . . . ?

FRANK (*alarmed*): My God, what is it?

RITA: I had to come an' tell y', Frank, last night, I went to the theatre! A proper one, a professional theatre.
FRANK *gets up and switches off the radio and then returns to the swivel chair.*

FRANK (*sighing*): For God's sake, you had me worried, I thought it was something serious.

RITA: No, listen, it was. I went out an' got me ticket, it was Shakespeare, I thought it was gonna be dead borin' . . .

FRANK: Then why did you go in the first place?

RITA: I wanted to find out. But listen, it wasn't borin', it was bleedin' great, honest, ogh, it done me in, it was fantastic. I'm gonna do an essay on it.

FRANK (*smiling*): Come on, which one was it?
RITA *moves upper right centre.*

RITA: '. . . Out, out, brief candle!
Life's but a walking shadow, a poor player
That struts and frets his hour upon the stage
And then is heard no more. It is a tale

Told by an idiot, full of sound and fury
Signifying nothing.'

FRANK (*deliberately*): Ah, *Romeo and Juliet*.

RITA (*moving towards* FRANK): Tch. Frank! Be serious. I learnt that today from the book. (*She produces a copy of* Macbeth.) Look, I went out an' bought the book. Isn't it great? What I couldn't get over is how excitin' it was.

FRANK *puts his feet up on the desk.*

RITA: Wasn't his wife a cow, eh? An' that fantastic bit where he meets Macduff an' he thinks he's all invincible. I was on the edge of me seat at that bit. I wanted to shout out an' tell Macbeth, warn him.

FRANK: You didn't, did you?

RITA: Nah. Y' can't do that in a theatre, can y'? It was dead good. It was like a thriller.

FRANK: Yes. You'll have to go and see more.

RITA: I'm goin' to. Macbeth's a tragedy, isn't it?

FRANK *nods.*

RITA: Right.

RITA *smiles at* FRANK *and he smiles back at her.*

Well I just — I just had to tell someone who'd understand.

FRANK: I'm honoured that you chose me.

RITA (*moving towards the door*): Well, I better get back. I've left a customer with a perm lotion. If I don't get a move on there'll be another tragedy.

FRANK: No. There won't be a tragedy.

RITA: There will, y' know. I know this woman; she's dead fussy. If her perm doesn't come out right there'll be blood an' guts everywhere.

FRANK: Which might be quite tragic —

He throws her the apple from his desk which she catches.

— but it won't be a tragedy.

RITA: What?

FRANK: Well — erm — look; the tragedy of the drama has nothing to do with the sort of tragic event you're talking about. Macbeth is flawed by his ambition — yes?

RITA (*going and sitting in the chair by the desk*): Yeh. Go on. (*She starts to eat the apple.*)

FRANK: Erm — it's that flaw which forces him to take the inevitable steps towards his own doom. You see?

RITA *offers him the can of soft drink. He takes it and looks at it.*

FRANK (*putting the can down on the desk*): No thanks. Whereas, Rita, a woman's hair being reduced to an inch of stubble, or — or the sort of thing you read in the paper that's reported as being tragic, 'Man Killed By Falling Tree', is not a tragedy.

RITA: It is for the poor sod under the tree.

FRANK: Yes, it's tragic, absolutely tragic. But it's not a tragedy in the way that *Macbeth* is a tragedy. Tragedy in dramatic terms is inevitable, pre-ordained. Look, now, even without ever having heard the story of *Macbeth* you wanted to shout out, to warn him and prevent him going on, didn't you? But you wouldn't have been able to stop him would you?

RITA: No.

FRANK: Why?

RITA: They would have thrown me out the theatre.

FRANK: But what I mean is that your warning would have been ignored. He's warned in the play. But he can't go back. He still treads the path to doom. But the poor old fellow under the tree hasn't arrived there by following any inevitable steps has he?

RITA: No.

FRANK: There's no particular flaw in his character that has dictated his end. If he'd been warned of the consequences of standing beneath that particular tree he wouldn't have done it, would he? Understand?

RITA: So — so Macbeth brings it on himself?

FRANK: Yes. You see he goes blindly on and on and with every step he's spinning one more piece of thread which will eventually make up the network of his own tragedy. Do you see?

RITA: I think so. I'm not used to thinkin' like this.

FRANK: It's quite easy, Rita.

RITA: It is for you. I just thought it was a dead excitin' story. But the way you tell it you make me see all sorts of things in it. (*After a pause.*) It's fun, tragedy, isn't it? (*She goes over to the window.*) All them out there, they know all about that sort of thing, don't they?

FRANK: Look how about a proper lunch?

RITA: Lunch? (*She leaps up, grabs the copy of* Macbeth, *the can of drink and the apple and goes to the door*.) Christ — me customer. She only wanted a demi-wave — she'll come out looking like a friggin' muppet. (*She comes back to the table*.) Ey' Frank, listen — I was thinkin' of goin' to the art gallery tomorrow. It's me half-day off. D' y' wanna come with me?

FRANK (*smiling*): All right.

RITA *goes to the door*.

FRANK (*looking at her*): And — look, what are you doing on Saturday?

RITA: I work.

FRANK: Well, when you finish work?

RITA: Dunno.

FRANK: I want you to come over to the house.

RITA: Why?

FRANK: Julia's organized a few people to come round for dinner.

RITA: An' y' want me to come? Why?

FRANK: Why do you think?

RITA: I dunno.

FRANK: Because you might enjoy it.

RITA: Oh.

FRANK: Will you come?

RITA: If y' want.

FRANK: What do you want?

RITA: All right. I'll come.

FRANK: Will you bring Denny?

RITA: I don't know if he'll come.

FRANK: Well ask him.

RITA (*puzzled*): All right.

FRANK: What's wrong?

RITA: What shall I wear?

Blackout.

RITA *goes out*.

Scene Seven

FRANK *is sitting in the armchair listening to the radio.*

RITA *enters, goes straight to the desk and slings her bag on the back of her chair.*

She sits in the chair and unpacks the note-pad and pencil-case from her bag. She opens the pad and takes out the pencil-sharpener and pencils and arranges them as before. FRANK gets up, switches off the radio, goes to the swivel chair and sits.

FRANK: Now I don't mind; two empty seats at the dinner table means more of the vino for me. But Julia — Julia is the stage-manager type. If we're having eight people to dinner she expects to see eight. She likes order — probably why she took me on — it gives her a lot of practice —
RITA *starts sharpening her pencils.*

FRANK: — and having to cope with six instead of eight was extremely hard on Julia. I'm not saying that I needed any sort of apology; you don't turn up that's up to you, but . . .

RITA: I did apologize.

FRANK: 'Sorry couldn't come', scribbled on the back of your essay and thrust through the letter box? Rita, that's hardly an apology.

RITA: What does the word 'sorry' mean if it's not an apology? When I told Denny we were goin' to yours he went mad. We had a big fight about it.

FRANK: I'm sorry. I didn't realize. But look couldn't you have explained. Couldn't you have said that was the reason?

RITA: No. Cos that wasn't the reason. I told Denny if he wasn't gonna go I'd go on me own. An' I tried to. All day Saturday, all day in the shop I was thinkin' what to wear. They all looked bleedin' awful. An' all the time I'm trying to think of things I can say, what I can talk about. An' I can't remember anythin'. It's all jumbled up in me head. I can't remember if it's Wilde who's witty an' Shaw who was Shavian or who the hell wrote *Howards End*.

FRANK: Ogh God!

RITA: Then I got the wrong bus to your house. It took me ages to find it. Then I walked up your drive, an' I saw y' all through the window, y' were sippin' drinks an' talkin' an' laughin'. An' I couldn't come in.

FRANK: Of course you could.

RITA: I couldn't. I'd bought the wrong sort of wine. When I was in the off licence I knew I was buyin' the wrong stuff. But I didn't know which was the right wine.

FRANK: Rita for Christ's sake; I wanted *you* to come along. You weren't expected to dress up or buy wine.

RITA (*holding all the pencils and pens in her hands and playing with them*): If you go out to dinner don't you dress up? Don't you take wine?

FRANK: Yes, but . . .

RITA: Well?

FRANK: Well what?

RITA: Well you wouldn't take sweet sparkling wine, would y'?

FRANK: Does it matter what I do? It wouldn't have mattered if you'd walked in with a bottle of Spanish plonk.

RITA: It was Spanish.

FRANK: Why couldn't you relax? (*He gets up and goes behind RITA's chair, then leans on the back of it.*) It wasn't a fancy dress party. You could have come as yourself. Don't you realize how people would have seen you if you'd just — just breezed in? Mm? They would have seen someone who's funny, delightful, charming . . .

RITA (*angrily*): But I don't wanna be charming and delightful; funny. What's funny? I don't wanna be funny. I wanna talk seriously with the rest of you, I don't wanna spend the night takin' the piss, comin' on with the funnies because that's the only way I can get into the conversation. I didn't want to come to your house just to play the court jester.

FRANK: You weren't being asked to play that role. I just — just wanted you to be yourself.

RITA: But I don't want to be myself. Me? What's me? Some stupid woman who gives us all a laugh because she thinks she can learn, because she thinks that one day she'll be like the rest of them, talking seriously, confidently, with knowledge, livin' a civilized life. Well, she can't be like that really but bring her in because she's good for a laugh!

FRANK: If you believe that that's why you were invited, to be laughed at, then you can get out, now. (*He goes to his desk and grabs the pile of essays, taking them to the window desk. He stands with his back to RITA and starts pushing the essays into his briefcase.*) You were invited because I wished to have your company and if you can't believe that then I suggest you stop visiting me and start visiting an analyst who can cope with paranoia.

RITA: I'm all right with you, here in this room; but when I saw
those people you were with I couldn't come in. I would have
seized up. Because I'm a freak. I can't talk to the people I live
with any more. An' I can't talk to the likes of them on
Saturday, or them out there, because I can't learn the
language. I'm a half-caste. I went back to the pub where
Denny was, an' me mother, an' our Sandra, an' her mates.
I'd decided I wasn't comin' here again.
    FRANK *turns to face her.*

RITA: I went into the pub an' they were singin', all of them
singin' some song they'd learnt from the juke-box. An' I stood
in that pub an' thought, just what the frig am I trying to do?
Why don't I just pack it in an' stay with them, an' join in the
singin'?

FRANK: And why don't you?

RITA (*angrily*): You think I can, don't you? Just because you
pass a pub doorway an' hear the singin' you think we're all
O.K., that we're all survivin', with the spirit intact. Well I did
join in with the singin', I didn't ask any questions, I just went
along with it. But when I looked round me mother had
stopped singin', an' she was cryin', but no one could get it out
of her why she was cryin'. Everyone just said she was pissed
an' we should get her home. So we did, an' on the way I asked
her why. I said, 'Why are y' cryin', Mother?' She said, 'Because
— because we could sing better songs than those.' Ten minutes
later, Denny had her laughing and singing again, pretending she
hadn't said it. But she had. And that's why I came back. And
that's why I'm staying.

Blackout.

RITA *goes out.*

Scene Eight

FRANK *is seated in the swivel chair at the desk reading* RITA's
Macbeth *essay.*

RITA *enters slowly, carrying a suitcase.*

FRANK (*without looking up*): One second.
    *She puts down the suitcase and wanders slowly with her back
    to* FRANK.
    (*He closes the essay he has been reading, sighs and removes his*

glasses.) Your essay. (*He sees the suitcase.*) What's that?

RITA: It's me case.

FRANK: Where are you going?

RITA: Me mother's.

FRANK: What's wrong? (*After a pause.*) Rita!

RITA: I got home from work, he'd packed me case. He said either I stop comin' here an' come off the pill or I could get out altogether.

FRANK: Tch.

RITA: It was an ultimatum. I explained to him. I didn't get narked or anythin'. I just explained to him how I had to do this. He said it's warped me. He said I'd betrayed him. I suppose I have.

FRANK: Why have you?

RITA: I have. I know he's right. But I couldn't betray meself. (*After a pause.*) He says there's a time for education. An' it's not when y' twenty-six an' married.
FRANK *gets up and goes towards* RITA *who still faces away from him.*

FRANK (*after a pause*): Where are you going to stay?

RITA: I phoned me mother; she said I could go there for a week. Then I'll get a flat. (*She starts to cry.*) I'm sorry, it's just . . .
FRANK *takes hold of her and tries to guide her to the chair.*

FRANK: Look, come on, sit down.

RITA (*breaking away from him*): It's all right — I'll be O.K. Just give me a minute. (*She dries her eyes.*) What was me *Macbeth* essay like.

FRANK: Oh sod *Macbeth*.

RITA: Why?

FRANK: Rita!

RITA: No, come on, come on, I want y' to tell me what y' thought about it.

FRANK: In the circumstances . . .

RITA (*going and hanging her bag on the back of the swivel chair*): It doesn't matter, it doesn't; in the circumstances I need to go on, to talk about it an' do it. What was it like. I told y' it was no good. Is it really useless?
FRANK *sits in the chair.*

FRANK (*sighing*): I — I really don't know what to say.

RITA: Well try an' think of somethin'. Go on, I don't mind if y' tell me it was rubbish. I don't want pity, Frank. Was it rubbish?

FRANK: No, no. It's not rubbish. It's a totally honest, passionate account of your reaction to a play. It's an unashamedly emotional statement about a certain experience.

RITA: Sentimental?

FRANK: No. It's too honest for that. It's almost − erm − moving. But in terms of what you're asking me to teach you of passing exams . . . Oh, God, you see, I don't . . .

RITA: Say it, go on, say it!

FRANK: In those terms it's worthless. It shouldn't be, but it is; in it's own terms it's − it's wonderful.

RITA (*confronting him across the desk*): It's worthless! You said. An' if it's worthless you've got to tell me because I wanna write essays like those on there. (*She points to the essays on the desk.*) I wanna know, an' pass exams like they do.

FRANK: But if you're going to write this sort of stuff you're going to have to change.

RITA: All right. Tell me how to do it.

FRANK (*getting up*): But I don't know if I want to tell you, Rita, I don't know that I want to teach you. (*He moves towards the desk.*) What you already have is valuable.

RITA: Valuable? What's valuable? The only thing I value is here, comin' here once a week.

FRANK: But, don't you see, if you're going to write this sort of thing − (*He indicates the pile of essays.*) − to pass examinations, you're going to have to suppress, perhaps even abandon your uniqueness. I'm going to have to change you.

RITA: But don't you realize, I want to change! Listen, is this your way of tellin' me that I can't do it? That I'm no good?

FRANK: It's not that at . . .

RITA: If that's what you're tryin' to tell me I'll go now . . .
FRANK *turns away from her.*

FRANK (*moving away from the desk*): No no no. Of course you're good enough.

RITA: See I know it's difficult for y' with someone like me. But you've just gorra keep tellin' me an' then I'll start to take it in; y' see, with me you've got to be dead firm. You won't hurt me feelings y' know. If I do somethin' that's crap, I don't want pity, you just tell me, that's crap. (*She picks up the essay.*) Here, it's crap. (*She rips it up.*) Right. So we dump that in the bin, (*She does so.*) an' we start again.

ACT TWO

Scene One

FRANK *is sitting at his desk typing poetry. He pauses, stubs out a cigarette, takes a sip from the mug at his side, looks at his watch and then continues typing.*

RITA *bursts through the door. She is dressed in new, second-hand clothes.*

RITA: Frank! (*She twirls on the spot to show off her new clothes.*)

FRANK (*smiling*): And what is this vision, returning from the city? (*He gets up and moves towards* RITA.) Welcome back.

RITA: Frank, it was fantastic.
She takes off her shawl and gives it to FRANK *who hangs it on the hook by the door.* RITA *goes to the desk.*
(*Putting down her bag on the desk.*) Honest, it was — ogh!

FRANK: What are you talking about, London or summer school?

RITA: Both. A crowd of us stuck together all week. We had a great time: dead late every night, we stayed up talkin', we went all round London, got drunk, went to the theatres, bought all sorts of second-hand gear in the markets . . . Ogh, it was . . .

FRANK: So you won't have had time to do any actual work there?

RITA: Work? We never stopped. Lashin' us with it they were; another essay, lash, do it again, lash.
FRANK *moves towards the desk.*

RITA: Another lecture, smack. It was dead good though. (*She goes and perches on the bookcase.*)
FRANK *sits in the swivel chair, facing her.*

RITA: Y' know at first I was dead scared. I didn't know anyone. I was gonna come home. But the first afternoon I was standin' in this library, y' know lookin' at the books, pretendin' I was dead clever. Anyway, this tutor come up to me, he looked at the book in me hand an' he said, 'Ah, are you fond of Ferlinghetti?' It was right on the tip of me tongue to say, 'Only when it's served with Parmesan cheese', but, Frank, I didn't. I held it back an' I heard meself sayin', 'Actually, I'm not too familiar with the American poets'. Frank, you woulda been dead proud of me. He started talkin' to me about the American poets — we sat around for ages — an' he wasn't even

one of my official tutors, y' know. We had to go to this big
hall for a lecture, there must have been two thousand of us
in there. After he'd finished his lecture this professor asked if
anyone had a question, an', Frank, I stood up! (*She stands.*)
Honest to God, I stood up, an' everyone's lookin' at me.
I don't know what possessed me, I was gonna sit down again,
but two thousand people had seen me stand up, so I did it,
I asked him the question.
There is a pause and FRANK *waits.*

FRANK: Well?

RITA: Well what?

FRANK: What was the question?

RITA: Oh, I dunno, I forget now, cos after that I was askin'
questions all week, y' couldn't keep me down. I think that
first question was about Chekhov; cos y' know I'm dead
familiar with Chekhov now.
He smiles. RITA *moves to the chair by the desk and sits.*
FRANK *swivels round to face her.*
Hey, what was France like? Go on, tell us all about it.

FRANK: There isn't a lot to tell.

RITA: Ah go on, tell me about it; I've never been abroad. Tell me
what it was like.

FRANK: Well — it was rather hot . . . (*He offers her a Gauloise.*)

RITA: No, ta, I've packed it in. Did y' drink?

FRANK: Ah — a little. (*He puts the cigarettes on the table.*)

RITA: Tch. Did y' write?

FRANK: A little.

RITA: Will y' show it to me?

FRANK: Perhaps . . . One day, perhaps.

RITA: So y' wrote a bit an' y' drank a bit? Is that all?

FRANK (*in a matter of fact tone*): Julia left me.

RITA: What?

FRANK: Yes. But not because of the obvious, oh no — it had
nothing whatsoever to do with the ratatouille. It was actually
caused by something called *oeufs en cocotte.*

RITA: What?

FRANK: Eggs, my dear, eggs. Nature in her wisdom cursed me
with a dislike for the egg be it cocotte, Florentine, Benedict
or plain hard-boiled. Julia insisted that nature was wrong.
I defended nature and Julia left.

RITA: Because of eggs?

FRANK: Well — let's say that it began with eggs. (*He packs away the typewriter.*) Anyway, that's most of what happened in France. Anyway, the holiday's over, you're back, even Julia's back.

RITA: Is she? Is it all right?

FRANK (*putting the typewriter on the window desk and the sheets of poetry in the top left drawer*): Perfect. I get the feeling we shall stay together forever; or until she discovers *oeufs à la crécy*.

RITA: *Oeufs à la crécy*? Does that mean eggs? Trish was goin' on about those; is that all it is, eggs?

FRANK: Trish?

RITA: Trish, me flatmate, Trish. God is it that long since I've seen y', Frank? She moved into the flat with me just before I went to summer school.

FRANK: Ah. Is she a good flatmate?

RITA: She's great. Y' know she's dead classy. Y' know like, she's got taste, y' know like you, Frank, she's just got it. Everything in the flat's dead unpretentious, just books an' plants everywhere. D' y' know somethin', Frank? I'm havin' the time of me life; I am y' know. I even feel — (*Moving to the window.*) — I feel young, you know like them down there.

FRANK: My dear, twenty-six is hardly old.

RITA: I know that; but I mean, I feel young like them . . . I can be young. (*She goes to her bag.*) Oh listen — (*She puts the bag on the desk and rummages in it, producing a box.*) — I bought y' a present back from London — it isn't much but I thought . . .
She gives him a small box.
Here.
FRANK *puts on his glasses, gets the scissors out of the pot on the desk, cuts the string and opens the box to reveal an expensive pen.*

RITA: See what it says — it's engraved.

FRANK (*reading*): 'Must only be used for poetry. By strictest order — Rita' . . . (*He looks at her.*)

RITA: I thought it'd be like a gentle hint.

FRANK: Gentle?

RITA: Every time y' try an' write a letter or a note with that pen, it won't work; you'll read the inscription an' it'll make you feel dead guilty — cos y' not writing poetry. (*She smiles at him.*)

FRANK (*getting up and pecking her on the cheek*): Thank you — Rita. (*He sits down again.*)

RITA: It's a pleasure. Come on. (*She claps her hands.*) What are we doin' this term? Let's do a dead good poet. Come on, let's go an' have the tutorial down there.

FRANK (*appalled*): Down where?

RITA (*getting her bag*): Down there — on the grass — come on.

FRANK: On the grass? Nobody sits out there at this time of year.

RITA: They do — (*Looking out of the window.*) — there's some of them out there now.

FRANK: Well they'll have wet bums.

RITA: What's a wet bum. You can sit on a bench. (*She tries to pull him to his feet.*) Come on.

FRANK (*remaining sitting*): Rita, I absolutely protest.

RITA: Why?

FRANK: Like Dracula, I have an aversion to sunlight.

RITA: Tch. (*She sighs.*) All right. (*She goes to the window.*) Let's open a window.

FRANK: If you must open a window then go on, open it. (*He swivels round to watch her.*)

RITA (*struggling to open the window*): It won't bleedin' budge.

FRANK: I'm not surprised, my dear. It hasn't been opened for generations.

RITA (*abandoning it*): Tch. Y' need air in here, Frank. The room needs airing. (*She goes and opens the door.*)

FRANK: This room does not need air, thank you very much.

RITA: Course it does. A room is like a plant.

FRANK: A room is like a plant?

RITA: Yeh, it needs air. (*She goes to her chair by the desk and sits.*)

FRANK: And water, too, presumably? (*He gets up and closes the door.*) If you're going to make an analogy why don't we take it the whole way? Let's get a watering-can and water the carpet; bring in two tons of soil and a bag of fertilizer. Maybe we could take cuttings and germinate other little rooms.

RITA: Go way, you're mental you are.

FRANK: You said it, distinctly, you said, a room is like a plant.

RITA: Well!

There is a pause.

FRANK: Well what?

RITA: Well any analogy will break down eventually.

FRANK: Yes. And some will break down sooner than others. (*He smiles, goes to the bookcase and begins searching among the books.*) Look, come on . . . A great poet you wanted — well — we have one on the course . . .
RITA *sits on the desk watching* FRANK.

I was going to introduce you to him earlier. (*As he rummages a book falls to one side revealing a bottle of whisky which has been hidden behind it.*) Now — where is he . . . ?
RITA *goes over and picks up the whisky bottle from the shelf.*

RITA: Are you still on this stuff?

FRANK: Did I ever say I wasn't?

RITA (*putting the bottle down and moving away*): No. But . . .

FRANK: But what?

RITA: Why d' y' do it when y' ve got so much goin' for y', Frank?

FRANK: It is indeed because I have 'so much goin' for me' that I do it. Life is such a rich and frantic whirl that I need the drink to help me step delicately through it.

RITA: It'll kill y', Frank.

FRANK: Rita, I thought you weren't interested in reforming me.

RITA: I'm not. It's just . . .

FRANK: What?

RITA: Just that I thought you'd started reforming yourself.

FRANK: Under your influence?
She shrugs.
(*He stops searching and turns to face her.*) Yes. But Rita — if I repent and reform, what do I do when your influence is no longer here? What do I do when, in appalling sobriety, I watch you walk away and disappear, my influence gone forever?

RITA: Who says I'm gonna disappear?

FRANK: Oh you will, Rita. You've got to. (*He turns back to the shelves.*)

RITA: Why have I got to? This course could go on for years. An' when I've got through this one I might even get into the proper university here.

FRANK: And we'll all live happily ever after? Your going is as inevitable as — as . . .

RITA: *Macbeth*?

FRANK (*smiling*): As tragedy, yes: but it will not be a tragedy, because I shall be glad to see you go.

RITA: Tch. Thank you very much. (*After a pause.*) Will y' really?

FRANK: Be glad to see you go? Well I certainly don't want to see you stay in a room like this for the rest of your life. Now. (*He continues searching for the book.*)

RITA (*after a pause*): You can be a real misery sometimes, can't y'? I was dead happy a minute ago an' then you start an' make me feel like I'm having a bad night in a mortuary.
FRANK *finds the book he has been looking for and moves towards* RITA *with it.*

FRANK: Well here's something to cheer you up — here's our 'dead good' poet — Blake.

RITA: Blake? William Blake?

FRANK: The man himself. *You* will understand Blake; they over complicate him, Rita, but you will understand — you'll love the man.

RITA: I know.

FRANK: What? (*He opens the book.*) Look — look — read this . . . (*He hands her the book and then goes and sits in the swivel chair.*)
RITA *looks at the poem on the page indicated and then looks at* FRANK.

RITA (*reciting from memory*):
    'O Rose, thou art sick!
    The invisible worm
    That flies in the night,
    In the howling storm,

    Has found out thy bed
    Of crimson joy:
    And his dark secret love
    Does thy life destroy.'

FRANK: You know it!

RITA (*laughing*): Yeh. (*She tosses the book on the desk and perches on the bookcase.*) We did him at summer school.

FRANK: Blake at summer school? You weren't supposed to do Blake at summer school, were you?

RITA: Nah. We had this lecturer though, he was a real Blake freak. He was on about it every day. Everythin' he said, honest, everything was related to Blake — he couldn't get his

dinner in the refectory without relating it to Blake — Blake
and Chips. He was good though. On the last day we brought
him a present, an' on it we put that poem, y' know, 'The Sick
Rose'. But we changed it about a bit; it was — erm —
　　'O Rose, thou aren't sick
　　Just mangled and dead
　　Since the rotten gardener
　　Pruned off thy head.'
We thought he might be narked but he wasn't, he loved it.
He said — what was it . . . ? He said, 'Parody is merely a
compliment masquerading as humour'.

FRANK (*getting up and replacing the book on the shelf*): So . . .
　　you've already done Blake? You covered all the *Songs of
　　Innocence and Experience*?

RITA: Of course; you don't do Blake without doing innocence
　　and experience, do y'?

FRANK: No. Of course. (*He goes and sits in the swivel chair.*)

Blackout.

RITA *picks up her bag and shawl and exits.*

Scene Two

FRANK *is sitting at his desk marking an essay. Occasionally he
makes a tutting sound and scribbles something. There is a knock
at the door.*

FRANK: Come in.
　　RITA *enters, closes the door, goes to the desk and dumps her
　　bag on it. She takes her chair and places it next to FRANK
　　and sits down.*

RITA (*talking in a peculiar voice*): Hello, Frank.

FRANK (*without looking up*): Hello. Rita, you're late.

RITA: I know, Frank. I'm terribly sorry. It was unavoidable.

FRANK (*looking up*): Was it really? What's wrong with your
　　voice?

RITA: Nothing is wrong with it, Frank. I have merely decided to
　　talk properly. As Trish says there is not a lot of point in
　　discussing beautiful literature in an ugly voice.

FRANK: You haven't got an ugly voice; at least you *didn't* have.
　　Talk properly.

RITA: I am talking properly. I have to practise constantly, in everyday situations.

FRANK: You mean you're going to talk like that for the rest of this tutorial?

RITA: Trish says that no matter how difficult I may find it I must persevere.

FRANK: Well will you kindly tell Trish that I am not giving a tutorial to a Dalek?

RITA: I am not a Dalek.

FRANK (*appealingly*): Rita, stop it!

RITA: But Frank, I have to persevere in order that I shall.

FRANK: Rita! Just be yourself.

RITA (*reverting to her normal voice*): I am being myself. (*She gets up and moves the chair back to its usual place.*)

FRANK: What's that?

RITA: What?

FRANK: On your back.

RITA (*reaching up*): Oh — it's grass.

FRANK: Grass?

RITA: Yeh, I got here early today. I started talking to some students down on the lawn. (*She sits in her usual chair.*)

FRANK: You were talking to students — down there?

RITA (*laughing*): Don't sound so surprised. I can talk now y' know, Frank.

FRANK: I'm not surprised. Well! You used to be quite wary of them didn't you?

RITA: God knows why. For students they don't half come out with some rubbish y' know.

FRANK: You're telling me?

RITA: I only got talking to them in the first place because as I was walking past I heard one of them sayin' as a novel he preferred *Lady Chatterley* to *Sons and Lovers*. I thought, I can keep walkin' and ignore it, or I can put him straight. So I put him straight. I walked over an' said, 'Excuse me but I couldn't help overhearin' the rubbish you were spoutin' about Lawrence'. Shoulda seen the faces on them, Frank. I said tryin' to compare *Chatterley* with *Sons and Lovers* is like tryin' to compare sparkling wine with champagne. The next thing is there's this heated discussion, with me right in the middle of it.

FRANK: I thought you said the student claimed to 'prefer'
Chatterley, as a novel.

RITA: He did.

FRANK: So he wasn't actually suggesting that it was superior.

RITA: Not at first — but then he did. He walked right into
it . . .

FRANK: And so you finished him off, did you Rita?

RITA: Frank, he was asking for it. He was an idiot. His argument
just crumbled. It wasn't just me — everyone else agreed with
me.
FRANK *returns to reading the essay.*

RITA: There was this really mad one with them; I've only been
talkin' to them for five minutes and he's inviting me to go
abroad with them all. They're all goin' to the South of France
in the Christmas holidays, slummin' it.

FRANK: You can't go.

RITA: What?

FRANK: You can't go — you've got your exams.

RITA: My exams are before Christmas.

FRANK: Well — you've got your results to wait for . . .

RITA: Tch. I couldn't go anyway.

FRANK: Why? (*He looks at her.*)

RITA: It's all right for them. They *can* just jump into a bleedin'
van an' go away. But I can't.
He returns to the essay.
Tiger they call him, he's the mad one. His real name's Tyson
but they call him Tiger.

FRANK (*looking up*): Is there any point me going on with this?
(*He points to the essay.*)

RITA: What?

FRANK: Is there much point in working towards an examination
if you're going to fall in love and set off for the South of . . .

RITA (*shocked*): What! Fall in love? With who? My God, Frank,
I've just been talkin' to some students. I've heard of match-
making but this is ridiculous.

FRANK: All right, but please stop burbling on about Mr Tyson.

RITA: I haven't been burbling on.
He returns to the essay.
What's it like?

FRANK: Oh — it — erm — wouldn't look out of place with these.

(He places it on top of a pile of other essays on his desk.)

RITA: Honest?

FRANK: Dead honest.

Blackout.

FRANK *exits.*

Scene Three

RITA *is sitting in the armchair by the window, reading a heavy tome. There is the sound of muffled oaths from behind the door.*

  FRANK *enters carrying his briefcase. He is very drunk.*

FRANK: Sod them — no, fuck them! Fuck them, eh, Rita? *(He goes to the desk.)*

RITA: Who?

FRANK: You'd tell them wouldn't you? You'd tell them where to get off. *(He gets a bottle of whisky from his briefcase.)*

RITA: Tell who, Frank?

FRANK: Yes — students — students reported me! *(He goes to the bookcase and puts the whisky on the shelf.)* Me! Complained — you know something? They complained and it was the best lecture I've ever given.

RITA: Were you pissed?

FRANK: Pissed? I was glorious! Fell off the rostrum twice. *(He comes round to the front of his desk.)*

RITA: Will they sack you?

FRANK *(lying flat on the floor)*: The sack? God no; that would involve making a decision. Pissed is all right. To get the sack it'd have to be rape on a grand scale; and not just the students either.
  RITA *gets up and moves across to look at him.*

FRANK: That would only amount to a slight misdemeanour. For dismissal it'd have to be nothing less than buggering the bursar . . . They suggested a sabbatical for a year — or ten . . . Europe — or America . . . I suggested that Australia might be more apt — the allusion was lost on them . . .

RITA: Tch. Frank, you're mad.

FRANK: Completely off my cake. I know.

RITA: Even if y' don't think about yourself, what about the students?

FRANK: *What* about the students?

RITA: Well it's hardly fair on them if their lecturer's so pissed that he's falling off the rostrum. (*She goes to her chair by the desk and replaces the book in her bag.*)

FRANK: I might have fallen off, my dear, but I went down talking — and came up talking — never missed a syllable — what have they got to complain about?

RITA: Maybe they did it for your own good.

FRANK: Or maybe they did it because they're a crowd of mealy-mouthed pricks who wouldn't know a poet if you beat them about the head with one. (*He half-sits up.*) 'Assonance' — I said to them — 'Assonance means getting the rhyme wrong . . .' (*He collapses back on to the floor again.*) They looked at me as though I'd desecrated Wordsworth's tomb.

RITA: Look Frank, we'll talk about the Blake essay next week, eh?

FRANK: Where are you going? We've got a tutorial. (*He gets up and staggers towards her.*)

RITA: Frank, you're not in any fit state for a tutorial. I'll leave it with y' an' we can talk about it next week, eh?

FRANK: No — no — you must stay — erm . . . Watch this — sober? (*He takes a huge breath and pulls himself together.*) Sober! Come on . . .
He takes hold of RITA *and pushes her round the desk and sits her in the swivel chair.*
You can't go. I want to talk to you about this. (*He gets her essay and shows it to her.*) Rita, what's this?

RITA: Is there something wrong with it?

FRANK: It's just, look, this passage about 'The Blossom' you seem to assume that the poem is about sexuality.

RITA: It is!

FRANK: Is it?

RITA: Well it's certainly like a richer poem, isn't it? If it's interpreted in that way.

FRANK: Richer? Why richer? We discussed it. The poem is a simple, uncomplicated piece about blossom, as if seen from a child's point of view.

RITA (*shrugging*): In one sense. But it's like, like the poem about the rose, isn't it? It becomes a more rewarding poem when you see that it works on a number of levels.

FRANK: Rita, 'The Blossom' is a simple uncomplicated . . .

RITA: Yeh, that's what you say, Frank; but Trish and me and some others were talkin' the other night, about Blake, an' what came out of our discussion was that apart from the simple surface value of Blake's poetry there's always a like erm — erm —

FRANK: Well? Go on . . .

RITA (*managing to*): — a like vein. Of concealed meaning. I mean that if that poem's only about the blossom then it's not much of a poem is it?

FRANK: So? You think it gains from being interpreted in this way?

RITA (*slightly defiantly*): Is me essay wrong then, Frank?

FRANK: It's not — not wrong. But I don't like it.

RITA: You're being subjective.

FRANK (*half-laughing*): Yes — yes I suppose I am. (*He goes slowly to the chair of the desk and sits down heavily.*)

RITA: If it was in an exam what sort of mark would it get?

FRANK: A good one.

RITA: Well what the hell are you sayin' then?

FRANK (*shrugging*): What I'm saying is that it's up to the minute, quite acceptable, trendy stuff about Blake; but there's nothing of you in there.

RITA: Or maybe Frank, y' mean there's nothing of your views in there.

FRANK (*after a pause*): Maybe that is what I mean?

RITA: But when I first came to you, Frank, you didn't give me any views. You let me find my own.

FRANK (*gently*): And your views I still value. But, Rita, these aren't your views.

RITA: But you told me not to have a view. You told me to be objective, to consult recognized authorities. Well that's what I've done; I've talked to other people, read other books an' after consultin' a wide variety of opinion I came up with those conclusions.
He looks at her.

FRANK (*after a pause*): Yes. All right.

RITA (*rattled*): Look, Frank, I don't have to go along one hundred per cent with your views on Blake y' know. I can have a mind of my own can't I?

FRANK: I sincerely hope so, my dear.

RITA: And what's that supposed to mean?

FRANK: It means — it means be careful.

RITA *jumps up and moves in towards* FRANK.

RITA (*angrily*): What d' y' mean be careful? I can look after myself. Just cos I'm learnin', just cos I can do it now an' read what I wanna read an' understand without havin' to come runnin' to you every five minutes y' start tellin' me to be careful. (*She paces about.*)

FRANK: Because — because *I* care for you — I want you to care for yourself.

RITA: Tch. (*She goes right up to* FRANK. *After a pause.*) I — I care for you, Frank . . . But you've got to — to leave me alone a bit. I'm not an idiot now, Frank — I don't need you to hold me hand as much . . . I can — I can do things on me own more now . . . And I am careful. I know what I'm doin'. Just don't — don't keep treatin' me as though I'm the same as when I first walked in here. I understand now, Frank; I know the difference between — between — Somerset Maugham an' Harold Robbins. An' you're still treating me as though I'm hung up on *Rubyfruit Jungle.* (*She goes to the swivel chair and sits.*) Just . . . You understand, don't you Frank?

FRANK: Entirely, my dear.

RITA: I'm sorry.

FRANK: Not at all. (*After a pause.*) I got round to reading it you know, *Rubyfruit Jungle.* It's excellent.

RITA (*laughing*): Oh go way, Frank. Of its type it's quite interesting. But it's hardly excellence.

Blackout.

RITA *exits.*

Scene Four

FRANK *is sitting in the swivel chair.*

RITA *enters and goes to the desk.*

RITA: Frank . . .
He looks at his watch.
I know I'm late . . . I'm sorry.
He gets up and moves away.

Am I too late? We were talkin'. I didn't notice the time.

FRANK: Talking?

RITA: Yeh. If it'll go in my favour we were talking about Shakespeare.

FRANK: Yes . . . I'm sure you were.

RITA: Am I too late then? All right. I'll be on time next week. I promise.

FRANK: Rita. Don't go.

RITA: No — honestly, Frank — I know I've wasted your time. I'll see y' next week, eh?

FRANK: Rita! Sit down!

RITA *goes to her usual chair and sits.*

FRANK (*going to the side of her*): When you were so late I phoned the shop.

RITA: Which shop?

FRANK: The hairdresser's shop. Where you work. Or, I should say, worked.

RITA: I haven't worked there for a long time. I work in a bistro now.

FRANK: You didn't tell me.

RITA: Didn't I? I thought I did. I was telling someone.

FRANK: It wasn't me.

RITA: Oh. Sorry. (*After a pause.*) What's wrong?

FRANK (*after a pause*): It struck me that there was a time when you told me everything.

RITA: I thought I had told you.

FRANK: No. Like a drink?

RITA: Who cares if I've left hairdressin' to work in a bistro?

FRANK: I care. (*He goes to the bookshelves and takes a bottle from an eye-level shelf.*) You don't want a drink? Mind if I do?

RITA: But why do you care about details like that? It's just boring, insignificant detail.

FRANK (*getting a mug from the small table*): Oh. Is it?

RITA: That's why I couldn't stand being in a hairdresser's any longer; boring irrelevant detail all the time, on and on . . . Well I'm sorry but I've had enough of that. I don't wanna talk about irrelevant rubbish anymore.

FRANK: And what do you talk about in your bistro? Cheers.

RITA: Everything.

FRANK: Everything?

RITA: Yeh.

FRANK: Ah.

RITA: We talk about what's important, Frank, and we leave out the boring details for those who want them.

FRANK: Is Mr Tyson one of your customers?

RITA: A lot of students come in; he's one of them. You're not gonna give me another warning are y', Frank?

FRANK: Would it do any good?

RITA: Look for your information I do find Tiger fascinatin', like I find a lot of the people I mix with fascinating; they're young, and they're passionate about things that matter. They're not trapped — they're too young for that. And I like to be with them.

FRANK (*moving and keeping his back to her*): Perhaps — perhaps you don't want to waste your time coming here anymore?

RITA: Don't be stupid. I'm sorry I was late. (*After a pause she gets up.*) Look, Frank, I've got to go. I'm meeting Trish at seven. We're going to see a production of *The Seagull*.

FRANK: Yes. (*He turns to face her.*) Well. When Chekhov calls . . .

RITA: Tch.

FRANK: You can hardly bear to spend a moment here can you?

RITA (*moving towards him a little*): That isn't true. It's just that I've got to go to the theatre.

FRANK: And last week you didn't turn up at all. Just a phone call to say you had to cancel.

RITA: It's just that — that there's so many things happening now. It's harder.

FRANK: As I said, Rita, if you want to stop com—

RITA (*going right up to him*): For God's sake, I don't want to stop coming here. I've got to come here. What about my exam?

FRANK: Oh I wouldn't worry about that. You'd sail through it anyway. You really don't have to put in the odd appearance out of sentimentality; (*He moves round to the other side of the desk.*) I'd rather you spared me that.
FRANK *goes to drink.*

RITA: If you could stop pouring that junk down your throat in

the hope that it'll make you feel like a poet you might be able
to talk about things that matter instead of where I do or don't
work; an' then it might be worth comin' here.

FRANK: Are you capable of recognizing what does or does not
matter, Rita?

RITA: I understand literary criticism, Frank. When I come here
that's what we're supposed to be dealing with.

FRANK: You want literary criticicm? (*He looks at her for a
moment and then goes to the top drawer of his desk and takes
out two slim volumes and some typewritten sheets of poetry
and hands them to her.*) I want an essay on that lot by
next week.

RITA: What is it?

FRANK: No sentimentality, no subjectivity. Just pure criticism.
A critical assessment of a lesser known English poet. Me.

Blackout.

RITA *exits.*

Scene Five

FRANK *is sitting in a chair by the window desk with a mug in his
hand and a bottle of whisky on the desk in front of him listening
to the radio. There is a knock at the door.*

FRANK: Come in.

RITA *enters and goes to the swivel chair behind FRANK's
desk.*

FRANK (*getting up and switching off the radio*): What the —
what the hell are you doing here? I'm not seeing you till
next week.

RITA: Are you sober? Are you?

FRANK: If you mean am I still this side of reasonable
comprehension, then yes.

RITA (*going and standing next to him*): Because I want you to
hear this when you're sober. (*She produces his poems.*) These
are brilliant. Frank, you've got to start writing again. (*She goes
to the swivel chair and sits.*) This is brilliant. They're witty.
They're profound. Full of style.

FRANK (*going to the small table and putting down his mug*):
Ah . . . tell me again, and again.

RITA: They are, Frank. It isn't only me who thinks so. Me an' Trish sat up last night and read them. She agrees with me. Why did you stop writing? Why did you stop when you can produce work like this? We stayed up most of the night, just talking about it. At first we just saw it as contemporary poetry in its own right, you know, as somethin' particular to this century but look, Frank, what makes it more — more . . . What did Trish say — ? More resonant than — purely contemporary poetry is that you can see in it a direct line through to nineteenth-century traditions of — of like wit an' classical allusion.

FRANK (*going to the chair of the desk and standing by the side of it*): Er — that's erm — that's marvellous, Rita. How fortunate I didn't let you see it earlier. Just think if I'd let you see it when you first came here.

RITA: I know . . . I wouldn't have understood it, Frank.

FRANK: You would have thrown it across the room and dismissed it as a heap of shit, wouldn't you?

RITA (*laughing*): I know . . . But I couldn't have understood it then, Frank, because I wouldn't have been able to recognize and understand the allusions.

FRANK: Oh I've done a fine job on you, haven't I?

RITA: It's true, Frank. I can see now.

FRANK: You know, Rita, I think — I think that like you I shall change my name; from now on I shall insist upon being known as Mary, Mary Shelley — do you understand that allusion, Rita?

RITA: What?

FRANK: She wrote a little Gothic number called *Frankenstein*.

RITA: So?

FRANK: This — (*picking up his poetry and moving round to RITA.*) — this clever, pyrotechnical pile of self-conscious allusion is worthless, talentless, shit and could be recognized as such by anyone with a shred of common sense. It's the sort of thing that gives publishing a bad name. Wit? You'll find more wit in the telephone book, and, probably, more insight. Its one advantage over the telephone directory is that it's easier to rip. (*He rips the poems up and throws the pieces on to the desk.*) It is pretentious, characterless and without style.

RITA: It's not.

FRANK: Oh, I don't expect you to believe me, Rita; you

recognize the hallmark of literature now, don't you? (*In a final gesture he throws a handful of the ripped pieces into the air and then goes to the chair and sits.*) Why don't you just go away? I don't think I can bear it any longer.

RITA: Can't bear what, Frank?

FRANK: You, my dear — you . . .

RITA: I'll tell you what you can't bear, Mr Self-Pitying Piss Artist; what you can't bear is that I am educated now. What's up, Frank, don't y' like me now that the little girl's grown up, now that y' can no longer bounce me on daddy's knee an' watch me stare back in wide-eyed wonder at everything he has to say? I'm educated, I've got what you have an' y' don't like it because you'd rather see me as the peasant I once was; you're like the rest of them — you like to keep your natives thick, because that way they still look charming and delightful. I don't need you. (*She gets up and picking up her bag moves away from the desk in the direction of the door.*) I've got a room full of books. I know what clothes to wear, what wine to buy, what plays to see, what papers and books to read. I can do without you.

FRANK: Is that all you wanted. Have you come all this way for so very, very little?

RITA: Oh it's little to you, isn't it? It's little to you who squanders every opportunity and mocks and takes it for granted.

FRANK: Found a culture have you, Rita? Found a better song to sing have you? No — you've found a different song, that's all — and on your lips it's shrill and hollow and tuneless. Oh, Rita, Rita . . .

RITA: RITA? (*She laughs.*) Rita? Nobody calls me Rita but you. I dropped that pretentious crap as soon as I saw it for what it was. You stupid . . . Nobody calls me Rita.

FRANK: What is it now then? Virginia?
RITA *exits.*
Or Charlotte? Or Jane? Or Emily?

Blackout.

Scene Six

FRANK *talking into the telephone. He is leaning against the bookshelf.*

FRANK: Yes . . . I think she works there . . . Rita White . . . No, no. Sorry . . . erm. What is it? . . . Susan White? No? . . . Thank you . . . Thanks . . .
He dials another number.
Yes . . . Erm . . . Trish is it? . . . Erm, yes, I'm a friend of Rita's . . . Rita . . . I'm sorry Susan . . . yes . . . could you just say that — erm — I've . . . it's — erm — Frank here . . . her tutor . . . Yes . . . well could you tell her that I have — erm — I've entered her for her examination . . . Yes you see she doesn't know the details . . . time and where the exam is being held . . . Could you tell her to call in? . . . Please . . . Yes . . . Thank you.

The lights fade to blackout.

Scene Seven

RITA *enters and shuts the door. She is wrapped in a large winter coat. She lights a cigarette and moves across to the filing cabinet and places a Christmas card with the others already there. She throws the envelope in the waste-bin and opens the door revealing FRANK with a couple of teachests either side of him. He is taken aback at seeing her and then he gathers himself and, picking up one of the chests, enters the room. RITA goes out to the corridor and brings in the other chest.*

FRANK *gets the chair from the end of his desk and places it by the bookcase. He stands on it and begins taking down the books from the shelves and putting them into the chests. RITA watches him but he continues as if she is not there.*

RITA: Merry Christmas, Frank. Have they sacked y'?

FRANK: Not quite.

RITA: Well, why y' — packing your books away?

FRANK: Australia. (*After a pause.*) Some weeks ago — made rather a night of it.

RITA: Did y' bugger the bursar?

FRANK: Metaphorically. And as it was metaphorical the sentence was reduced from the sack to two years in Australia.

Hardly a reduction in sentence really — but . . .

RITA: What y' gonna do?

FRANK: *Bon voyage.*

RITA: She's not goin' with y'?

FRANK shakes his head. RITA begins helping him take down the books from the shelves and putting them in the chests.

RITA: What y' gonna do?

FRANK: What do you think I'll do. Aussie? It's a paradise for the likes of me.

RITA: Tch. Come on, Frank . . .

FRANK: It is. Didn't you know the Australians named their favourite drink after a literary figure? Forster's Lager they call it. Of course they get the spelling wrong — rather like you once did!

RITA: Be serious.

FRANK: For God's sake, why did you come back here?

RITA: I came to tell you you're a good teacher. (*After a pause.*) Thanks for enterin' me for the exam.

FRANK: That's all right. I know how much it had come to mean to you.

RITA perches on the small table while FRANK continues to take books from the upper shelves.

RITA: You didn't want me to take it, did y'? Eh? You woulda loved it if I'd written, 'Frank knows all the answers', across me paper, wouldn't y'? I nearly did an' all. When the invigilator said, 'Begin', I turned over me paper with the rest of them, and while they were all scribbling away against the clock, I just sat there, lookin' at the first question. Y' know what it was, Frank? 'Suggest ways in which one might cope with some of the staging difficulties in a production of *Peer Gynt*.'

FRANK gets down, sits on the chair and continues to pack the books.

FRANK: Well, you should have had no trouble with that.

RITA: I did though. I just sat lookin' at the paper an' thinkin' about what you'd said. I tried to ignore it, to pretend that you were wrong. You think you gave me nothing; did nothing for me. You think I just ended up with a load of quotes an' empty phrases; an' I did. But that wasn't your doin'. I was so hungry. I wanted it all so much that I didn't want it to be questioned. I told y' I was stupid. It's like Trish, y' know me flatmate, I thought she was so cool an' together — I came home the other night an' she'd tried to top herself. Magic, isn't it? She spends half her life eatin' wholefoods an' health foods to make her live longer, an' the other half tryin' to kill herself. (*After a pause.*) I sat lookin' at the question, an' thinkin' about it all. Then I picked up me pen an' started.

FRANK: And you wrote, 'Do it on the radio'?

RITA: I could have done. An' you'd have been proud of me if I'd done that an' rushed back to tell you — wouldn't y'? But I chose not to. I had a choice. I did the exam.

FRANK: I know. A good pass as well.

RITA: Yeh. An' it might be worthless in the end. But I had a choice. I chose, me. Because of what you'd given me I had a choice. I wanted to come back an' tell y' that. That y' a good teacher.

FRANK (*stopping working and looking at her*): You know — erm — I hear very good things about Australia. Things are just beginning there. The thing is, why don't you — come as well? It'd be good for us to leave a place that's just finishing for one that's just beginning.

RITA: Isn't that called jumpin' a sinkin' ship?

FRANK: So what? Do you really think there's any chance of keeping it afloat?
She looks at him and then at the shelves.

RITA (*seeing the empty whisky bottles*): 'Ey, Frank, if there was threepence back on each of those bottles you could buy Australia.

FRANK (*smiling*): You're being evasive.

RITA (*going and sitting on a tea-chest*): I know. Tiger's asked me to go down to France with his mob.

FRANK: Will you?

RITA: I dunno. He's a bit of a wanker really. But I've never been abroad. An' me mother's invited me to hers for Christmas.

FRANK: What are you going to do?

RITA: I dunno. I might go to France. I might go to me mother's. I might even have a baby. I dunno. I'll make a decision, I'll choose. I dunno.
FRANK *has found a package hidden behind some of the books. He takes it down.*

FRANK: Whatever you do, you might as well take this . . .

RITA: What?

FRANK (*handing it to her*): It's erm — well, it's er — it's a dress really. I bought it some time ago — for erm — for an educated woman friend — of mine . . .
RITA *takes the dress from the bag.*

FRANK: I erm — don't — know if it fits, I was rather pissed when I bought it . . .

RITA: An educated woman, Frank? An' is this what you call a scholarly neckline?

FRANK: When choosing it I put rather more emphasis on the word woman than the word educated.

RITA: All I've ever done is take from you. I've never given anything.

FRANK: That's not true you've . . .

RITA: It is true. I never thought there was anythin' I could give you. But there is. Come here, Frank . . .

FRANK: What?

RITA: Come here . . . (*She pulls out a chair.*) Sit on that . . .
FRANK *is bewildered.*

RITA: Sit . . .
FRANK *sits and* RITA, *eventually finding a pair of scissors on the desk, waves them in the air.*

RITA: I'm gonna take ten years off you . . .
She goes across to him and begins to cut his hair.

Blackout.

*Further titles in the
Methuen Modern Plays series
are listed overleaf.*

/